DARK EDGE PRESS

A Deadly Inheritance

Jane McParkes

Published in 2022 by Dark Edge Press

Y Bwthyn
Caerleon Road,
Newport,
Wales.

www.darkedgepress.co.uk

A CIP catalogue record for this book is available from the British Library.

ISBN (eBook): B0B5M3K5S4
ISBN (Paperback): 979-8-3574-2654-3

For my mum.
Who taught me to read and to love books.

CONTENTS

CHAPTER ONE

It had been another night full of frantic, desperate dreams, but this time when Olivia forced her eyes open, her body was still swaying, still fighting the waves that had been pulling and spinning her round all night. She lifted her head and immediately regretted it. The room was swaying now. Like she had the worst hangover in the world. And yet she hadn't even had that much to drink the night before. Had she?

A surge of nausea propelled her out of bed and across the wooden floorboards to the bathroom, wincing at the early morning light forcing itself between the closed shutters.

'You are not going to vomit. You are not going to vomit . . .' She told herself, easing open the window and inhaling carefully. The salty, Cornish air edged with a hint of seaweed helped a little, but as she stood there, memories of the previous day began to download in her mind. Fragments of the Trustees' meeting, Libby's uncharacteristic snarky attitude towards her, and then the vicious words she'd hurled at her afterwards rushed into her throbbing head.

Oliva stumbled into the shower, her face turned up to the pounding, hot jets as she tried to coax her body and brain back to life and wash herself clean of Libby's cruel words. More snippets of the evening began to surface. Martin had appeared by magic, ready to help as she'd rushed to get away from the Goods Shed and everyone who had seen her humiliation. His kind face and gentle tone had weakened Olivia's resolve to stay strong and cope with the fall-out by herself. And they had come back to Tresillian, where they'd eaten supper together and she had drunk enough wine to loosen her tongue and confide in Martin about feeling as if everything was falling apart. She remembered swallowing a third glass of Malbec, but after that everything was a blur.

Olivia turned the temperature dial to cold and forced herself to stand there for fifteen seconds, then dried herself and shuffled back to the bedroom. Two pairs of round dark eyes observed her solemnly from the bed. Lowering her head gingerly, she kissed each dog gently on the nose.

'I don't suppose you guys can tell me what happened last night?' Two feathery tails wagged tentatively as she eased on her black running tights and top, still careful not to make any sudden movements. 'No, I thought not. Okay, let me just make one of Mollie's cure-alls and then we'll go deal with this crap the way we always do.'

***

Five minutes later Olivia was sipping a mug of milk thistle tea sweetened with honey while she watched the dogs rush around the garden, checking out the new smells that had arrived overnight. The rich nutty flavour of the tea was soon working its magic and Olivia pulled on her running jacket and slid her feet into her favourite trail running shoes; even managing to bend to tie the laces without feeling too sick. The thought of scraping her thick curls up into a scrunchie was a step too far, and she settled for her running headband instead. Letting herself out of the back door she whistled to the dogs and set off, slowly at first, into the bright light of the Cornish dawn. Once she reached the lane, she picked up speed, slowly but steadily, and began to feel better. She could do this. Running was the one thing that helped settle her mind, and she much preferred the burning in her lungs and the screaming of her muscles to the cocktail of emotions that had taken up residence in her stomach for the last eight weeks.

Subtle streaks of pink, orange and yellow spread across the sky above her as she ran down the quiet lane which wound its way along the south bank of Penbartha creek. For once, Olivia was impervious to the sounds, sight and smells of a spectacular sunrise, but excited barking soon brought her out of her worries. A familiar, elderly figure, carrying a posy of flowers was marching towards her. Olivia groaned. Normally, she was happy to stop and listen to Mrs Chynoweth's reminiscences, but today she did not feel up to small talk. And this old lady, who had run the village post office for the past sixty years could talk for Cornwall.

'Morning Olivia!' The cheery greeting cut through the fug of Olivia's slowly receding headache. 'How are you feeling today, my bird?'

Unable to avoid or ignore her, Olivia slowed her pace to a gentle jog as they met on the path. While the older woman bent to fuss the dogs, Olivia used the time to recover her breath and take a sip of water from the bottle in her running belt. She forced a smile onto her face that quickly faded when Mrs Chynoweth launched into the morning's news.

'Your blazing row with that piece of work from upcountry was all over the village by eight o'clock last night.' Mrs Chynoweth straightened up slowly. 'I couldn't believe what my grandson told me about the way Libby spoke to you, after all you've done since you got back. And to suggest you'd let George and Mollie down? What a cheek! I'm not surprised you shouted at her.'

A mixture of hurt and anger swirled around Olivia's stomach, its intensity surprising her. She'd forgotten that super-fast broadband had nothing on the speed of gossip in these small Cornish villages, with everyone adding their own spin, opinions and little extras. She avoided the old lady's gaze by shaking out her arms and legs to keep her muscles warm and closed her eyes.

'Can't say I was surprised though.' Mrs Chynoweth stepped closer. 'She hasn't really grasped the way we do things down here. Always coming into my post office acting proper teasy and expecting the impossible as far as deliveries for her fancy business are concerned. Or complaining when something she's ordered hasn't arrived yet. I've tried to explain that even Amazon won't guarantee next day delivery for our postcodes.' She paused for a moment and Olivia jumped in, anxious not to fan the flames.

'Oh, Libby's okay. It just takes some people longer to adapt to the slower pace of life down here.' She spoke with feeling. 'And we both said things in the heat of the moment that we probably shouldn't. We'll sort it.' Olivia was now more embarrassed by being the subject of village gossip than she was by her outburst, and hastily changed the subject. 'You're out early this morning, Mrs C.'

Mrs Chynoweth gestured at the posy. 'Just going to put these on my Alan's grave. It's his birthday today. He'd have been eighty-five.'

'Really?' Olivia managed a smile. 'Mr C was always so lovely to me when I was little.' Her smile grew as she remembered. 'He'd slip a little white paper bag full of sweets into my pocket whenever he could and say I need feeding up.'

She could feel Mrs Chynoweth's gaze looking her up and down. It was still as sharp as in the days of Olivia's childhood when she could spot a potential child shoplifter as soon as they walked through her door and fix them with a glare that soon changed their mind. Olivia tuned back into the comforting thick Cornish accent rolling over her words.

'You still do. You've spent too many years in New York. All the women there are too thin if you ask me.'

The dogs were now sniffing in the hedgerow and Olivia whistled to them to hide her smile. Mrs Chynoweth nodded at the smaller of the two dogs at Olivia's heels

'Unlike young Zennor here. She's putting her weight back on nicely, I'm glad to say. It was so sad to see her grieving after George died, I thought she'd fade away.'

Olivia bent and patted Zennor. 'It's all the steamed chicken and fish I'm feeding her. She much prefers that to the kibble she was on before.'

'I bet she does! You're a kind girl, Olivia.' Mrs Chynoweth's face wrinkled into a smile. 'And it's true what they say . . . My Alan's been gone five years now and I still miss him every day. But time heals.'

Olivia remained silent. She wasn't so sure.

'It's only been eight weeks, Olivia. You'll heal too. Trust me.' The sharp eyes held hers for a moment. 'That nice Carol on the telly just said we were getting a storm today and by the look of those clouds coming in, she was right. There'll be a mist as thick as a hedge before long, you mark my words. And I must get back . . .'

'You'd better hurry then.' Olivia pulled out her water bottle for another sip. The aftereffects of last night's argument and wine were still leaving a nasty taste in her mouth.

Mrs Chynoweth took a few steps and then stopped and turned back, a worried frown on her plump face. 'I know you've been finding things a bit tough since you got back, but I just wanted you to know that Mollie would be proper proud of you.' She must have seen the tears pooling in

Olivia's eyes as she hurried on. 'She always knew she could depend on you to do the right thing.'

Olivia gulped back her tears. 'She did?'

'Yes, my bird. Whenever I asked how she coped with you living in different places all over the world, she'd just smile and say that you were looking for your place in life and that you'd come back. And you always did. More often than some folk who only live in Plymouth. And now you're back where you're most needed.'

The old lady cocked her head on one side, her eyes bright. 'And don't you worry about what happened last night. No one who matters around here'll take any notice of what was said. A few loose words can't do that much harm, can they?' She waved her posy at Olivia. 'Look on the bright side, bird. At least no one died.'

Mrs Chynoweth was right. No one had died. But the reason she was so upset, Olivia admitted to herself as she ran on with the salt-scented breeze filling her lungs, was because Libby had questioned her integrity. And her timing had been terrible. Olivia needed all the members of the Goods Shed and the trustees to have faith in her ability to see the next phase of the Penbartha station renovation through. Yes, she was mad at Libby, but she was also angry with herself for losing her temper rather than calmly refuting all the accusations thrown at her. She picked up her pace subconsciously. She hadn't lost her temper like that for years and it couldn't have happened at a worse time.

By the time Olivia and the dogs reached the end of the lane, patchy sea mist was drifting in and curling itself around the trunks of the ancient trees and bushes lining the creek. They turned inland along the disused railway line that formed part of a network of well-maintained paths popular with walkers, cyclists and runners. As predicted by Mrs Chynoweth, the mist had begun to thicken into a dense fog, rolling silently in from the creek and covering the landscape in front of her, suffocating all the usual sounds of the distant water and the cries of the seabirds. Olivia briefly considered taking the path to her right, where the air was still clear, to head into the safety of the village. Alternatively, she could stay on the main track, which would lead her to the old Penbartha railway station buildings and the source of her most current worries. Her hesitation was only brief. She ran this way every morning, come rain or shine. Libby Walsh wasn't going to stop her doing what she loved. No matter what she said.

The fog soon swirled around Olivia's body and sucked at her face, getting heavier and denser with every step. She ran on, caught in its cold, suffocating grip, through a silent and empty, alien landscape where the mist grew thicker. Then, suddenly, she was lost. The old station buildings she had thought were in front of her had vanished. Even the huge trees that lined the track were invisible. And where were the dogs? Panic rising and heart pounding, Olivia stopped. She spun round and called out, her voice high-pitched and anxious. She felt a rush of relief as two cold, wet noses butted her legs and she bent to pat them, running her hands through their damp fur and talking calmly to them, as much to convince herself as them that everything was all right.

Taking a deep breath, she straightened up and peered ahead into the gloom. For a fanciful moment, she could imagine she had slipped through the mist into another time, back to the heyday of this once busy railway line when the trains ran through Penbartha to the larger stations at Falmouth and Truro. How good would time travel be, if she could have another attempt at yesterday? Boy, would she have done things differently . . .

Cursing Libby and herself again, she pulled up her hood and forced herself to press on along the walkway, aware only of the dogs' collar tags tinkling beside her. Before long, Olivia's eyes fastened with relief on a high yellow smudge of light in the distance as the first of the station buildings slowly loomed into view through the shadows. Her relief plummeted when she realised the light was coming from the Signal Box. Of all the people to be up and about, did it have to be Mr I-know-it-all Trevithick? At least there were no trustee meetings scheduled for today so she wouldn't have to face him in person, she reassured herself, put her head down and ran on.

As expected, the renovated Goods Shed, which comprised the heart and hub of the Penbartha Station Heritage Trust, was in total darkness as she approached. Few of the members made it into the workplace this early, but a light seeping from a window of the nearby Weighbridge Hut was most unusual at this time of day. The Studio, as its tenants officially called it, or the Hut, as it was more commonly known, was Libby Walsh's workplace.

The shadows created by the dim light from the Hut window mingled with the mist and hung heavily across the walkway as she got nearer. The dogs ran eagerly ahead to the main door, knowing Libby would have treats for them. Olivia called them away. She had no desire to attract Libby's attention and risk a repeat performance of last night's hostilities. Not until she'd worked out what to say.

Both dogs scratched at the door and whined, heads on one side expectantly, tails wagging. Olivia's instinct was telling her to keep running and get home and out of her muddy gear, but the kinder part of her wondered whether Libby, too, had been unable to sleep and was now regretting their argument. She stood for a moment, unsure. Then she knocked tentatively on the door and listened. The dogs, bored with waiting and now thinking of their breakfast, whined more loudly.

'Just a minute, guys. You stay out here. Let me see what's going on.'

She tried the handle. The door was open. Weird.

Knowing Libby would never leave her workplace unsecured, Olivia pushed her cold, wet hood down, nudged the door wider and stepped inside the studio. Her gaze swept the two tan leathers facing each other in front of an exposed brick wall full of artistic photographs of successful events, weddings and parties. A vintage silver wine cooler sat on the low coffee table, alongside empty bottles of wine and two cut glass wine goblets on a tray. Eventually her gaze reached the slouched figure of Libby, sitting at her desk by the far wall, beneath artfully festooned mood boards planning future events. She had fallen asleep in her chair, with her head resting on the chrome and glass desk. Olivia thought back to her own wine consumption a few hours earlier and frowned. By the look of it, Libby had also drowned her anger in wine.

'And I'm the one who's the complete waste of space, am I?' Olivia muttered, as Libby's vicious words sliced through her again. 'Which of us is functioning right now?' She turned away. 'Oh, forget it. I'll leave you to sober up.'

No longer caring whether her actions woke Libby, she strode across the studio to turn off the music playing in the background and gradually realised that other than her own footsteps on the polished concrete floor, there were no sounds in the room. A thousand hot pinpricks began marching up Olivia's spine, through her neck and into her hair. Something was wrong.

She reached out an unsteady hand and touched Libby's back. There was no movement. No body warmth. No breath.

'Shit. Libby!?' Olivia whipped her hand away and staggered back.

Forcing herself nearer, she moved the swivel chair round with a squeak. For a moment she just gaped, short sharp breaths escaping through her mouth, looking away and back again repeatedly, hoping the scene in front of her would change.

It didn't. Libby's silver jewel-encrusted letter opener, fashioned in the form of a stiletto dagger and used to protect her long fingernails, was embedded up to its hilt in her ribs.

CHAPTER TWO

Jago Trevithick leant back in his chair, feet resting on the desk, sipping his early morning cup of tea, and relishing his favourite news and current affairs programme on the radio. He wondered, not for the first time, why anyone ever agreed to appear on this particular show, though he held a grudging respect for the interviewer's technique. He'd even adopted it himself on occasion. Setting his tea aside, he glanced through the legal section of *The Times.* His chocolate Labrador lay snuffling softly at his feet, chasing rabbits in her dreams, both of them savouring the peace of the early morning before the Goods Shed tenants and builders arrived.

Steren's head shot up, her ears pricked.

Jago shushed her, turning the page and taking another sip of tea.

'It's okay, Steren. Go back to sleep.'

Steren, always open to the idea of visitors, wagged her tail and whined.

With a frustrated sigh, Jago unfolded his legs off the desk and turned down the radio. Over Steren's whining, a woman's voice was shouting, getting closer. And louder. And dogs were barking.

Footsteps hammered up the eighteen wooden steps of

the external stairway, followed by what sounded like at least two sets of clattering dog paws. He crossed to the door and opened it just as a dishevelled figure with wild, dark hair raised a fist to knock. He folded his arms across his chest and glanced at his watch. Not even seven-thirty and already his peace was shattered.

'Bit early for a social call, isn't it?'

His gaze shifted to the woman in front of him as she recoiled from his words. This was far from the calm and collected Olivia Wells he had come to know. He lowered his voice, taking her arm to guide her inside. 'What on earth's the matter?'

She shook him off, her voice rising as panic took over. 'It's Libby ... something's happened ...'

He looked back at his mug of tea cooling in the morning air she was letting in to his cosy room, his mind still on the radio interview.

'Please ...' Icy cold fingers gripped his wrist and jolted his attention back to her. 'You must come ...'

Olivia turned to head back down the stairs. 'I don't have my mobile or keys to get into the Goods Shed. Can you call 999?'

That got his attention.

'Is Libby hurt? Do we need an ambulance?'

She grabbed at the handrail to steady herself. 'I think it might be too late for that.'

'Right.' His mood switched and he shepherded the dogs inside, grabbing his mobile. By the time he pulled the door shut behind him, Olivia was already at the bottom of the stairs. 'Where is she?'

'The Hut.' Her breath rattled in her throat as she broke into a run.

They sprinted along the walkway that connected the Signal Box to the other renovated station buildings. Olivia stopped abruptly at the Hut door. She turned to him, eyes wide, visibly shaking.

Jago's pulse quickened as he saw her fear and he just nodded. 'You wait here.'

***

When Jago stepped back outside, Olivia was exactly where he'd left her, hunched up against the cold, her face even paler than before and her hair twisted into wild, medusa curls. He pulled out his mobile, turning away from her as he stabbed out three digits.

'Is she . . .?' Olivia's voice wobbled.

'Dead? Definitely.' He held the mobile to his ear. 'And if I can get any bloody signal, I'd say we need the police.'

***

Blue and white police tape fluttering in the morning wind declared the Weighbridge Hut and the surrounding area a crime scene. A large blue and white forensics tent sealed the entrance. The usually peaceful walkway was busy with uniformed officers, paramedics, and men and women in white overalls, overshoes, face masks and blue gloves bustling about.

By the time Jago and Olivia had been allowed to return to the Signal Box, she was visibly shivering in her lightweight running gear. She'd reluctantly accepted Jago's fleece and now shrank back against the wall as far away as possible from the tall windows and their full view of the walkway and the grisly scene below. As Jago busied himself making them both a hot drink, he watched out of the corner of his eye as her legs crumpled beneath her and she slid to the floor. In a swift movement she drew her knees up to her chin and wrapped her arms tightly round them, looking like she was physically trying to hold herself together. Eventually an enormous shudder ran through her body and a low moan escaped her lips. Her two dogs immediately rushed to her side and nudged their noses under her arms, tails tentatively wagging in support. Olivia gathered them to her and buried her face in their fur. Only when her breathing had eased did he place a steaming mug at her side.

'Here's some tea. It'll help warm you up.'

She took a sip and gagged at its sweetness. 'Urgh!' Dark eyes squinted up at him.

'I thought sweet tea was supposed to be good for shock.' His voice was gruff. 'Shall I make you another one?'

She shook her head and forced herself to take another sip. 'No worries. I'll try it.'

Jago retreated behind his desk with his newspaper as Olivia forced herself up from the floor and walked across the room to the windows, mug still in hand. Behind her, the slowly dissolving mist still shrouded the view. Everything was grey: the local granite of the station buildings, the sky and even the creek in the distance. But it was the same view that countless of railway signalmen would have enjoyed over the years and Jago loved it.

Olivia took several sips of tea and then set the mug on the windowsill. 'How long do you think they will be?' She didn't turn round.

'Who knows? They'll have loads of procedural stuff to do before they speak to us. The policeman said someone would be here as soon as they can. We're first on their list apparently.' He chose not to add that the uniformed officer had taken one look at Olivia's green face and obviously decided it would be better to get her way from the crime scene before she contaminated it even more than she already had with her footprints.

'I just don't know how anyone could do such a crazy thing as that to another human being. I can't believe anyone round here is that psycho, can you?'

Even though Olivia kept her back to him, Jago could sense her increasing distress. In trustees' meetings she

14

usually spoke in a calm, modulating voice with a British accent that had only a slight American twinge to it. Her voice always stood out a little, even in the melting pot of accents that made up the members of the Goods Shed. Now it was getting stronger, more American, with every syllable.

He turned a page of his newspaper.

'Statistics would tell you that most murders aren't committed by random psychopaths Olivia. But by people who know them well. Partners, lovers, family members.' He paused. 'Even friends.'

Olivia spun round then, two spots of colour bright against her pale cheeks and Jago regretted his choice of words.

'I'm sorry?' Her hands went automatically to her throat, as if to clutch something, but her neck was bare. 'I can't believe you just said that...' Olivia couldn't even finish the sentence and she turned her face away quickly, but not before Jago saw her eyes filling with fresh tears. She marched over to the chesterfield sofa that fitted snugly against one wall of the room, called the dogs to her and sat, letting her damp ringlets fall across her face and denying Jago any chance to read her expressions.

Jago returned to his newspaper but found his mind wandering back to the troubled young woman in front of him. Although he'd heard a great deal about Olivia from her godfather, he'd only met her for the first time when she returned to Penbartha after George's sudden death. He had gone to see her at Tresillian to give his condolences and tell her about the pleasant evening he'd spent with George the evening before he died and how he'd been so full of plans for the Goods Shed, the station building and the future. And although Olivia had been every bit as attractive as George had described with her dark, almost exotic, looks, he'd found her surprisingly cold and unfriendly towards him. As though she didn't want to share her memories of George and it was taking every last ounce of her composure to accept his sympathy. And since then, she had limited her contact with him to trustees' meetings and never once engaged him in conversation. Unlike every other member of the Goods Shed – local or incomer – with whom she chatted with easily and had quickly proved herself to be a popular and respected figure. Jago still had absolutely no idea what he had done to upset her or why she unsettled him the way she did.

He followed Olivia's gaze as she took in her surroundings. Although he had seen her almost every morning since her return, running down the walkway, upright and lithe, he doubted she'd given any thought to what had happened to the inside of the Signal Box since she had drawn up all the plans for the various buildings on the station site. And as much as he found her hard to warm to personally, he had to grudgingly admit, as an architect, she had fantastic vision.

He recalled George's photographs which had shown how the sad, old Signal Box had looked before Olivia had worked her magic on it from New York. There had been holes in the roof, rotten laths hanging down from the high-pitched ceiling and lumps of plaster crumbling between the open rafters. No daylight could get through the broken, boarded up windows and there had been inches of dust and huge black cobwebs everywhere. All the old signalling equipment had been removed by British Rail and sold for scrap, leaving empty spaces behind on both floors, filled with unidentifiable objects over the intervening years. But the basic structure of the building, being made of local granite was sound and deemed worthy of renovation by both George and Olivia. Rocky Berryman, their main contractor, had replaced the original slate roof with reclaimed matching tiles, and all the old wooden windows, doors and stairs with new and sustainably sourced fittings. The main floor now boasted a wood burning stove which warmed the entire, newly insulated building and a neat internal spiral staircase gave access to the lower floor, now used as safe storage for Jago's railway memorabilia business.

He tried to see the renovated building through Olivia's eyes and wondered if she approved of what he had done with it. At a relatively generous three meters by six metres, he had been careful not to overfill the room with unnecessary furniture. An oak stationmaster's desk and chair, similar to the one in George's study at Tresillian, provided Jago with a workstation and a Great Western Railway oak-cased clock kept time above the doorway. Various pieces of attractive railway memorabilia and books filled two bookcases. His only concessions to comfortable luxury were the vintage dark brown chesterfield sofa which took pride of place beneath the wall of windows opposite the desk and a large oriental wool rug which mostly covered the reclaimed wooden floorboards. It suited him and his needs and was a warm and comfortable place to spend his working days.

A quick glance at Olivia's face showed that her gaze now rested on the wall behind Jago's desk, where his most prized collection hung.

'They're interesting.' She commented as she stood to examine the six large but slim rectangular cast iron nameboards that graced the walls. She ran her fingers over the lettering on the signs; Padstow, Wadebridge, Camelford and Delabole, Tresmeer – all lost railway stations like Penbartha.

'Thanks. They're my own personal collection.'

She squinted at the green background. 'But not GWR signs, I see?'

Jago nodded. 'No, these are signal box nameboards from the North Cornwall Railway line. Hence the green background rather than black. I know George was a GWR devotee, but I made it a personal ambition to collect all the boards from that particular line as my family are from Launceston.'

'How many are there?'

'Thirteen. So I'm almost halfway there.' His voice lightened. 'I managed to pick up the Launceston sign at an online auction last week, and I'm waiting for its delivery. That's the jewel in my crown.' He sobered his voice as soon as he saw the look on Olivia's face. 'Sorry, bad timing.'

She waved away his apology. 'I'm used to the excitement things like that generate, from George.'

She sat back down on the sofa. Any brief connection they may have shared at the memory of George was immediately replaced by a spear of pain flickering in her dark eyes and he realised he'd triggered a whole lot of sad memories for her.

He suddenly remembered the promise he'd made to her godfather and ran a hand across his face. 'I haven't had a chance to speak to you properly since the funeral, but I've been meaning to ask . . . how are you doing up at Tresillian . . . on your own?'

'I'm fine, thank you. And I'm not on my own.' Olivia's reply was automatic. 'I have Cassie next door. And the dogs.'

Jago watched as pain flickered in her eyes and she clasped her arms round her waist again.

'Well, obviously I'm not fine.' She corrected herself and her voice rose. 'Particularly now I've just found my friend's body.'

Jago noticed her clenched fists and the tears in her eyes, but she held his gaze for a moment. A sudden whine broke the awkward silence.

'The dogs are hungry,' she said, turning away from him. 'I need to take them back to Tresillian. I always feed them straight after our morning run. Mylor will be okay for a while longer, but Zennor needs to eat small meals regularly.'

Jago looked at the two dogs and chuckled. 'It was so typical of George to end up with those mongrels, when he could have any pedigree that he wanted. I never really understood that.'

Olivia's mood changed and she squared her shoulders, her chin automatically lifting. 'If you knew George half as well as you're always telling people you did, you would know why he ended up with them. No-one wanted Mylor because he wasn't the pedigree he was supposed to be. And the same went for Zennor.' She shot him a fierce look. 'Because that is exactly the sort of thing that George and Mollie did.'

Hearing his name, Mylor nudged Olivia with his nose; his tail giving a hesitant wag in solidarity.

'Ah yes. The famous, but uncontrollable stud dog, Romeo, and his unregulated love matches.' Jago commented mildly. 'A classic example of George and his rescue projects. You and I know all about those, don't we Olivia?'

Another flash of pain crossed her face then and she stood up quickly and pulled off his fleece. She hung it on a hook by the door before opening it and whistling to the dogs. 'Thanks for your help, Jago.' Her voice was icily polite again. 'If you could just tell the police I've . . .'

Two dark-suited men met her at the top of the stairs. 'Tell the police you've what, Miss Wells?

'I . . .' Olivia floundered. 'My dogs . . .'

Jago stood and walked to the door. 'May I help?'

'I'm Detective Inspector Trenow and this is Detective Sergeant Burridge,' the taller of the two men said. 'Thank you both for your patience. We'd like to ask you a few questions.'

CHAPTER THREE

Olivia sat, surrounded by paperwork at the once-tidy desk in her godfather's study, lost in her thoughts. A hot shower on her return home had helped warm her up and a mug of strong tea, washed down with two ibuprofen and some toast made a slight but noticeable impact on her headache. Mylor and Zennor had no trouble switching off the unsettling events of the morning and snoozed in front of the wood burner which filled the room with the serious heat that only comes from a proper fire. Olivia, on the other hand had to keep pulling her thoughts back from what she had seen in the Weighbridge Hut. Whirling images of Libby slumped over her desk, thoughts of how she had died violently, in her studio and all alone, kept spinning through her mind. Although she hadn't been looking forward to the day ahead when she'd set out on her run, never in a million years had she thought it would turn out like this. Calls and messages of support on her voicemail went unanswered, although every now and then she felt a sudden urge to check her phone for Libby's number, to call her up, just to hear her voice and prove to herself that she was still alive.

Why, Olivia kept asking herself, hadn't she just gone and sorted things out with Libby straight away? Because, a little voice whispered, she'd been angry and embarrassed that Libby had betrayed her secrets and she'd wanted to run and hide and lick her wounds until she had decided what to do about it. And then Martin had persuaded her to leave it until everyone had calmed down. She shouldn't have listened to him. If she had gone to the Hut instead of going home, Libby might still be alive. But it was too late now. Libby was dead.

In the eight weeks since Olivia had been back in Penbartha, she'd been operating on autopilot. She had done all the essential things; registering George's death, arranging his funeral, settling whatever business affairs and dealings she could and trying to keep everything functioning as usual, alongside her work for 2Olivarez Architecture & Preservation Partnership in New York. Not to mention overseeing the renovation works on the Penbartha station building, and the final snagging list for the Goods Shed. By staying so busy she had avoided falling apart. Eighteen months ago, Mollie's death had broken her heart, but her godmother had been ill for some time and Olivia and George had been there for her and each other at the end. But this was different. George's death could easily still break her completely if she allowed herself to think about him too much.

A familiar ache for New York, her adopted home, swept through her. She loved Cornwall, but if she were back in America, she could pretend that nothing had happened; that everything was as it always had been in Penbartha, and that George and Mollie were still here, just a phone call away. And now she could add Libby to that picture, busy in her Hut, organising her fantastic events, laughing and being outrageous. If only . . .

Outside, bud-laden branches whipped against the windowpanes, jolting her out of her thoughts. To calm herself, Olivia slowly breathed in the evocative scent of wood and pipe smoke she always associated with this room. Her eyes rested briefly on George's tweed jacket, still resting on his favourite wing-backed chair. Neither she nor Cassie could bring themselves to move it yet and just by touching it now, she could hear George's calm, deep voice with his gentle rolling accent, reminding her that there was nothing like throwing oneself into a job for getting over emotional upsets. And he had always been right. Olivia's ability to distract herself with hard work was one of the reasons she was still here. Like running, or drawing or painting, work made her focus completely on the one thing she was doing. It made her concentrate and meant that her mind was occupied and unable to dwell on anything else.

Olivia eyed the various piles of paperwork on the desk, threatening to engulf her laptop; queries from private clients, planning reports and the most recent accounts from the Goods Shed. Taking a deep breath and straightening her shoulders, she called Alice to tell her she wouldn't be coming into the Goods Shed, though she doubted much work would be done there today with everything else that was going on. Then she pulled the various papers detailing the renovation and refurbishment works to the station building towards her and reached for her reading glasses. Before long she had dealt with her emails, amended a planning application and annotated some complex drawings for Rocky's next big eco-refurbishment project. Only then did Olivia feel calm enough to deal with the schedules, spreadsheets and calculations for the station building renovation, soothed by the slow, lazy tick of the grandfather clock standing guard in the hall and the dreamy snuffles of two sleeping dogs.

***

Olivia was so engrossed in her work that she barely

noticed the jangling of the heavy front doorbell. The dogs' stranger-alert bark eventually brought her back to the moment. Propping her reading glasses in her curls, Olivia went to answer it, rolling her shoulders and wincing as her neck muscles twinged. Both dogs rushed ahead, barking excitedly, unaccustomed to the very non-Cornish practice of using the front door and eager to greet any friend, or repel any foe. Olivia felt her pulse quicken. It was the police.

'Miss Wells. Sorry we had to cut short our discussion earlier. And thanks for agreeing to see us this afternoon.' DI Trenow spoke for both men. 'May we come in?'

'Sure. Come through.' Olivia glanced at the grandfather clock, amazed to see that four hours had passed since she'd left Jago at the Signal Box. She shushed Zennor's low growl, amused to see a nervous look settle on the younger detective's solemn face as she led the way down the wide hallway, eight sets of claws clattering against the stone-flagged floor. As they passed an antique oak hall stand, the musky, exotic scent of homemade potpourri in a large, old floral china bowl suffused the air. She remembered gathering various herbs and flower petals throughout the year to create Mollie's popular mixture. Taking a deep breath of the fragrance to gain comfort and strength, she looked around and wondered if the old house felt as abandoned and lonely as she did.

'Miss Wells,' a voice rang out from behind her, 'could you please keep your dogs under control? This one is baring its teeth at me in quite a menacing manner.'

Olivia twisted round. Mylor, although barely reaching much above the sturdy detective's knee, was sending mixed messages. The black crossbreed's tail was wagging wildly, but he was showing two rows of gleaming white teeth, his top lip curled right back. She bent and patted the dog before straightening up.

'He's smiling, DS Burridge. Have you never seen a dog

smile before? You don't need to worry about Mylor hurting you. He was way down the line when the canine god was handing out brains. It's this one you have to watch.' She pointed to Zennor who was sitting prettily at Olivia's feet, fluffy white tail tucked neatly round her and eyeing the visitors beadily.

'Get through here, Burridge, and don't be so pathetic.' Trenow's eyes twinkled with mirth. 'I can see now why you didn't apply to the Dog Unit and why I've got the pleasure of you instead.' He leant down to pat Mylor and looked up at Olivia with clear grey eyes. 'This is his first case in CID, and I've been told to be gentle with him.'

Surprised by the indiscretion, Olivia ushered them through a final archway into the huge kitchen which merged seamlessly into a green oak orangery, built across the entire rear of the house. Two roof lanterns flooded light into the large, open-plan space, discretely zoned into cooking, dining and sitting areas. She had designed it herself so that the windows framed uninterrupted views over the gardens and the creek in both directions like an ever-changing landscape painting. Although Mollie had decorated everywhere in muted tones of coastal colours, she had furnished the whole house with quirky and unusual finds collected over the years from street-markets and house-clearance sales. Her knack of putting together unlikely combinations of colours and objects involved bright patchwork quilts and crocheted throws covering the sofas, a vintage railway trunk, serving as a coffee table, and various lamp stands fashioned out of driftwood. The overall effect made the house warm, comforting and welcoming.

Olivia left the detectives standing in front of the windows, admiring the view, and occupied herself with making their requested coffee. Noticing her hands were shaking slightly as she arranged the homemade cookies Cassie had dropped off the day before, she pressed her palms down on the cool granite surface of the island unit and took a moment to observe the two men. Trenow was the older of the two, tall and thin in his crumpled suit with dark, sharp eyes. Burridge was stocky with ginger hair, a beard trimmed close to his pale freckled skin and pale, almost translucent eyes. She thought the police were supposed to inspire trust in people, but this one certainly didn't. They stood, gazing at the view stretching out over the widest part of the creek to the patchwork of farmland and tree-covered slopes in the distance, rising from the water.

Olivia watched purple clouds gathering over the opposite bank and listened to the sound of the sea getting restless at the mouth of the creek. The noise of clinking boat masts clashed with shrieking gulls and birds that wheeled and whirled overhead, calling to each other to seek sanctuary on dry land. The storm, promised earlier by Mrs Chynoweth, was brewing. As the detectives' conversation turned into a debate about whether the snow-white bird that they could see standing with its shoulders hunched in the shallows on the other side was a heron or an egret, Olivia put the tray on the table.

'It's an egret. It's got a black beak and black legs. Herons are much bigger and have yellow feet and beaks.'

Burridge scowled. 'Well, we're not here to discuss ornithology.'

Olivia winced. Another mark against her in that detective's book.

A slight smile played round Trenow's mouth. 'C'mon now, Burridge, I told you that we learn something new every day in this job. He cast his gaze around the room admiringly. 'It's a delightful place you've got here, Miss Wells. I understand you inherited it from your godparents. Along with everything at Penbartha station.'

Olivia busied herself with pouring coffee and offering cookies and let her hair fall across her face for a moment.

'That's right. I see you've done some homework.'

'We're investigating a murder, Miss Wells. Which took place on your property. We have to ask certain questions.' Burridge eased the collar of what was obviously a new shirt with his fingers.

Olivia caught a look pass between the two detectives.

Trenow helped himself to a biscuit, without offering one to his colleague, and sat down, obviously more comfortable in his own, well-worn suit.

'I realise this has been an ordeal for you, Miss Wells, but we need to clear up one or two things about Miss Walsh.'

The lump of lead that had lain in her chest for the past two months rose and pressed itself behind her eyes. She tried to blink it away but failed.

'We could do this at Truro police station if you prefer . . .' DS Burridge butted in.

Another look passed between the two men.

'But we're here now, so we'll press on.' Trenow turned his full gaze on Olivia, 'We don't need you to repeat everything you told us earlier, about how you found the victim, but we would like to ask you some more questions about Libby Walsh and who she mixed with, what you knew of her. That sort of thing.'

Olivia swallowed. 'Okay.'

'Would you say you were good friends with Libby? You'd known her for what? Two months?'

Olivia's fingers went automatically to her throat and clutched at the shiny, smooth brown gemstone on a slim leather cord that now hung in its usual place, around her neck. 'That's right. Yes.'

'And did she have many other close friends? From talking to the other members of the Goods Shed, it doesn't seem she mixed socially with many of them. Was that your impression?'

Olivia frowned. 'I think she mainly socialised with Clara, her business partner. And Martin Lambert, our business mentor.' She took a sip of her coffee. 'She had lots of friends away from the Goods Shed, but I don't know who they were.'

'So you didn't meet any of them?'

'No. I've been busy. I've had other things on my mind. I'm sorry I can't help you there. I've only been back here a short while. Since my godfather died.'

'Ah yes,' Trenow consulted his notebook. 'I've heard a lot about Mr George Stevenson. Tell me about him.'

Olivia's gaze rested involuntarily on a picture on the mantlepiece. It was a photograph of her godparents taken in the garden, in the summer, judging by the blooming flowers and their casual clothes, with their arms round each other and laughing alongside a third person in the picture. Olivia looked at her ten-year-old self; her long, dark hair loose in a riot of curls and her face lit up with joy. They were all laughing at something, or someone, just out of shot. Probably Aidan, she thought, and something twisted deep inside her. Her eyes shifted to another photograph of George and Mollie with her teenage self. The wild mane of hair was unchanged but the joy from the childhood photo had gone from her dark eyes. She gulped down some coffee.

Trenow cleared his throat while he waited for her to continue.

'They loved rescuing unwanted things and either restoring them to their former glory or just breathing fresh life into them to fulfil their potential. They did it with this house and they did it with the station buildings. George was passionate about the environment and our heritage, and about old, neglected industrial buildings being protected or converted into something else if it was impossible to use them for their original purpose.'

Trenow searched through his pocketbook, and then turned back to her.

'Mrs Greville, your administrator, explained briefly

how the Goods Shed operates. But she said you were the person to ask for more details about it.'

Olivia nodded. 'George and Mollie visited me every year in New York, and it was there that George learned about the idea of affordable and quality shared workspaces for young businesses and creative entrepreneurs. And being George, he immediately saw that there was a need for such a concept in Cornwall, particularly as it was already attracting creative and artistic types from all over the country.'

'And I gather there's more to it than that, with the green and eco side of things?'

'Yes. George was quite unusual for his generation and was a lifetime advocate of sustainability. He really believed in championing young eco businesses.'

'And the premises at the old Penbartha railway station? He owned them?'

'Yes. He bought them years ago, from British Rail, for a ridiculously small amount of money. And when he decided to go for the co-working idea, he was able to combine the renovation of the station buildings with his commitment to sustainability and the community.' Olivia spoke more freely now she was on familiar territory. 'His biggest dream was to make the entire site as environmentally friendly as possible and help all the members and tenants bring greener practices into their businesses. But it was more important to him that he was helping eco-conscious and creative people to break with the traditional ways of working and giving them more freedom by providing them with an affordable shared workspace. He won a Cornish Heritage Award for his work on the Goods Shed.' She stopped, realizing she'd been on her hobbyhorse and pulled an awkward face. 'It's basically about reducing people's carbon footprints and working towards a more sustainable future.'

Trenow nodded. 'And how did Libby Walsh come to be

involved in the Goods Shed?'

Olivia took another sip of coffee.

'I'm not sure, really. I was in New York when she and Clara took over the Weighbridge Hut once it had been renovated.'

Trenow consulted his notebook. 'Mrs Clara Yates? You mentioned her earlier. She's currently in Glasgow for family reasons, isn't she?'

Olivia nodded. 'Her husband's sister was taken ill about three weeks ago, and they've gone up to help with her children.'

'Leaving Libby to run the business?'

She nodded. 'Yes. And they've got a local student who helps out.'

Trenow turned a page. 'Sarah Santos?'

'Yes.'

'May I ask how an events and planning business fits into a set-up like this?'

'How do you mean?'

'Well, most of the people we've met have been green or creative entrepreneurs, not your run-of-the-mill party planners.'

Olivia hesitated before replying.

'I don't think either Clara or Libby would thank you for that description.' Trenow acknowledged her admonition. 'They prefer to call themselves sustainable event consultants.' She ignored Burridge's smirk. 'They specialise in quality events that create lasting memories for their clients in a way that leaves minimal impact on the environment. All their work is creative and eco-conscious, and it meets a real need down here. People want environmentally friendly parties and weddings these days. Clara concentrates on the wedding and party side of the business while Libby's expertise is in corporate events.' Her voice wobbled at her automatic use of the present tense.

'Such as?'

Olivia shrugged. 'Business and product launches, conferences, networking events, company awaydays, small festivals . . . that sort of thing. Their business involves a lot of curation and organisation and client meetings, which is why they've got the Weighbridge Hut. There are meeting rooms at the Goods Shed, but there's a booking system and that wouldn't work for the way they operate.'

Trenow scribbled more notes before returning his gaze to Olivia.

'You said you were in New York when Clara and Libby moved into the Weighbridge Hut?'

Olivia nodded.

'Mrs Greville told us all about your successful career as an architect there.'

She felt herself redden. 'Alice is very loyal. I hope she didn't bore you.'

'Not at all. It was most interesting and informative.'

Olivia looked away and shifted in her seat, uncomfortable with the idea of being the subject of a police discussion.

Trenow put down his pen. 'Did you mind giving up everything in New York to come back here?'

Olivia stared at him as a fresh wave of anxiety swept through her.

'I don't think I would have been thrilled if I had to leave a great job and apartment behind in New York.' The tone of Burridge's voice made his opinion obvious.

'I have an awesome boss and he understands it's something I have to do.' She opened her mouth to continue but closed it quickly.

'But you'd made a life there, according to Mrs Greville.' The note of envy was audible in the detective sergeant's voice. 'And you certainly sound more of a New Yorker than a local.'

'Do I?' Olivia regarded him with a cool brown stare. 'I

think I just absorb accents. It's the chameleon in me. I guess I'm not always comfortable being the odd one out. Give me another few weeks here and I'll have the strongest Cornish accent you've ever heard.'

'Forgive Burridge, Miss Wells. He's from Devon. And still dazzled by the bright lights of London and New York and doesn't appreciate what we've got down here in Cornwall.'

Once again Olivia witnessed a hostile glance pass between the two men and was reminded that the West Country Wars were still being fought.

'So, were you happy to come back to Cornwall, Miss Wells?' Burridge repeated.

'Not exactly happy, given that it meant my godfather was dead.' She stared at him.

'Aren't you due a big promotion at your New York firm soon?' Burridge persisted.

The knot in Olivia's stomach tightened, and she gathered the coffee cups together and moved away from the table. 'I'm sorry. But what exactly has this got to do with Libby's death? My friend has been murdered and you only seem interested in my career.'

Burridge frowned. 'We're just trying to find out more about you. As one of the last people to see Miss Walsh alive.'

Olivia dropped the cups onto the island unit with a crash. 'But there were loads of us in the Goods Shed after the trustees' meeting, hanging round and just chatting. Are you asking everyone else all these questions? I told you everything earlier. What more is there to say?'

Trenow got to his feet and helped her right the cups.

'These are just routine questions, Miss Wells, to help us get a feel for things. Can we sit down again, please?'

Olivia reluctantly followed him to the table and sat staring out of the window as fat raindrops patterned the creek with concentric circles, leaving increasingly larger rings as the rain fell more heavily. Her insides churned in synchronicity.

Trenow cleared his throat.

'Mrs Greville said all the different buildings on the station site are run as a trust?'

'Yes. The Penbartha Station Heritage Trust. George didn't want me to have to make the major decisions all by myself, as I wasn't living in the UK at the time, and wasn't all that involved right from the beginning, apart from architectural designs for the renovations.' Olivia shifted her gaze from the window and picked at a loose thread on the knee of her pale jeans.

'And who are the other trustees?'

'I'm sure Alice will give you all the details of their names and addresses.' Olivia's gaze fell on the sheet of paper with familiar names that Trenow was easing out of a file. 'Ah'

'And what's their role?'

'They have the responsibility of directing the Trust's affairs under the overall mission statement's objectives. And they manage the assets of the Trust, including the property and investments on behalf of the beneficiary.'

'And that is?'

'Me.' Olivia held his gaze.

'So you can't make decisions unilaterally?'

'No.' She wrapped the thread around her finger and tugged a bit harder.

'Are you usually all in agreement?'

She looked away for a moment while she considered his question. There had been more tension among the trustees at recent meetings; Jess Hopkins could be difficult, and Jago was . . . well Jago. She thought briefly about mentioning their names and then decided not to. 'Usually. Well, I thought so. Some of them have been getting antsy about membership levels and a few other incidental things. But nothing major. Until yesterday . . .'

Trenow looked up sharply. 'Yes?'

Olivia chose her words carefully. 'It was always in the long-term strategic plan that we would open the main station building itself, which includes the ticket office and waiting rooms and so on, as a café. In this kind of set-up, it's considered good practice to have a third income stream.'

She read the lack of comprehension on Burridge's pale, ginger-freckled face and sighed. His interest in the finer details seemed to have waned, and he was now keeping a careful eye on Mylor.

'We have income from more professional type tenants who rent permanent offices on the mezzanine in the Goods Shed, and then there's the membership income from the members who use the main co-working space,' she explained. 'So, we need a third source of income to help pay for all the set-up costs and so on to be able to carry on next year.'

'And who will use the café? Just the members?' At least Trenow was trying to keep up.

'No. It's totally and physically separate but will follow the same principles regarding the environment and sustainability. So, besides members, we expect villagers, walkers, cyclists, tourists. And the old railway path network brings passers-by from nearby villages and the harbour. So, anyone, really. And there will be an area within the café available for individual groups to use in the day, or the entire building can be used for large village events in the evenings We feel it's important for our community to have a dedicated gathering place. Especially since the parish council, in their infinite wisdom, sold the Village Hall for development.' Olivia didn't feel the need to elaborate.

'So not all the trustees were in agreement with the decision to go ahead with the café?'

'Only one was against. When it went to the vote, the

original plan, put in place by George, was upheld.'

Trenow's pen was poised above his notebook. 'And who objected?'

A movement outside caught her eye and a tall, blond floppy-haired man battling with a golfing umbrella appeared at the door. Relief surged through her, and Olivia rushed to open it. At the same time, Trenow's mobile rang, and he moved away to answer it.

'Martin. Thank God you're here!' She restrained herself from throwing her arms round him, but he caught her up in a hug.

'I've only just heard the awful news about Libby. I literally just stopped in at the Goods Shed to drop some information off for Alice. Poor, poor Libby.'

Olivia leaned in to his embrace and then stood back, furiously blinking away the tears that burned against her eyelids. Martin's face was puffy, his eyes damp and swollen. She pulled him through to the kitchen and hugged him again, whispering into his ear. 'These are the detectives in charge of the case.'

Martin took a moment to compose himself, blowing his nose, and busied himself by straightening the coffee cups abandoned on the island unit until all their handles pointed to 5 o'clock. Trenow finished his call and pushed his mobile back into his pocket.

Olivia made the introductions. 'This is Martin Lambert,' she paused for a moment, 'the friend of mine and Libby's I was telling you about. He's our business mentor and has an office at the Goods Shed. He's also a trustee and was at the meeting yesterday.'

Martin reached for a tumbler from a glass-fronted cabinet and filled it with iced water from the dispenser on the stainless-steel fridge. He took a long drink before shaking each detective's hand firmly and returning to stand at Olivia's side, looking more like his old self.

He cleared his throat. 'I'm sorry. It's just been such a

horrible shock. We were all so close . . .' his voice trailed off.

'That's perfectly understandable, Mr Lambert.' Trenow was gracious. 'Are things still busy at the Goods Shed?'

Martin nodded. 'The local press and even some nationals apparently have descended on the village and the Goods Shed, but Alice is sending them all away and has forbidden everyone to gossip with strangers.' He managed a slight smile. 'She has made the dire consequences of going against her orders very clear.'

Trenow flicked his pen against his notebook.

'If we could return to the question, Miss Wells,' he said. Martin turned to her expectantly. 'Who objected to the proposal about the café?'

With her impeccable timing, Zennor placed her paw on Olivia's foot, and she scooped her up and held her close, burying her face in the little dog's soft fur. She could feel Trenow's eyes boring into the top of her head.

'Miss Wells?'

'Libby Walsh.' She lifted her head slowly and saw a triumphant look flash across Burridge's face. She tried to ignore the huge tremor rolling through her stomach that was telling her this wasn't going well.

'Ah.'

Olivia remained still and silent, watching Trenow as he consulted his notebook and then leant back in his seat and pursed his lips.

'Yet you told us earlier that you and she had been good friends?'

Olivia felt her heart tighten at the memory of their argument and then horror flooded her mind as prickles started marching up her spine. 'We were.' Her mouth was dry.

'We were all good—' Trenow's hand silenced Martin.

'We'll come to you later, Mr Lambert, we're asking Miss Wells questions at the moment.' He turned back to her.

'Are you happy for Mr Lambert to remain here?'

Olivia felt the blood drain from her face. She nodded.

'You used the past tense, Miss Wells. Would you like to expand on that?'

She swallowed. 'Libby was good to me when I first came back. I'd only really been involved with the architectural side before, and I was suddenly confronted with all the day-to-day operational stuff of the Trust. But Libby was on the ball and helped me get up to speed. And she, Martin, and I socialised a fair bit. Libby was good fun and we seemed to have a lot in common.'

'Really?'

She paused, unwilling to divulge too much personal information. 'We'd had some similar life experiences. She'd lost people she was close to and threw herself into work to cope. We seemed to share many likes, dislikes, opinions and attitudes.' Hot tears suddenly pricked at her eyelids at the loss of her friend. 'I really thought we were coming from the same place.'

'Can you think of anyone who would have wanted to kill her?'

A new, clearer vision of Libby's mottled face and blank, staring eyes crept into Olivia's mind and she swallowed hard. 'No.'

Trenow tapped his pocket. 'One of our team undertaking interviews at the Goods Shed has just reported that you and Libby were seen having a heated exchange yesterday afternoon after the trustees' meeting.'

Olivia closed her eyes and clutched her pendant as painful memories came rushing back. When she opened them, Trenow was watching her closely.

'I'd confided in Libby about some personal stuff. And she betrayed my confidences, and other things, in front of a lot of people. So I found myself drawn into it. I didn't make a conscious decision to have a blazing row in public, Inspector.'

He checked back at his notebook 'And was that betrayal of confidence about you not planning on staying here? A lot of the members mentioned their concerns about that.'

'Among other things. Yes.' She bit her lip to stop more words tumbling out.

'And apparently, according to our source, you threatened Miss Walsh in front of witnesses.'

She felt a sudden heat rush to her cheeks and her stomach churned as she realised the full implication of his words. 'I might have said something in anger, Inspector, under provocation. About her keeping out of my way for a while. About not being responsible for my actions. But that's the sort of thing you say in anger, isn't it? A figure of speech. I didn't mean it.'

'Is it?' Trenow's eyebrow rose. 'Exactly how angry were you with Miss Walsh?'

A cold fist closed itself round Olivia's heart and she reached an arm out towards Martin. He was by her side instantly.

'Oh please. Inspector. Really?' Martin's voice was sharp.

Trenow ignored him and changed tack. 'Did you threaten to kill Libby Walsh?'

Olivia gasped again, her eyes stinging with hot tears. 'No! I'm horrified by what happened to her. No one should ever have to die like that.'

Trenow closed his notebook and looked directly at her.

'Where did you go last night, Miss Wells? After you left the Goods Shed?'

The silence in the room was so loud it hurt her ears.

'I can help you there, Inspector.' Martin turned to Trenow and Burridge. 'We had to get out of the situation, and so we came straight back here to calm down. I've never seen Olivia so upset and angry before, and I couldn't possibly have left her on her own in a state like that.' He sat down heavily at the table and the others all followed suit. Olivia's eyes never left Trenow, who was busy scribbling in his notebook.

'And what did you do after you got back here, sir?'

Martin thought for a moment.

'I opened a bottle of wine,' he nodded at the recollection. 'We just chatted until Olivia had calmed down and then I cooked supper for us both.'

'And what time were you here until, sir?'

Martin held Olivia's gaze. 'I stayed the night.'

'And what time did you leave this morning?' Trenow's eyes were bright.

Olivia lowered her head, her heart hammering with confused relief.

Martin paused. 'Probably about six o'clock. I had to get to a breakfast meeting in Plymouth.'

'And how do you know that Miss Wells didn't slip out of the house in the night to return to the Weighbridge Hut?'

Olivia bit her bottom lip until she could taste blood.

Martin sent Olivia a slightly embarrassed look. 'I'm a light sleeper, Inspector. I can assure you she didn't leave the bed all night.'

'And you, Miss Wells, can you confirm that Mr Lambert didn't leave the house until six o'clock this morning?'

'If that's what Martin says.' Her hand went to head. 'I must have had quite a lot to drink.'

Martin turned to Trenow. 'Olivia's answered all your questions, Inspector, can we take it you've finished with us now?'

'Not quite.' Trenow flicked back through his notes. 'Miss Wells, you said that you, Miss Walsh and Mr Lambert socialised together. Would that have been in the Weighbridge Hut?'

Olivia thought back to the many evenings the three of them had spent chatting and drinking wine together in the Hut. She looked anxiously at Martin.

'Among other places.' He answered the question for

her. 'Yes.'

'Are your fingerprints on the police database?'

'No,' they answered in unison.

'In which case, we will need you to provide fingerprints and mouth swabs for DNA. And, as we explained earlier, we'd like to collect the clothes and shoes you were wearing when you found the body this morning, Miss Wells.'

Olivia nodded towards a bag in the corner of the room.

Trenow continued. 'The Crime Scene Investigators will be lifting lots of prints and samples from the Weighbridge Hut during their examination. If you were regularly there, we'll need your samples for elimination purposes.'

The two detectives got to their feet and headed down the hall. Olivia and the dogs followed them.

'Don't go anywhere too far away, Miss Wells. We will more than likely need to speak to you again if any fresh evidence comes to light.'

Olivia blinked. 'What sort of evidence?' she asked, her voice not quite steady.

Mylor's hackles rose, and he let out a low growl.

Burridge stopped and fixed her with a stare.

'Any evidence we find at the scene that might link you to the crime.'

CHAPTER FOUR

Olivia ran south around the headland and along the coastal path with the dogs, her feet pounding the ground furiously, trying to escape Trenow's implications. The storm of the previous night, when the lightning had zigzagged its way across the creek and up through the gardens, had blown itself out and in the early spring morning the sky and sea merged into pale, subtle streaks of silver-blue and aquamarine, all rinsed sparklingly clean by the rain. A flock of kittiwakes dotted the calm sea ahead of her, their yellow bills and black wingtips marking them out from other gulls bobbing between dinghies and fishing boats in the shallows.

Despite the freshness of the cool air and the sharp tang of sea salt on her lips, Olivia was weary. Throughout the night, she had tossed and turned in time with the waves crashing in the distance, her mind spinning through every worry she'd ever had and adding all her new ones. After little sleep, she had woken with a racing heart and a sick feeling in her stomach. Her first thought was that Libby was dead. As was George. And Mollie. And everyone who'd ever truly loved her. The only way to escape from the painful emotions swirling around her heart was to do what she'd done since she was ten years old; run hard.

The south-easterly winds were strong on the exposed cliff path, and Olivia concentrated on stretching her legs out to the steady beat of a fishing boat engine chugging along offshore. Her thoughts turned to Libby and how they'd become friends. Olivia had been working ridiculously long hours when she'd first arrived; concentrating on the Goods Shed membership plans and building works during the day and then staying late into the evenings to deal with her American clients. She had been grateful that Libby and Martin, who were more like the people she socialised with in New York than many other members, had noticed her long working hours. They'd quickly befriended her and often persuaded her to go out with them after they had finished their own long days.

At any other time, Olivia now admitted to herself, she would have been more cautious about confiding in someone she barely knew, but she had gauged that Libby was a free spirit and not the sort of person to sit in judgement on her long-term plans. She hadn't for a moment thought Libby would tell other people at the Goods Shed. Then she gave herself a mental shake. She should never have trusted Libby and now she was paying the price. But nothing could make her friend's death any less awful. Who would do such a horrific thing?

The memory of Trenow's enquiries as to her whereabouts on the night of Libby's death propelled Olivia to the highest point of that stretch of the coast path, her initial feelings of panic and fear subsiding. It was ridiculous of the detectives to suggest that she could murder anyone. The memory of Martin's voice, calmly telling the police how he had stayed the night with her, sent a shiver down her spine. It scared her that she couldn't remember anything that had happened after Martin had cooked her supper. She remembered eating the risotto he'd cooked and her foolish decision to try and numb the raw pain of betrayal and humiliation with alcohol. Now, in the cold light of day her heart tightened at the thought of the honest and potentially embarrassing conversation she needed to have with Martin.

***

After she'd showered., Olivia pulled on her day-to- day black skinny jeans and flat boots. For some much-needed comfort she selected one of Mollie's many vintage Liberty cotton shirts from her closet. She wore them a lot in New York when she wanted to feel close to her godmother and they had become her trademark work uniform. Back at Tresillian there was another wardrobe full of them and she buried her nose in their soft fabric, fancying she could still smell Mollie's perfume on them. Adding a fleece, she and the dogs weaved their way through the garden to the converted coach house at the top of the drive, stopping occasionally to survey the damage caused by the storm. Twigs and branches scattered the lawn, but the daffodils and snowdrops had survived the battering of the wind and stood tall and proud in the morning breeze. In true Cornish style, the storm had marched off to the east, and it was clear that the sun would be today's victor in the battle of the elements. The sky was a perfect blue with only a few small, steam-train puffs of delicate white cloud drifting out towards the horizon. Olivia took several deep breaths of the fortifying fresh sea air that Mollie had always told her would give her the courage to face anything and prayed that they would at least get her through the next few hours.

Cassie's substantial, round figure swathed in taupe and cream linen layers bustled out of the coach house and gathered Olivia to her ample bosom in a swift and single movement. 'I'm so sorry, my lovely. How are you doing?'

The older woman's familiar embrace was too much for

42

Olivia, and the tears she had been fighting all morning started trickling down her cheeks.

'I can't believe she'd dead, Cass. It's just all so awful . . .' her voice broke.

Cassie put both arms round Olivia's shoulders, her voice calm and comforting. 'It's okay to be upset, my lovely.' Cassie's local accent was warm and soothing as she ushered her inside. 'You've had a terrible shock. You're allowed to cry.'

Olivia leant into her much sturdier friend's shoulder and breathed in the comforting smell of home baking and fresh coffee and felt herself relax for a moment, thanking the universe again for sending Cassie to them. Olivia's concern about her godparents' uncharacteristic impulsiveness at hiring Cassie as a live-in housekeeper and gardening assistant had soon been eased by regular positive updates and then vanished completely on meeting her. With her blinding smile, engaging charm and can-do attitude, they were all soon left wondering how they had ever managed without her. She hugged Cassie and then moved away to stare at the birdfeeder outside, teeming with garden birds lured to the garden with her special seed.

Sighing, Cassie rearranged one of the linen scarves draped artistically around her neck and then poured two mugs of steaming coffee. She gesticulated for Olivia to sit down. 'You're putting too much pressure on yourself, my lovely. You need to slow down.' She looked more closely at Olivia and tutted to herself. 'You also need to eat something. Willow's dropped off some of your favourites in case you came over for breakfast, as she didn't feel she could intrude up at the house. She wanted me to let you know that your meeting is still on if you're feeling up to it. But I told her she should postpone it.'

'No, it's okay.' Olivia blew her nose. 'I know how anxious she is for the café to open. A lot hangs on it for her and Fraser, so we need to press on if we're going to meet our deadline.' She pushed her uneaten croissant aside.

'You can't carry on like this, Olivia. You've just had another awful shock and you're not a robot. You need to grieve. For Mollie, George and now Libby . . .'

A sudden volley of barking announced another visitor.

'Take that disgusting thing off, Kitten. I've told you countless times not to bring it into my house,' Cassie snapped at her daughter with untypical impatience.

'Hi, Mum.' Kitten dropped an affectionate kiss on her head and threw her rather dubious coat into a nearby corner. The dogs took an immediate interest in it. Zennor quickly turned her pointy nose up and sat as far away from it as possible. Mylor sniffed it and began circling enthusiastically, looking as though he was about to add to its already pungent smell. That led to more squealing from Kitten until Cassie made a very pointed show of removing the offending item and taking it downstairs to the laundry room.

Kitten took advantage of her mother's brief absence to take a quick sip from her mug and settle herself down opposite Olivia. She helped herself to a croissant, before looking directly at her, narrowing her mascara-spiked eyelashes.

'How's it going, Olive?' There were only two people in the world who were allowed to call her Olive, and Kitten was one of them.

'Not great.' Olivia didn't elaborate.

'So I've heard.' Kitten's voice was muffled by croissant as she brushed flaky crumbs from her T-shirt emblazoned with the slogan 'There is no Planet B'. 'And I should think the rest of Cornwall has heard by now, judging by the rumblings in the village. I'm not really sure how we can combine our aims for the café of focusing on community and kindness with one of the members being murdered on the premises. How's that going to be good for business?'

Olivia winced. 'Not funny, Kitten.'

'It's not meant to be.' Kitten ran her hand through her pink cropped hair. 'And I'm sorry for what's happened, but this could have a negative impact on everything we're working towards.' She reddened. 'Oh, I know she was your friend, but Libby and I never really had much that I common.'

'Really?' Olivia tilted her head to one side. 'I thought everyone round here was singing from the same hymn sheet?'

'Let's just say the tune was the same, but some of our words were different.' Kitten looked down at her croissant. and wiped her mouth, carefully dabbing between her lip and nose piercings. 'Martin was always much more her type. And talking of Martin, the word around the Goods Shed is that the police are checking out everyone's alibi, and Martin is apparently yours. That's a bit of a turn up for the books, isn't it?'

'Stop your smutty innuendos right there, young lady,' Cassie interrupted as she returned, preventing Olivia from asking her own question. 'It's nice to know Olivia's got Martin looking after her.'

Olivia ran her finger round the rim of her mug, not looking at either of them. 'Martin's just being a good friend.'

'Exactly.' Cassie declared. 'He's an honourable man. And a kind one too. He was good to George in his last few months. He even went out of his way to bring his post down the drive every single day to save him the walk.'

While Olivia allowed herself a small smile at Martin's typical act of kindness, Kitten pulled a face at her mother's back as she topped up the coffee and winked at Olivia.

'I didn't know that. Why didn't you just take George's post down to him, and save Martin the job?'

Cassie's face developed a slightly pink flush, and she picked up a croissant and examined it appreciatively.

'Well, we sort of got into the routine of Martin popping in here for coffee and a chat.'

Kitten burst into laughter.

'Mum! You are way too old for him. I get that he's a nice guy and good-looking and all that, but I would have thought you'd learnt your lesson about younger men from Dad.'

Anxious to stop a familiar family argument from starting, Olivia jumped in quickly.

'Don't read too much into it, Kitten, Martin just happened to be there when I needed him. Fortunately. And I hope you don't think I've been spending all my time with Martin and Libby at the expense of my other friends.' She paused. 'I think they made me miss New York a little less . . .'

Kitten nodded. 'I guessed that, Olive.' She looked down at her mismatched ripped tights, oddly shaped miniskirt, and huge boots and grimaced. 'Like I said . . .'

Olivia shook her head sadly. 'Yeah well, look where it got me.' She pulled herself together. 'I should have finished the final amendments to the plans for your flat the weekend. Rocky's already up to second fix in the café, so when he's finished, he can just move upstairs and carry on.'

Kitten brightened. 'So, d'you reckon I'll be in before we open?' She flashed a smile at Cassie. 'As much as I love being here with Mum, it will be good to have my own place again.'

'If all goes to plan, yes.' Olivia was unsure which woman looked more relieved. 'I promised you, Kitten. And you know I never renege on a promise.'

'Thanks.' Kitten's small, cat-shaped face suddenly hardened, and her amber eyes flashed. 'Talking of promises, was what Libby said in the Goods Shed, true? About you selling up and going back to New York?'

Heat flooded Olivia's face. 'That's not what I said. I

would never sell!'

'Just about everyone in the Goods Shed is talking about what Libby said, that you'd told her it was your plan—'

'Libby said lots of things that were completely out of order and untrue from what I've heard,' Cassie interrupted her daughter once more. 'You know better than to believe Olivia would do that to everyone here after all George and Mollie worked for.'

'Do I, Olivia?' Kitten poured herself more coffee, stirred in milk and two sugars.

Like a mouse being slowly tortured, Olivia was unable to move from the gleaming hazel eyes.

'Okay, so I might have confided to Libby about how overwhelmed I was feeling, and how much easier it would be if I could just go back to Manhattan and my life there, and not have to worry about anyone else. Can you blame me for that?' She took a deep breath. 'There's a massive difference between feeling protective towards a place like Penbartha station and then finding myself completely responsible for it. Not to mention all the people who have given up their old lives upcountry to come down to Cornwall to start afresh. And the villagers and others who will benefit.' She paused to draw breath. 'But Libby took my words out of context and embroidered what I had said to make it look really bad.' Olivia's voice broke. 'I'm sorry, Kitten, but I didn't say those things Libby accused me of. You've got to believe me.'

'She does believe you, love,' Cassie jumped in. 'Everyone who knows you will believe you.'

Olivia forced herself to look away from Kitten's challenging gaze. 'Everyone saw me get angry and lose my temper. And now the person who said all those things is dead.'

'People would have believed you over Libby any day of the week.' Kitten drained her mug. 'You're one of us in a way she never was, Olive. No one thinks you're anything other than the unfortunate person who found her.'

'But what I said is like toothpaste coming out of the tube. You can't ever put it back in. Those words can never be unsaid. And too many people heard them.' Olivia shook her head sadly. 'And they also heard Libby say I wasn't up to the job, and she didn't know why George had any faith in me. That I was only paying lip service to sustainability so I could charge premium rents and that I didn't have an ethical bone in my body. And now she's dead!'

Kitten narrowed her eyes. 'We can't do anything about that, Olive. Yes, it's awful that she's dead. But we have to leave it to the police to track down whoever it was who killed her. In the meantime, you have to prove that everything she said about you was wrong. Isn't that the obvious thing to do?'

'I don't really have a choice, do I?' Olivia ran her fingers over the smooth surface of the stone hanging round her neck.

'Not from where I'm standing, Olive. You owe George and Mollie. They took you in when your parents couldn't cope. They gave you a home. Supported you through school, uni and everything. You owe them. This is what they dreamed about for Penbartha and you're the one they trusted to do it.'

'And what if I can't?' Panic made her voice rise.

'This isn't just about you, Olive.'

'I know that, and I'm here, aren't I?' Olivia watched Cassie's tame blackbird fly down to perch on the balcony outside the window where it started tapping his foot impatiently for his sultanas. 'It's just not the same without George and Mollie.'

Kitten's mouth fell open. 'How can you say that? You've got such a connection to this village, to the station and to Tresillian. It's in your DNA. You're living in George and Mollie's home, looking at the same views they looked at all day. All their hopes and dreams for you and for Penbartha station are embedded in the walls. How can you not feel close to them?'

Her words sliced through Olivia, and she struggled to hold on to her tears. Once again, Kitten went in for the kill.

'But perhaps Libby had a point.' The hazel eyes flashed again. 'You only stick around when things are going your way, don't you? That's exactly what you've always done in the past. When the going gets tough, you go running. As far away as possible.'

'That's not fair.' Olivia struggled to keep calm. 'I've said I'll see this through, and I meant it.'

'Good.' Kitten got to her feet and gathered her stuff together. 'And I suggest we keep this conversation strictly between the three of us. You don't want to unsettle the members any further, or there won't be anything left to save.'

CHAPTER FIVE

The blue and white police tape, wound around the bent tree trunks, flapped like ticker tape across the walkway as Jago walked towards the old station building. He felt an old familiar tingling of curiosity as his mind sorted facts, snippets of conversation and all the information he'd just heard into clearly defined compartments. He wondered how far the police had got in their investigations. He didn't envy Ross Trenow's job of getting the locals to talk. But if he wanted to find out what had happened, or what people thought had happened, he could do worse than spend a morning in the Goods Shed and the village shops like he just had, listening to the gossip that was still swirling around.

'It's looking good!' he called up to Rocky, who was balancing on top of a ladder that was leaning precariously against the side of the station building, hammer in hand. Tool belt slung casually around his hips; he was pounding the nails with a force that seemed unnecessary even to Jago's limited knowledge of woodwork. The midday sun streamed through the budding branches of the trees and softened the edges of the attractive old granite building. 'I've just been into the village and Willow's sent you some lunch.'

Rocky stopped hammering and looked down, his scowl lifting. 'Now you're talking. I haven't stopped yet today.'

He shoved his hammer back into his tool belt and slipped effortlessly down the ladder, landing next to Jago. Both men gazed upwards to admire his latest handiwork.

'What do you think?'

Jago inspected the cream, decorative wooden awning that now stretched the entire length of the station roof and overhung the platform, just as it would have done in its prime. Rocky had reproduced the fancy wooden darting that fringed the canopy, an exact replica of the original detail so distinctive of the Great Western Railway.

'It's the perfect finishing touch,' Jago said. 'You were right about those old station photos from George's stash coming in handy. He'd have been delighted with it.'

Rocky grinned. 'I hope so. I only remember this old girl at her worst, from when I was a kid. She's been neglected for too long. It's been great working to get her back to looking like she did in her heyday.'

'You can hardly tell the difference between the old and the new roof tiles now it's all finished.' Jago's hand shielded his eyes against the sun. 'Even the PV and solar water panels don't look too obtrusive, and I wasn't convinced about them.'

'Well, that's what I'm all about now,' Rocky said. 'As Kitten keeps reminding me, we only have one planet, and we have to look after it.'

Jago had attended a few Goods Shed meetings where Kitten had shared her views, at some length and with enormous zeal, on environmental topics, so he moved on quickly.

'And you're onto the inside now? May I look?'

'As you've brought me lunch, I will allow you a sneaky peek, just don't tell Olivia or Kitten. And watch where you put your feet. I've only just had the lads carry all the wood panelling over from the workshop this morning. It's taken me weeks to get it finished with everything else going on and it's all over the place, waiting to be fitted.'

Jago followed Rocky, stepping carefully through the entrance doors. He breathed in the clean smell of new plaster and fresh paint. Dazzling sunlight poured in from the eight arched windows either side of the huge open room. The old wood panelled interior, previously divided into six different dark areas, including the booking hall, waiting rooms and stationmaster's office, had been transformed. Despite his original misgivings about the change of use of the old building, he had to admit it looked good and said so.

'Thanks. I know you weren't convinced to begin with,' Rocky said. 'But all the original panelling had been ripped out before George bought it and the waiting rooms and offices were far too small as they were. I accept you purists don't like this much change but there's no point in preserving a building in aspic if you can't use it for anything. And we've got so many of these beautiful old industrial buildings in Cornwall whose original purpose is redundant that it makes sense to give them a new purpose.' Rocky paused for a moment. 'They call it adaptive re-use in America,' he pulled a face. 'And it's Olive's speciality over there. She's done a fantastic job of reimagining the space here, if you ask me, without compromising its sense of history.'

Jago nodded. 'Does both of you doing the same kind of work help, or do your ideas clash?' He couldn't imagine ever working with Olivia.

Rocky grinned. 'Rarely, if at all. We've both always liked buildings with history, with stories to tell. And we both really enjoy the eco-renovation side of things, like we've done here.' He waved his arm around. 'It's pure coincidence we ended up doing the same kind of work. But Olive's work is on a much larger scale than mine. She deals with ten, twenty storey Manhattan warehouses and other massive buildings.'

'And big teams of builders, I presume?'

Rocky sighed and walked across to a pile of timber. 'Lucky her.' He paused, suddenly looking harassed. 'I have so much work on, Jago, and not just here. I can't tell you how pushed I am at the moment. We got those old railways sleepers to make the counter area and the furniture. If I can get it all done in time ... And Kitten's on at me all the time to get this finished ASAP, as it will be her baby. Not to mention the flat upstairs.'

Jago glanced round the cluttered room. 'You can't have too much heavy stuff left to do now?'

'Not heavy stuff, no. But it's always the small things that take the time. The sparks have just finished the low energy electrics, and now we need to get all this panelling in and painted, not to mention the underfloor heating, fitting the kitchen out and finishing all the furniture. I really should have outsourced that bit of the job.' He leant against the nearest pile of timber and the bright light from the windows showed up the dark rings under his eyes.

'Oh, God. I hate jobs with such strict deadlines.' His face was glum. 'Deadlines are very upcountry.'

Jago laughed and gestured outside, into the sunshine. Despite the brightness there was a cooling breeze now coming off the creek, bringing its usual scent of salt and seaweed.

'Come over to the Signal Box for a cup of tea and your lunch from Willow. You need a change of scene.'

They wandered outside together.

'What do you reckon to all this business with Libby Walsh?' Jago asked casually.

Rocky tossed his hard hat to one side, and they strolled across to the Signal Box, nodding hello to passing dog walkers making the most of the spring sunshine.

'Most people think she probably had a tiff with some upcountry boyfriend, and it went too far.' He eventually spoke. 'That's what I've heard. And folk hope that whoever did this will have left Cornwall by now.'

Jago frowned. 'People certainly don't seem to be that upset or troubled about it all. Or even think anyone else might be in danger.'

'Well, that probably tells you all you need to know about Libby Walsh.' Rocky's retort was sharp. 'She really didn't have much to do with anyone other than Martin Lambert before Olive came back. She didn't mix with the other members or us locals like most of the Goods Shed lot do. I must say I was a bit surprised when she became so pally with Olive. And even more so when Olive went along with it.' His voice hardened.

'But Olivia got on well with her?'

Rocky grunted. 'Olive's moved around so much she's learned how to get on with most people.'

Present company excepted, Jago mused. He turned and led the way up the steps into the Signal Box and tossed a treat to a welcoming Steren, who demolished it in a single gulp before retreating to her basket. Rocky settled himself on the sofa as Jago made two pint-sized mugs of tea.

'That was a big argument they had in the Goods Shed from what I've heard.'

Rocky narrowed his eyes, and Jago cursed himself for being so blunt. 'Depends who you listen to.'

'Alice gave me the edited highlights.'

'You know more than me then.'

Jago tried again. 'Apparently, Libby told Olivia she wasn't up to the job and that everyone thought the same, or words to that effect.'

Rocky snorted. 'I doubt Olive would have been bothered by that. She deals with contractors and builders all the time. She'll have heard worse.'

Jago took a long sip of tea. 'She got quite personal, according to Alice. And then revealed that Olivia was planning on selling up and going back to New York as soon as she could.'

'No way.' Rocky's knuckles tightened round his mug.

'According to Alice, Olivia told Libby to keep out of her way until she had calmed down. Or she wouldn't be responsible for her actions. And I reckon Alice really thought she meant it.'

Rocky shook his head and took a loud swallow of tea. 'No way. But Libby must have really pushed her buttons to get her to say that.' He glared at Jago. 'I hear you've been sniffing around. What else have you discovered?'

'Nothing.' Jago was honest. 'People round here are tight-lipped when it comes to their own. I might be Cornish, but because I'm from the north of the county, I may as well be from Pluto as far as the villagers here are concerned.' He frowned. 'The police will find it tough getting to the bottom of a murder in a place like this. It's small, off the beaten track, and everyone knows everyone else.'

The scowl was back on Rocky's face. 'Exactly. They need to stop poking around as well. Local folk all respect Olive and won't like the police asking questions about her. They'll close ranks.'

'Do you think most of the villagers are in favour of what's going on at the Goods Shed and station?' Jago asked.

Rocky set down his mug. 'Why wouldn't they be? It's boosting the local economy and bringing more life to the village. And what folk really like about it is a lot of the members go home at night and leave Penbartha to us locals.'

'So, you don't think Libby was murdered because she was connected to the Goods Shed?'

'No, I don't,' Rocky spoke through gritted teeth. 'I'm not going to pretend I have the first idea about what's going on, but what I do know is that what she said to Olive will have caused a shit-load of problems we can do without.'

Jago persisted. 'Do you know anything about this upcountry boyfriend?'

Rocky shrugged. 'No. And I'm not interested. But if Libby had taken against Olive, despite making out to be her best friend, I reckon he did us all a favour.'

The harshness of Rocky's tone surprised him into silence. He handed Rocky a brown paper bag containing his lunch from Willow, and the two men munched their fresh baguettes in peace. Jago screwed up his bag, threw it into the recycling section of the bin and, conscious of the touchiness of the other man, swallowed hard.

'How can you be so sure Olivia didn't do it?' He could almost feel Rocky bristling.

'Look, Jago, I don't understand your sudden interest in Olive.' He scrunched his own bag. 'But you'll just have to trust me. I've known Olive practically all my life. And she wouldn't hurt a fly. We played together as kids when the Wells family came down here in the holidays, staying at Tresillian. They were always down here in the early years. The four of us kids were as thick as thieves.'

'The four of you?'

'Yeah. Me and my brother Jory. Olive and her brother, Aidan. She was a real tomboy and up for anything, no matter how risky or crazy. One of the boys. With bollocks.' Rocky's face clouded over. 'Things were different after Aidan died.'

Jago sat up straighter. 'How did he die?'

Rocky growled. 'It was a tragic accident. Nothing to do with Oliva, if that's what you're getting at.'

'How were things different after he died?'

'We were kids. Three's an odd number. My brother moved on to other friends. But Olive and I always stayed close. Like siblings, really. We even looked alike back then and had the same colouring and everything. Aidan was fair with blue eyes, like their mum and dad. And when Olive came down here to live with George and Mollie, we spent even more time together. Even though she went to the posh school in Truro, and I went to the local school here, we've stayed close mates for all these years.'

'And you don't think Olivia would be capable of something like this?'

Rocky knocked over his mug as he sprang to his feet. He stood right in front of Jago, his jaw tight. 'Read my lips. No Way. I know she didn't do it. And I'll do anything I can to protect her. So back off!'

Jago raised both hands. He was in no doubt about how protective Rocky felt towards Olivia.

'No problem. Can I ask you one more thing, though?'

'Depends what it is.' Rocky glared and sat back down.

'Why on earth do you call her Olive?'

Rocky threw back his head and laughed, his strong white teeth gleaming in his tanned face, and he suddenly looked years younger and happier.

'It was my grandad's name for her. He was a great fan of the cartoon *Popeye* and had all the old VHS videos, which he made us all watch again and again. Olive Oyl was tall and skinny with dark hair and dark eyes, so the name sort of stuck.'

'She really doesn't look anything like an Olive though,' Jago said.

'That was the point,' Rocky said, draining the dregs from his mug. 'She wore prescription glasses from about fourteen, but as soon as she could afford it when she qualified as an architect, she had laser eye surgery. Problem now is that she can't read a damn thing up close and has to wear reading glasses.'

Jago nodded, recalling that she usually had a pair hooked through her curls at the trustees' meetings, and often another pair on her nose or around her neck.

'She's hopeless with them though,' Rocky commented fondly. 'Loses them all the time. She now buys cheap ones by the dozen from QVC or somewhere, in all colours, shapes and sizes and leaves pairs everywhere. I always say that you can tell where she's been by just following the trail of discarded reading glasses. But whenever I feel guilty about her nickname, I remind myself that it was her who started calling me Rocky.'

Jago raised an eyebrow.

'You don't think I was christened Rocky, do you? Petroc is my proper name. When I came up with Olive, she took her sweet revenge and thought of the most equally inappropriate name she could for a short, skinny and puny boy.' He sighed. 'I hated those bloody films.'

Jago observed Rocky's arm and shoulder muscles straining the seams of his Falmouth Eagles Rugby T-shirt. 'No need for you to worry now though.'

Rocky shrugged. 'Like I said, Olive's like a sister to me and anyone who messes with her has me to answer to.'

Jago nodded firmly and ventured to ask another question, choosing his tone carefully.

'How is she coping with all of this?'

Rocky's glare swept round the Signal Box and finally rested on Jago.

'She seems okay. Her first instinct may have been to do a bunk, but she's come back from New York to see this thing through and that is what she'll go all out to do. Now, can I ask you a question?'

'Fire away.'

'Why the sudden interest in Olivia? She's been back for weeks, and I haven't noticed you paying her the slightest attention before now.' Rock's black eyes didn't move from Jago's face.

He decided to be honest. 'I don't know really. Perhaps because I get a bad feeling about what's going on here and I . . .'

Steren jumped to her feet, sniffing the air anxiously and growling deep in her throat. Jago looked out of the window and stiffened. 'What the hell's going on out there?'

Rocky rushed over to the window. 'Oh, my God! It looks like smoke!'

They both charged towards the door. Rocky got there first, shouting over his shoulder. 'It's definitely smoke. Coming from the station . . . Shit! The timber and panelling . . . Shit, shit, shit! Call 999.'

CHAPTER SIX

Olivia followed the grassy spine of the quiet lane that wound its way from Tresillian House down the south bank of the creek towards the village, happy to let the spring beauty of her surroundings distract her from thoughts of Libby and Kitten's own harsh words. Years of experience had taught her to neatly side-step the damp and marshy places which developed every year as the hedgerows thickened and little streams and natural fountains appeared by magic. A delicious waft of vanilla fragrance made her stop and inhale the scent from a huge branch of magnolia, brought down by the night storm and lying where it had been tossed in a garden alongside the lane. Its gigantic white blooms, with delicate pink tips were in stark contrast to the swaying daffodils and bright tulips and the riot of bright blues, purples, pinks and orangey reds of the rhododendrons and azaleas that filled the well-tended gardens. As a child, Mollie had entertained her for hours with tales of the historic Cornish plant hunters who set sail for distant lands, braving strong seas and unfriendly natives to bring back wonderful subtropical plants and trees that grew as huge in Cornwall as they had in their indigenous countries. Olivia had devoured all her tales and was secretly sure they were responsible for some of her wanderlust.

Birdsong, fresh air, and a glimpse of nautical life had been one of Mollie's favourite remedies for most ills. And Olivia was a great believer in getting outside and reassuring herself that nature was still ticking along at its own pace, regardless of what was going on in the newspapers. By the time she reached the end of the lane, pausing only to wave at the postman as he drove past her at speed, she felt calmer, more grounded, and ready to face whatever the day threw at her. The tide was coming in too quickly to take the shortcut into the village across the glistening creek via the steppingstones, so Olivia followed her preferred path past the boatyard with its pungent smell of tar, round the playing field and across the old stone bridge which had been the scene of many an enthusiastic game of Pooh Sticks throughout her childhood. As she crossed the bridge, she watched a mother duck round up her seven very new ducklings, and a sudden gust of wind blew down the cobbled incline in front of her. She sniffed appreciatively at the mouth-watering smells of freshly baked bread, savoury pastries and delicious cakes wafting on the breeze from her destination.

Olivia was secretly glad that Penbartha was less dependent on tourism than many other Cornish villages. With only one pub, no fancy restaurants and only a scattering of holiday homes, tourists weren't attracted there in large numbers. Most of the permanent residents were local landowners, or worked in fishing, farming and other local industries, so the village remained a quiet, hidden creek-side gem with a close-knit community. And, unusually for many small villages, Penbartha still had several traditional shops. The butcher and fishmonger, post office and newsagent all stood on the creek side of the street, and were dotted among old cottages with thatched roofs, small windows, and latticed porches. Further up the hill, and opposite the stone war memorial, a general store stood slightly back from the pavement, its dark green awning shaded tiered wooden crates displaying brightly coloured fruit, vegetables, plants, and flowers arranged attractively and neatly, with chalked signs declaring their provenance.

The Old Bakehouse stood at the bottom of the hill, in its original location next to the redundant, red village pump. Its two large, white bay windows were framed with immaculate black-and-white striped awnings, giving the bakery a smart and welcoming appearance. However, it was the wonderful smells and enticing window displays which tempted customers over the threshold throughout the day and enveloped them in its yeasty cocoon.

Olivia ran up the steps and through the glossy black door between the bay windows, its old-fashioned bell tinkling in her wake. Willow Jardine stood behind the counter tidying the display, looking like a Nordic goddess, in a freshly laundered and starched white apron embroidered with the Old Bakehouse logo over a black baker's tunic and black and white checked chef's trousers. Tall, slender, and elegant as her name suggested, she wore her sleek blonde hair – for which she had her Danish grandmother to thank – up in a neat twist under her matching checked baker's cap.

'Oh, Olivia!' she exclaimed, rushing to greet her friend. 'I'm so sorry about all the awful things that have been happening. Come and sit down and I'll get you some coffee.' She led Olivia over to the far side of the bakery to one of two small American diner-style booths, mostly used by local pensioners to sit and chat while they waited to be served. Olivia sank onto the bench seat and eased her laptop out of her bag. Willow quickly fetched a cup of coffee and placed it down in front of her friend as she sat opposite her.

'Try this. It's one of the fresh coffees we're trialling for the station café. It's from an amazing local roastery who seem to share our values about sustainability and fair trade. And they've just introduced a carbon neutral courier service—' The bell interrupted her mid-flow. 'Let me just serve this customer. Oh, and Kitten might be late for our meeting. The surfing action group in Falmouth have just called her to photograph the plastic litter dumped on the beaches by last night's storm.' Her face creased into a worried frown. 'They're roping all the local dog walkers to help clear it up, but we really need to stop the stuff getting into the sea in the first place.'

While Willow served her customer, Olivia sipped her coffee, enjoying its rich, smooth taste and took her time to admire the latest improvements to the bakery that Willow and her husband had worked so hard on. Just stepping over the threshold transported her back to the smartest of establishments in the Upper Eastside of Manhattan; all black, white and chrome, exactly the look she knew they had been trying to recreate, with shelves of French and Italian breads, mid-European grain breads, as well as pastries and cakes.

'Do you like the new lights? Rocky had them put in yesterday.'

Having served her customer, Willow returned to her seat and Olivia followed her gaze to the rows of lights hanging above the chrome display cabinets and clapped her lands in delight. A variety of large industrial stainless-steel whisks and beaters had been cleverly upcycled into light pendants that shone down on the displays.

'They're fantastic! Where are on earth did you find them?'

'Rocky, of course. Part man, part womble. He saw them in a skip and asked if he could have them. Then he cleaned them up, got an electrician friend to wire them up and voila! They're fab, aren't they?'

Olivia nodded, a smile on her face. 'That man just can't

help himself! He's a walking advert for the circular economy and has taken dumpster diving to a whole new level. I don't know what I'd do without him and his team.' She paused for a moment. 'Although without him I wouldn't have all this extra eco-renovation work and I'd be able to concentrate on the Goods Shed and the café. I've got a client of his to go to across on the north coast after our meeting here.'

Willow glanced at her watch and craned her neck to look out of the front window.

'Kitten shouldn't be long, and I've got a new focaccia in the oven for you both to try.' She looked again at her watch and sighed crossly. 'Heaven knows where Sarah is. She didn't turn up at all yesterday, and she's supposed to be covering my lunchtime shift so I can talk to you guys about the menu for the station café. I sometimes wish I'd never agreed with Clara to take her on.'

'I thought she'd be helping Libby out while Clara's away?' Olivia kept her voice steady as she opened her slim laptop and spread some drawings on the table.

Willow's face hardened, making her high cheekbones even more pronounced. 'Apparently, she didn't need her. So when Clara had to go up north, she asked me whether I could find some work for Sarah here in her absence. And as Clara had put in a kind word for us with so many catering companies when we first opened, I felt obliged to help.' Her voice took on a harsh tone. 'You know how they say that no good deed goes unpunished?' She left the sentence hanging, picked up a drawing and inspected it. 'This is looking good.'

Olivia decided to change the subject. 'Is Fraser here today?'

'He's had to pop out for a while. To see some suppliers.' Willow's usually shining blue eyes clouded, and Olivia thought she was about to say something else, but she reached across the table and took her hand. 'Do you want to talk about what's been happening with you? It might help.'

With a deep sigh, Olivia told Willow everything. The entire tale took a while to get through, with constant interruptions by local customers, all of whom insisted on making a point of talking to Olivia and making their unspoken support for her clear.

Willow's eyes widened once she finally recounted yesterday's events at Tresillian. 'Well, thank God for Martin! But I hadn't realised you and he were an item.'

'We're not,' Olivia wiped her eyes. 'Despite what you may have heard on the grapevine.' She managed a weak smile and rummaged about in her tote bag.

Willow caught hold of her friend's hands and examined them. 'I don't think I ever saw you in Manhattan without beautifully manicured nails.' She looked up. 'Or straight hair.'

Olivia looked down, sighed, and then instinctively touched her wild curls. 'I'm not sure many of my colleagues at Olivarez would recognise me at the moment, without my weekly trips to the nail bar, beautician and hairstylist.' She forced another small smile. 'I guess I just went along with it because it fitted better with my image at work there. Whereas those kinds of things don't really matter here.'

Willow examined her own short nails. 'You seem to have adapted really well to life back here after being in New York for so long. Even your accent has lessened. So, how are you finding it, honestly?'

Olivia remembered Kitten's warning words and just smiled. 'Okay, but it can be claustrophobic at times.'

Tears filled Willow's eyes. 'Oh, Olivia. I could never describe this village as claustrophobic. Sometimes I feel as though Fraser and I will never be truly accepted here. It's so tightly knit I reckon the only reason we've lasted this long is because we bake excellent bread and are friends with you, and Kitten, Cassie and George, bless him.' She pulled a pair of reading glasses out of her apron pocket and handed them to Olivia. 'You left them here the last time we met.'

Olivia took them gratefully and rested them in her curls, silently wishing she wasn't part of quite such a close community, where most people were related by either marriage or blood and were either best friends or sworn enemies. And where everything was shared and discussed, whether one liked it or not. She considered her friend's point, her head on one side. 'It's not that bad, is it?'

'Oh, they're friendly enough on the surface, but it's as if there's this thin but strong line between acquaintances and friends. And it's looking like it's impossible to cross. Even after more than a year.'

Olivia smiled. 'Uncle George always joked that the locals here don't trust anyone who dares to cross the Tamar until they've been here for at least fifteen years.'

The merry tinkling of the shop bell announced the arrival of a petite, dark-haired girl dressed in the bakery assistant's uniform of black cargo pants and polo shirt. She rushed through to the back of the bakery before re-emerging, tying the Old Bakehouse smart, white apron around her tiny waist. Only then did she seem to register the two women sitting in the booth, her eyes meeting Willow's with a challenging look and turning her back pointedly to occupy herself tidying the bread on the racks and neatening the piles of brown paper bags.

'Sorry I'm late, Willow.' Her voice contained absolutely no hint of apology. Neither did she bother looking up.

'And what about yesterday?' Willow's voice was uncharacteristically sharp. 'Were you too upset about Libby to put in an appearance?'

Sarah's head snapped up, and she glared at Willow through narrowed eyes. 'I thought you'd have heard that I was being questioned by the most obtuse detective I have ever met. Although, I reckon he was just going through the motions, as though he already knows who murdered Libby. He wasn't interested in anything I had to say. Ginger prat!'

Olivia watched Sarah, whose tone and facial expression matched her angry words, and silently agreed with her opinion of Burridge. Willow caught her friend's eye and shook her head and they returned to the plans for the station café, discussing menus and order levels, while Sarah served the lunchtime customers. Aware of Olivia's next appointment and unable to wait for Kitten any longer, Willow went out the back to fetch the bread she wanted her friend to taste. A lull fell in the shop and Sarah fiddled with the raffia used to tie cake boxes. As soon as Olivia caught her eye, she quickly checked that Willow was still busy and hurried over to the booth.

'Can I talk to you about Libby?'

'I thought the police were telling everyone not to discuss their investigation?' Olivia didn't want to get involved in village gossip.

'That Burridge is an idiot. Apparently, one of the members told the police about the bust-up you had with her, and that was all that interested him.'

Olivia's pulse quickened. 'Really?'

'Yes. He didn't ask me a single thing about any other part of Libby's life. Just went on and on about what happened between the two of you the other night.'

'And what did you say?'

Sarah waved the question away with her small hands. 'He wasn't interested in what I had to say. Just carried on asking stupid questions about you.' A crafty look crossed Sarah's face. 'Don't they say that the person who finds the body is usually the killer?'

Olivia could feel the acid churning in her stomach. 'Do they?'

'You seem to be the focus of his investigations so far,

and he's putting everyone's back up. He'll never get the information he needs to discover the killer the way he's going. He might have a West Country name, but he's from Devon and no more one of us than Willow or Fraser. People won't talk to him.'

'What information?'

'The information that's available. Folk round here will only answer the questions he asks, and he's not asking the right ones.'

'I don't understand . . .'

Sarah sighed impatiently. 'It's bad enough that someone has murdered Libby. The idea of the police not catching the right person, and just going with the easy option to help their clear-up rates makes it even worse.'

'But surely they need evidence?' Olivia's heart was still beating fast. Willow's approaching footsteps heralded her arrival. Before she appeared, Sarah spoke quickly.

'Will you help me? I think I can find out more than the police have so far.'

Olivia shook her head firmly. 'We should leave it to the police. I don't want to give them any reason to believe I'm involved. If I start asking questions, it will look suspicious. And I've already got enough on my plate.'

Sarah scowled and stood up. Then, as Willow came entered the shop, she bent down and whispered in Olivia's ear.

'Won't you even consider doing this for old times' sake? The good times you had with Libby? We owe it to her to find out who the murderer is. And hopefully save your neck in the process. Just think about it.'

Willow handed her a slate serving platter. She raised an eyebrow. Olivia, still reeling from Sarah's words, looked away.

'Try it,' Willow urged.

Olivia bit into the flat, oven-baked Italian bread, stuffed with sun-dried tomatoes and creamy feta cheese. She closed her eyes, transported to happier times spent on a sun-warmed Tuscan plaza with a glass of chianti in her hand. Forcing Sarah's words from her mind, she slowly opened her eyes and smiled.

'That,' she proclaimed, 'is Italy in a bite. Delicious. And definitely going on the menu.'

Willow grinned.

'Fraser's really enjoying developing our artisan bread range. And Jago liked it too. He tried some earlier when he popped in to pick up some lunch for him and Rocky.'

The smile vanished from Olivia's face. 'Please don't mention that man's name to me. He disapproves of everything I say or do. Especially at trustees' meetings. No one else is like that with me.'

'That's probably because you're always so antagonistic towards him.' Willow frowned. 'You seem to feel strongly about him.'

'I beg your pardon?' Olivia's voice rose and tears pricked at her eyes. 'Okay, I'll tell you why I feel antagonistic towards him. He's the one who . . .' She bit her lip, unable to continue.

'Who what?'

Olivia changed her mind and dodged the question. 'Everyone seems to think he's some superior being with his stuffy attitude and clever sentences. But we don't hear about all the good things he does for the Goods Shed, do we? Not like Martin.'

'Well, I'm not sure self-promotion is Jago's style.' Willow's tone was mild. 'Ask anyone at the Goods Shed about the help and practical advice he gives them. He has an amazing way of grasping ideas and coming up with brilliant suggestions. Fraser's always bouncing ideas off him. And he's kind.'

'Is he?' Olivia swallowed the last of her bite, licked the salt from her lips and scowled.

Willow chuckled. 'Oh, come on, Olivia, Jago's a nice guy.

And if I wasn't married, I'd consider him extremely attractive. A real silver fox.'

'Ugh. Willow. What would Fraser say?'

Her smile vanished. 'I'm not sure he'd even notice.'

Olivia looked at her friend with concern. 'What's the matter, Willow? You can tell me.'

'To be honest? I'm not sure, really. And you've got enough problems of your own. You don't need to hear mine.'

A gentle smile softened the worry on Olivia's face. 'That's what friends are for. What is it that Rocky always says? A problem shared is a problem dragged out until bedtime?'

'I can just imagine him saying that.' Willow laughed, and Olivia realised it was a sound she hadn't heard for a long time.

A fire engine flashed by the window, heading down the street, its siren harsh and ear-splitting. Then another. Both women darted to the window. As they rushed out of the door a wild, dishevelled figure with unmistakably pink hair was running down the street.

'Fire! Quickly! The station is on fire!'

CHAPTER SEVEN

'Out of the building! Get out! Leave it to us now.'

'It's nearly out!' Rocky yelled back. 'Don't ruin everything with loads of water. Please!'

Jago barely heard the reply as two firefighters grabbed him and physically hauled him out of the building. He sprawled on the walkway, coughing smoke from his lungs and gulping for fresh air. His clothes were filthy, his mouth tasted like an old ashtray, and he wondered if he would ever be able to smell anything again, other than the pungent soot that seemed to have adhered itself to the inside of his nostrils. Rocky was forcing himself to his knees beside him.

'Thanks for your help in there.' His voice rasped against the smoke in his throat. 'We needed both extinguishers. I couldn't have done it alone.'

Jago shrugged off his thanks, running his tongue around his lips, seeking moisture.

'You could have just walked away.'

Jago turned towards the other man, his eyes stinging and red. 'Why would I?' he croaked.

'Oh, God' Rocky turned his head towards a sound of shrieking voices and running footsteps. 'That's all we need.' He collapsed back onto the ground.

Jago pushed himself upright to face the three women running towards the station. Kitten, responsible for most of the shrieking, arrived first. Olivia was at her heels, while Willow, impeded by her black bakery clogs, brought up the rear. He was vaguely aware of a crowd gathering on the far side of the station and recognised two greenies from the Goods Shed and some local dog walkers being held back by the barriers hastily erected by the Fire and Rescue Service.

'Let me through! Let me through! I have water for those poor men. Let me through, now!'

Jago had never been so pleased to see Alice Greville. The fresh-faced firefighter, charged with the responsibility of keeping onlookers at bay, did not even attempt to hold her back. He gratefully snatched the bottles of water Alice handed to him, passed one to Rocky and the two men stood gulping thirstily, surveying the damage through streaming eyes.

Once he could swallow without pain, Jago tuned in to what was going on around him. Everyone's eyes were trained on the station building where all the windows and doors were being thrown open by the firefighters, and dark grey smoke was slowly seeping out. Kitten was still wailing, Rocky was trying to comfort her, while Willow stood wringing her hands in despair. Only Olivia was silent and still, slightly apart from the others.

'Who's in charge here?' A firefighter, wearing a white helmet with a black comb-like stripe stretching from its peak and down to the base, which Jago assumed meant he was the boss, emerged from the building, removing his breathing apparatus.

Kitten stepped forward, but Rocky pushed Olivia ahead of her. 'Olivia is.'

He nodded at Rocky and addressed Olivia. 'Max Gordon, the Watch Manager. It might not look it, but I think you've been lucky here. The fire didn't have time to take hold, thanks to the early intervention, but there is quite a lot of smoke damage.'

Jago had to strain to hear Olivia's response. 'Have you any idea how it started?'

The Watch Manager took off his helmet and shook his head. 'Not yet. We're still looking, and I've radioed for the Fire Investigator to come down ASAP. First, I must question the men who were working here.'

Rocky put his hand on Olivia's shoulder and stepped ahead of her. 'That's me. And my two lads. Who are over there.' He pointed to the diminishing crowd of onlookers, who were losing interest and wandering away once everything was under control. His apprentices were hopping from foot to foot on the far side of the barrier and looking worried.

'Right. We need to talk. Over here.' He led Rocky over to where they stood, and they were all soon huddled deep in conversation.

'When can we see the damage?' Kitten whimpered. 'All my plans and dreams may have gone up in smoke.'

'Oh, shut up, Kitten! You're not the only one whose future is on the line here. Why does everything always have to be about you?'

The harsh words, so unexpectedly from the gentle and kind Willow, stunned everyone into silence.

Alice recovered herself first. 'I think we all need a nice cup of tea.' She patted Willow's arm, her cheeks pink with worry.

'Let's wait in the Signal Box,' Jago suggested. 'We can keep our eye on things from up there until they let us back in.'

***

He guided Willow and Kitten to opposite ends of the chesterfield, ensuring that they sat as far away from each other as possible. For the second time in two days, Olivia sat on the floor, her back straight against the wall, arms folded tightly against her chest. She didn't take her eyes off the café opposite, doing a better job than Jago at blocking out the bickering going on around her. Once again, he was relieved to hear Alice scurrying up the wooden staircase. She came in bearing a tray holding a large teapot, milk jug, cups, and a plate of biscuits. Jago took it from her, smiling.

'Thanks Alice. You're a gem.'

She blushed an even brighter pink than usual. 'My pleasure, Mr Trevithick. If there's anything else I can do, you just have to ask.'

'You've already done more than enough, Alice.' He steered her to the door. 'I'll bring the tea things back later.'

Willow poured tea and passed the mugs around. Olivia sipped hers slowly, absently fondling Steren's short ears as the dog sat at her feet and rested her big gentle head on her knee, waiting for a biscuit. Jago retreated with his mug to his safe place, behind his newspaper and tried to ignore Kitten who was still mithering about her plans.

'I just need to know where I stand,' she repeated, for at least the sixth time.

'Don't we all.' Willow abandoned her mug, jumped up and stood right in front of the younger girl. Jago peered out from behind his newspaper.

'It's not so bad for you, Willow.' Kitten leapt to her feet too and glared upwards. 'You've already got a business which is doing well. And a home. This is a whole new start for me.'

Jago lowered a corner of *The Times* to watch Olivia's reaction, but her eyes were closed, her arms wrapped round her knees.

Willow flung her baker's cap to the floor and sank back down onto the sofa.

'Yes. We've got a business we've sunk all our life

savings into. And a home over the top of it so we can never get away. For which we gave up everything and everyone we knew in Edinburgh. To come down here where we're still treated as outsiders.'

Kitten waved her hand dismissively.

'You just have to work at that. Mum and I had to make an effort to get involved when we moved here, even though Mum's Cornish. It works both ways, you know.'

'And you don't think we haven't worked at it?' Willow's voice rose. 'When you work all the hours Fraser and I do, it's sometimes hard to muster up the energy to cook an evening meal, never mind go to a village Beetle Drive in someone's front room, or some other height of sophistication.'

'Well, don't complain if you can't be bothered.'

'I'm sure it's not a case of being bothered,' Olivia spoke up from her place at the window. She crossed the room and stood between the warring friends and took a deep breath.

'Come on, both of you. Let's not fight amongst ourselves. We need to pull together, now more than ever.' Her voice was firm, but Jago sensed she was battling to keep calm for her friends' sake. 'We'll soon find out what we are up against and then we can face it and make a plan. It's the not knowing that's the worst thing.'

Willow suddenly crumpled, tears trickling down her pale cheeks. 'I'm sorry, Olivia. It's just one or two things have been happening lately that have unsettled me.'

'That's understandable. Libby's murder has impacted everyone massively. We're all on edge.'

'It's not that.'

'What then?' Olivia knelt at her friend's knee and touched her arm. Jago leant forward.

'We've had a few incidents.'

'What sort of incidents?'

Willow plucked at her checked chef's trousers. 'Well, on

75

a couple of occasions our supplies haven't been delivered, so we couldn't bake certain items, and when we rang the suppliers, they said someone had called and cancelled the orders.'

'Did they say who? Male? Female?' The question slipped out of Jago without him even realising.

Willow turned tearful eyes to him, and he lowered his paper even further. 'We didn't ask. We were too anxious to get the orders reinstated as soon as possible. And although we lost some business, we thought it was just a mix-up to begin with.'

'And now?' Jago prompted.

'A couple of the restaurants we supply with bread and pastries just cancelled their orders for no reason. Sarah took that call. So, when Fraser didn't turn up with the delivery, they rang and got very upset that we had let them down.' She sniffed. 'And then we had to offer all sorts of discounts to get them to order with us again, so we hardly make any money from those customers now. That's why we are so desperate to secure this contract for the station café. It could be the making or breaking of us.'

Olivia looked horrified. 'Oh, Willow. Why didn't you tell me any of this?'

She burst into noisy tears. 'I didn't want to burden you with my problems. It's only been happening since you came back from New York, and you've got enough to deal with at the moment with everything else that's going on.'

Jago sat back in his chair. That was an interesting turn of events Fraser hadn't confided in him. Olivia put her arms round Willow. Much as he was reluctant to admit it, Olivia's handling of the situation impressed him. She could clearly do without two warring friends either side of her to add to everything else she was dealing with, yet she still managed to show concern and understanding for her friends. She moved away and spoke with what, to Jago's ears, was forced optimism.

'We'll sort it out, Willow, I promise. You may just need to build some extra checks into your order and sales processes. I'm sure it can be done, quite simply.'

Willow raised her tear-stained face to Olivia. 'Thanks. And I really am sorry to trouble you with our worries.'

Olivia waved her apologies away. 'That's what friends are for. Aren't they, Kitten?' She looked out of the window and over to the station, where Rocky was beckoning them across. 'It looks like they've finished. Let's go over.'

***

'Okay, what's your professional opinion about the damage?' Olivia took back control.

'Well,' Max Gordon said, 'it's nowhere near as bad as it would have been if Rocky hadn't noticed the smoke when he did. But I still don't think we should go in again just yet. You must leave the windows open for as long as possible. You need to get the air circulating to disperse the small particles of carbon that are swirling around.' He excused himself, as a man in a Fire Investigation uniform called him over.

'And I'll get some industrial fans in there overnight. Along with some dehumidifiers to combat the effects of the water.' Rocky spoke up. 'Although thankfully there isn't much water damage, as the fire didn't get much of a chance to take hold. We're lucky the retrofit work we've done so far hasn't been damaged. It's mainly just soot, and some charring to the panelling.'

'But isn't that even harder to get rid of?' Kitten's voice rose by several octaves.

Rocky winced and raised both hands in a gesture of peace.

'Don't panic. Max suggests we wipe all the walls down with white vinegar tomorrow and place big bowls of it around the room for two or three days to absorb the smell.

With lavender oil to make it smell sweeter.'

Olivia nodded. 'I can get you the lavender oil from Mollie's workroom.'

'Thanks, Olive. And apparently, it's a good idea to shake industrial quantities of baking soda all over the floor, to absorb the worst of any odour that may be trapped there.'

'I'll drop some round later,' Willow said.

'Cheers. We need to make sure we've got rid of the particles and odour before we put the screed down for the underfloor heating. We don't want a permanently singed smell in the café, do we?' Rocky's attempt at a smile didn't quite work.

'So how long do you reckon it's set us back by?' Jago noticed that it was Olivia who asked the question that everyone else was afraid to.

Rocky raked his finger through his black curls and down his cheeks, smearing soot across his face and adding to his already piratical appearance.

'In all honesty? At least a week or t—'

'But we haven't got that long,' Kitten's wail interrupted him. 'We open at Easter. Which is four weeks away and we're already up against the wire as it is.'

'Look KittiKat, I'll draft some of the lads in from my other jobs, so we can make up the time. I reckon we'll have to replace and repaint a lot of the woodwork we've already put in, but I'll work round the clock to carve the new panelling that we've lost today. And I doubt there'll be much damage upstairs, as we caught it so quickly, so your flat shouldn't be put back by too much. If we all pull together, we'll do it. I promise.' Rocky took her hands tenderly in his own black and sooty ones.

Jago stared at the tender scene. He hadn't realised there was anything between Rocky and Kitten, other than a common friendship with Olivia. He glanced quickly in her direction and noticed a look of surprise flit across her face, followed by a softening. As Olivia caught his eye and glowered, he allowed his gaze to move on to the others. Kitten looked anxious about the time delay, Willow and Fraser relieved that there was hope, Rocky stressed about all the extra work. His gaze returned to Olivia standing apart and alone, her entire body was rigid. Jago considered himself something of an expert at reading people, but Olivia mystified him. What was going on inside that mind of hers?

'Miss Wells?'

Olivia spun round at the sound of her name as Max Gordon and his colleague approached.

'Yes?'

'I think we've found the source of your fire.'

Everyone gathered round, their attention on the Investigation Officer's right hand. Max Gordon spoke first. 'Rocky here assured me that neither he nor any of his men smoke on or near the site. And a thorough search of the area has revealed no cigarette butts that would suggest otherwise.'

Rocky's sigh of relief blew his black curls away from his face.

'I sense there's a but,' Olivia said, voice unsteady.

The Investigation Officer uncurled the fingers of his right hand. Jago stood back to watch as the others bent forward.

'It's not obvious to the untrained eye, but this is the accelerant used to start this fire.' He registered the blank stares on the faces in front of him and separated out some charred remains in his hand, pointing to each one as he spoke. 'This is a book of matches, to which a cigarette has been attached and wrapped in some paper, and then a piece of cloth or wadding. All secured with a rubber band. When the cigarette is lit, it slowly burns down and ignites the matches which ignite the paper and cloth. It's a crude but very effective accelerant. You guys saw the smoke and got to the fire before it destroyed this evidence.'

'Evidence?' Fraser found his voice first.

'Evidence that this fire was not an accident. Evidence that someone who wanted to destroy this building deliberately started it. We need to get the police involved.'

CHAPTER EIGHT

Olivia drove back home across the narrowest part of the Cornish peninsular from her hastily rescheduled site visit on the north coast. Although Penbartha, which sat among the softer landscape and sandy beaches of the south coast, held a special place in Olivia's heart, she had always loved the dark, dramatic rocks and sheer ruggedness of this terrain. Enormous ancient stones lay scattered amidst scrubland, gorse and heather and the scenery was only saved from total bleakness by the glorious backdrop of the Atlantic Ocean.

Oliva always held her breath at this point of her return journey, before the road swept inland, and took her away from the blue, vast expanse of ocean, framed by craggy cliffs with the castle-like remains of old tin and copper mines clinging to their edges. And much to her delight, the sun performed its usual alchemy of turning the sea from forbidding grey through a palette of blues, from ultramarine to bright turquoise, with the distant, white-capped waves sparkling like diamonds. She opened her window, and taking a deep breath of sea air, called up Alice's number on her hands-free.

'Hey Alice. Everything went well with the Merricks at Wheal Senara, so no need to panic.'

'And were they happy with everything you managed to agree with the conservation officer?'

'Delighted. Rocky says they must have rubbed him up the wrong way somehow from the get-go.'

'I got the feeling they were expecting some resistance from him, which is why they were so anxious about the meeting being cancelled yesterday.'

'So did Rocky. But he was super helpful and agreed to all but one of our proposals, including extending the build across the original boiler house footprint, once he saw the research we'd carried out and the plans for the materials.'

'Well done, Olivia!' Alice's admiration was audible. 'Angus Webster is not known for being easy to please.'

Olivia chuckled. 'I'm used to dealing with the Landmark Preservation Commission in New York, remember? Believe me, Angus is a breeze in comparison. And I was particularly charming, as Rocky requested.'

'He needs to keep Mr Webster on his side if he wants to include the eco-renovation of old tin mines to his portfolio. This month engine, houses. Next month, who knows?'

Olivia thought longingly of the beautiful old engine house. 'It's going to be a wonderful place to live. With views to die for.' She forced her mind back to Alice. 'Has anything else cropped up this morning I need to know about?'

There was a pause. 'Er . . .'

Olivia could picture Alice biting her lip and wringing her hands. Her heart plummeted. 'What is it?'

'You've had a string of messages from Mr Olivarez on the answerphone here. Apparently, you haven't returned any of his calls for the last week or so and he needs to speak to you urgently. Some of your American clients are getting, to quote him, "pissed with you", if that makes sense?'

Olivia felt a twinge of guilt, but pressure from her boss was the last thing she needed. 'I'll deal with Joey. Don't worry. Look, I'm about to go through a dip . . . about to lose you . . . See you later . . . bye . . .' Olivia pressed the red button on her dashboard display to end the call. She needed to think about how to deal with Joey.

***

Twenty minutes later, Olivia pulled off the road onto a farm track and called Joey's number. He picked up straight away.

'Hello, Joey.'

'Hello, Olivia! How you doin'?' Joey bellowed in his thick New York accent and carried on without waiting for her reply. 'I guess I should be grateful to you for deigning to return my call. Even if it is practically the middle of the night here. I was beginning to think you'd dropped off the end of the goddam earth.' He spoke with his usual brusque tone, but Olivia knew that he got up very early to walk his dogs and would now be seated at his desk, gazing across the Lower Manhattan skyline. Like he was, six days a week. She also knew better than to take his sarcasm to heart.

'I'm sorry, Joey. Things are tougher than I expected. And it might take a bit longer than I thought to sort everything out.' She flinched at her understatement.

'Okay, okay, but I need you to check through a few items on the Rutherford account. They're getting a bit picky over the last bill.'

Olivia's heart sank. Brian Rutherford was one of her more demanding clients. 'How soon do you need me to do this?'

A sigh came down the line. 'Well, I don't expect you to pull an all-nighter on this one, but I have a conference call set for noon on Monday, local time, with Brian and his accountant, so I need to be up to speed.'

Olivia's mind flashed to the files of spreadsheets on her

laptop, including costs, timesheets and expenses, and sighed herself. It was going to take the entire weekend.

'I'm a bit tapped out Joey. Can't Drew help you?'

From his bark of laughter, she guessed that Joey hadn't learned to trust Drew any more in the time she'd been away.

'I'm not gonna even reply to that and I really hate to ask you to work this weekend, Olivia. But I promise that when Rutherford is sorted you can go back to enjoying your sleepy little seaside village where, to quote you, "nothing exciting ever happens".'

Olivia felt the colour drain from her face; thankful they weren't on a video call. Joey only read online newspaper headlines that affected him on a personal or professional level. There was no way he could know about Libby's murder. And she wanted to keep it that way.

'No problem. I'll shoot you an email by Sunday midday, your time. Okay?'

'I knew I could depend on you.' Joey's voice softened. 'Take whatever time you need to sort things out your end. Just make sure you continue to deal with all your clients remotely. And promise you'll be back here by Easter with an answer to my offer?'

Olivia felt another prick of guilt. 'I'll sort the Rutherford account over the weekend. And I'll do my best about Easter, Joey. When have I ever let you down?'

'Never,' he chuckled. 'And let's keep it that way. And, oh, Erin sends her love.'

Olivia smiled at the thought of her boss's wife, probably the closest thing she had to family in Manhattan. And although Erin had a tough, cynical New Yorker attitude to most of their employees, she had shown a surprisingly maternal side to Olivia, and she loved her for it.

'Back at her, Joey! And you. Bye.' And with all sorts of conflicting thoughts rushing through her mind Olivia hit the red button, took another deep breath and set off for

Penbartha.

***

She made her way through Tresillian's gardens, and headed straight to Mollie's krowji, to find the lavender oil she had promised Kitten for the café. For many years Mollie's garden workspace had been a large but humble garden shed where she'd spent hours drying, preserving and blending the herbs and plants that formed the basis of her lifelong interest in traditional plant medicine and herbal remedies. As her arthritis and heart problems worsened with age, George had insisted that she be warm and comfortable, and as a gift for her seventieth birthday had arranged for Rocky to build a contemporary wooden workspace with cedar cladding, now silvered with time and weather, and a sedum roof to blend in perfectly with its surroundings. As Olivia instinctively bowed her head to the plaque of the Cornish sun god Belenus, who guarded the entrance, she stepped inside and inhaled the tantalising air full of earthy smells and exotic scents that she would forever associate with her godmother.

Bunches of drying herbs and flowers hung down from special hooks screwed into the ceiling. Sturdy oak shelves lined the walls, filled with glass bottles and earthenware jars containing preserved herbs, tinctures, and other remedies. Below them were more cupboards and drawers full of enticing potions and lotions. A granite workbench took up one side of the krowji beneath a large window and, in pride of place on the opposite wall, was Olivia's favourite, a magnificent carved oak apothecary's cabinet that Mollie had owned for years. Four rows high, with eight small drawers along the top row, six larger drawers forming the second row, with the bottom two rows containing four even larger drawers. Each drawer had a brass name slot above the knob, and each slot bore a yellowing label with the Latin name of the exciting ingredients held within.

Today, the evocative smell of damp compost and rows of tiny plant pots filled with seeds on the granite workbench, waiting to burst into life, told Olivia that Cassie had been busy. She made a mental note to discuss Cassie's plans for the garden with her, and then closed her eyes for a moment, breathing in all the different smells held within the room: the floral scents with an underlying tone of citrus and the fresh green properties of herbs. Olivia always felt especially close to her godmother in this room where she could still feel her spirit and hear her wise words.

'Hello! Olivia?' An unfamiliar voice interrupted her thoughts, and she was frowning as she came face to face with Detective Inspector Trenow. He was bearing a tray with two mugs of tea and a plate of biscuits, closely followed by the two dogs who bounced around her legs, tails wagging in welcome. Her stomach tightened.

'Sorry to intrude.' Olivia glanced up from fussing over the dogs and didn't think he looked at all sorry. 'I called at the house and Cassie said you were in here. She sent some tea.' He looked round and sniffed appreciatively. 'Interesting place.'

'It is, yes.' Olivia took the tray from the detective and waved him toward two Lloyd Loom chairs by a window overlooking the herb garden, Mollie's pride and joy. 'No sergeant with you today?'

Trenow sat down heavily. 'Er, no. I got the feeling he'd rubbed you up the wrong way, so I thought we might get along better without him here. Look,' he paused, 'like I said, Burridge is new to CID. He's very ambitious, but he still has a lot to learn and I'm trying to manage his expectations. Apparently, his computer skills are second to none, but I can't say the same about his interpersonal ones.'

'So, what have you got him doing now?'

'Data input.' The hint of a smile pulled at his mouth, and Olivia almost liked the dishevelled, tired detective in front of her, despite her stomach rolling from the unexpected visit.

Trenow studied his surroundings. 'So, tell me about this place.'

Her defences momentarily lowered, Olivia obliged, happy to talk about her godmother rather than ask Trenow why he really was there.

'Mollie was born and brought up on the Penwith peninsular where her grandmother had been the local wise woman.' She ignored the quirk of Trenow's lips. 'She was always fascinated by the plants and herbs her grandmother used and did her PhD on the history of plants in medicine in Cornwall and the west country. She was working as a researcher at Kew Gardens when she met George, so when they moved back here, she carried on her research and developed her own practice as a local healer.'

'Like a white witch?'

Olivia bristled. 'That's rather an outdated term, if you don't mind me saying. Herbal medicine was traditionally practised by ordinary women without any superstition or magic. It's other people's ignorance that has caused the misunderstanding and suspicion.'

'I stand corrected.' Trenow was solemn. 'So what sort of things did she treat?'

'Pretty much anything. Let's just say I never suffered much from your usual complaints and illnesses. Mollie always had a cure for cuts, scratches, headaches, spots, period pains . . .' she paused for a moment . . . 'even hangovers.'

'Useful. But I think I'll stick with paracetamol.'

They drank their tea in an uneasy silence. Trenow ate the biscuits eagerly, ignoring Mylor's hopeful glances at the plate. Zennor settled down in her basket, her cocked ears and watchful eyes giving her a distinctly unfriendly air. Eventually Olivia could stand the suspense no longer. She clutched her mug between her hands and tried to keep her voice steady.

'Can we cut to the chase, Inspector?' She swallowed. 'Why are you here? Are you any closer to finding Libby's killer?'

Trenow placed his mug on the tray, then leant back, stretched his legs out in front of him, and took a bite of the final biscuit. 'I'm sorry, Olivia.' He checked himself. 'May I call you Olivia?'

She nodded, holding her breath.

'The investigation isn't going as well as we would have hoped. As you know there's no CCTV anywhere on the former station, or in the village, and there are no numberplate recognition cameras this side of the A39. The team's house-to-house enquiries in the village and among the Goods Shed members have come up with nothing concrete.' His eyes held Olivia's. 'Apparently no one saw or heard anything after your row.'

Olivia said nothing, but Sarah's words echoed in her mind.

'We've learnt all sorts of things, but nothing much about Libby.'

Olivia frowned.

'We found her mobile phone at the scene, and we've had her records fast-tracked. So far, they haven't thrown up any suspicious links – just what you'd expect between friends. So no leads there either, I'm afraid. We've also spoken at length to her business partner, so we know what Libby was working on. We're waiting for her bank to release her financial records, and that always takes time.' He sighed and then leant forward and pinned Olivia with his dark, sharp gaze.

'The first forty-eight hours after a death are crucial. I

would like to meet Libby's mother and tell her I've caught the person who killed her daughter. She sounds broken-hearted.'

'What?' Olivia gasped. 'Her mother died years ago! Libby told me all about it.'

Trenow frowned. 'Well, she was very much alive when I spoke to her yesterday. She told us that Libby hadn't been in touch a great deal in the last twelve months, with either her or her siblings.'

'Siblings?' She could feel the blood draining from her face. 'I thought she was an only child. That was why she understood how I felt about being on my own here.'

She was aware of Trenow's eyes still watching her closely.

'Afraid not. She has three siblings.'

A chill descended on Olivia, and she shivered. 'I don't understand. Why would Libby say . . . her poor family. Are they alright?'

Trenow's eyes didn't leave her face. 'They're in shock at the moment, obviously. They are keen to see Libby's killer brought to justice.'

Olivia bent to pat Zennor. 'Of course.'

'So can we go back to that last trustees meeting?'

She nodded.

'You said, and it has been corroborated by the other trustees, that Libby objected to the plan to go ahead with the café.'

'That's right.'

'Did Libby give you any indication that she was going to voice those concerns ahead of the meeting?'

'No. She'd gone quiet on me for a few days, didn't reply to texts and so on, but I just put that down to her being busy with the business while Clara was away . . .' Her explanation petered off.

'So you hadn't spoken to her before the meeting?'

'No.'

89

'Or after the meeting? Following your confrontation in the Goods Shed?'

'No.' She felt nausea rising slowly and fought it back.

'Are you aware of the Goods Shed App?'

The abrupt change in Trenow's questioning took her by surprise. 'Yes. Why?'

'Do you use it?'

'Rarely. The members use it for booking desks, meeting rooms, and accessing certain services.' She shrugged. 'Not stuff I need, really.'

'Do you ever use the members' chat room?'

'No.'

'So, you're not aware of what's being said?' His eyes were still fixed on her face.

'No. Why?' She paused for a moment. 'And how are you aware of it?'

Trenow rummaged in his pocket. 'One of the more helpful members showed me.'

'And?'

Trenow tapped his phone a few times and started flicking the screen with long, nail-bitten fingers. 'I screenshotted some of them. Take a look.'

Olivia rummaged for her reading glasses and then squinted at a succession of comments.

RIP Libby. Who'd have thought it in a place like this?

Libby was completely off her head, the way she spoke to Olivia. She's bound to be the police's main suspect, isn't she?

It was because Libby exposed her for what she really is. Not the guardian angel of this place like everyone makes out. Just wants to go back to New York.

Well, who could blame her?

She should do what George asked her. Lovely old man. Just after his money. Not worth going to prison for.

Have some respect people, Libby's dead. Olivia would never do a thing like that.

But what about the fire yesterday? An insurance job, surely? Or an attempt to divert our attention.

'Oh,' Olivia's voice was faint. 'They don't hold back, do they?'

'No. Have you got anything to say about these comments?'

She shook her head as she processed more of the comments and an icy finger traced slowly down her spine. 'Has the Fire Investigation Unit spoken to you yet? About what happened yesterday?'

Trenow nodded. 'Yes. And I'm waiting for the full report. In the meantime, we'll be following up some of these comments on the app, even if they are only opinions or rumours.'

Olivia's eyes widened, and her mind started doing somersaults.

'I've found from experience that often comments like this can lead you to the truth.' His dark eyes pierced into hers before he carried on. 'And you're sure you didn't go to the Weighbridge Hut the night Libby died?'

'Positive.' Her voice was only a squeak. 'I told you; I came back here with Martin.' Her pulse quickened at the memory. By her side, Zennor let out a low growl.

'Ah yes, you did.' Trenow leant forward, elbows resting on his knees. He ignored the dog. 'But a significant amount of forensic evidence has come back showing, firmly, that you were at the scene of the crime at the time of Libby Walsh's murder.'

CHAPTER NINE

'So, what sort of forensic evidence is he talking about?' Martin snapped the lid of his laptop closed and flashed concerned green eyes at Olivia.

'I have no idea. He wouldn't elaborate; just kept asking random questions, watching my reaction to them . . .' Olivia stood in front of his desk, still slightly out of breath from rushing to the Goods Shed to confide her fears in Martin. 'But I've got a really bad feeling about it. In here.' She pressed her hands to her stomach.

'This is absolutely ridiculous!' Martin walked across to the window and stared out at the darkening skies. 'Can't they see they're barking up the wrong tree? They're bound to find evidence that both of us have been in the Hut. We told him we'd spent loads of time in there with her, so whatever they find isn't going to tell them anything new.'

When he eventually turned to face Olivia, his own distress was clear. 'Have their enquiries thrown up anything at all?'

'Not really. Everyone's lips are sealed.' She shifted from foot to foot. 'Apart from the person who so kindly shared the members' chatroom details with him. And that was probably the same person who told him about my argument with Libby.'

He sat back down at his desk and held his head in his hands. 'You'd think the police would have found something by now. They seem to be making a real hash of this investigation.'

'Martin, do you really think they would try and pin Libby's murder on me just to make their job easier?' The words rushed out before she could stop them.

'How? You've got a cast iron alibi. Unless of course . . .' his green eyes, usually so bright, dulled suddenly.

'What?' She bit down so hard on her lower lip she could taste blood.

'Unless they think I was just making up my alibi to help you out. But no, they would have questioned me about it, and they haven't.' He visibly brightened. 'I think we're getting paranoid Olivia. Let's just hope the police get their act together and find Libby's killer quickly. Then we can concentrate on our jobs here. I hate to think what would happen to this place if you were taken away from it. It wouldn't last five minutes.'

Olivia's heart lurched. 'I'm sure the trustees could hold the fort for a while.' She couldn't keep the hopeful note out of her voice.

Martin snorted. 'I wouldn't bet on it. Wouldn't your father help out? After all, he is George's most direct descendant, isn't he?'

'His nephew, yes.' She swallowed. 'But he can hardly just pop over from Australia, can he?' She changed the subject. 'Trenow also told me some stuff about Libby.'

Martin looked up. 'Is that allowed in a murder investigation?'

'Who knows, but he was saying . . .'

She told him what the detective had said.

'Oh, Olivia, I'm so sorry. That must have been so hard for you to hear, especially as you were the one who found her.' Martin carried on. His voice thick with emotion. 'No one seems to think about that, do they? How you must be feeling? Even though you'd argued, you don't just forget friendship, do you, and all the things you've done together, the good times?'

Olivia sat down on the opposite side of the desk and stared at him, tears pricking her eyes. This was making her feel worse, not better.

'Do you mind if we don't talk about that please, Martin? I'd rather not.'

He caught hold of her hand across the desk. 'Of course not. I'm being insensitive and I'm sorry.'

'But I would like to talk about Libby. You knew her for much longer than I did.'

A sudden knock at the door interrupted her, and the door burst open, followed by a large, surfer-type man with a tanned face and sun-streaked hair.

'Hey, Martin! That grant you helped us get has just funded our new brochure as well as the website, and I wanted you to see it! Oh, hi, Olivia.' He thrust an arty brochure into their hands as he spoke, his face bright with excitement. He and his partner had set up a sea-swimming business, offering guided tours of all the best wild swimming spots of Cornwall and the Isles of Scilly, and had recently attracted the attention of a national newspaper.

'The website has had dozens of hits today and we've had loads of calls. What do you think?'

Martin and Olivia both switched their concentration to the impressive brochure.

'It looks great!' Martin was quick to praise. 'Well done, Joel.'

'Yes, congratulations. Those swims round the Scillies look beautiful.' Olivia couldn't help but smile at his enthusiasm.

Martin chuckled. 'And that's really saying something. I'm not sure Olivia's much of a swimmer if truth be told. She always says she prefers to keep her feet firmly on dry ground.' He turned to her with a smile. 'Don't you?'

Joel grinned at Olivia. 'You gotta learn, Olivia. We're thinking of doing beginners' classes. Want me to sign you up?'

Olivia wriggled a little in her seat. 'I don't think so. I prefer to look at the sea from the safety of dry land. But thanks for the offer.'

'No probs.' He turned to Martin. 'We couldn't have done it without you. If you hadn't known about that grant opportunity for coast-based businesses and helped us with our application . . .'

Martin waved away the thanks.

'Just doing my job. And it's always great when things work out. Makes everything worthwhile, doesn't it, Olivia?'

Olivia nodded and managed a forced smile.

'Well, I just wanted to let you know that we're having a bit of a celebration in the pub later and we'd like you to join us.' Joel stared down at his trainers for a moment and then glanced at Olivia. 'Both of you. We don't reckon you had anything to do with Libby's murder, Olivia. It must have been that upcountry boyfriend of hers that people are talking about.'

'Thanks, Joel.' Martin shook the other man's hand. 'That would be lovely, and it will show that Olivia has nothing to hide. We'll be there later.' He turned to Olivia. 'Let me see Joel out and make you a cup of tea. I think we could both do with one.'

Olivia walked to the door and looked around her, forcing her mind away from Libby and Trenow. Beneath her, the ground floor of the Goods Shed was where the creative, passionate and driven members who produced the dynamic and collaborative environment that George had wanted to attract mostly worked. A handful of more dedicated members were scattered throughout the workspace, where, even on a day as dull as this, the light flooded through the eight large multi-paned windows on each side of the ground floor and the sixteen smaller windows on the mezzanine floor above.

A dozen or so of the younger members, who had obviously finished work for the week were congregated on the sofas and armchairs grouped in clusters at the far end break-out area, separated by reclaimed galvanised metal water tanks planted with exotic ferns which acted as both physical and sound barriers from the more formal section of the workspace. This area was where the inspiration and sharing of ideas among like-minded people flourished. Olivia loved the way the Goods Shed members spoke about their work; buzzing with enthusiasm as they spoke about their dreams, their minds rapidly filling with even more ideas as they talked about the type of work they did, their plans, hopes and visions for the future.

Martin's office was on the mezzanine floor of the Goods Shed. This level housed six, self-contained offices with glass partitions separating them from the landing, carefully designed to enable their occupants to soak up the creative atmosphere from the open space downstairs, while retaining privacy. The arrangement of space worked well at the Goods Shed, and Olivia wondered if she could design something along similar principles for the former Methodist Episcopal Church in Greenwich Village that she was writing a proposal for. She was working hard to preserve the historic architectural and special features of the building, whose function was changing from a public worship space to a high-tech research and design facility, but there was still something missing. Why hadn't she thought of a mezzanine level before? *Because*, a little voice in her head whispered, *her creative mind seemed to work differently in Cornwall and especially here in the Goods Shed*. She immediately dismissed the voice, but nodded as she walked back to the sofa, and sat down to wait for Martin. *With a bit of tweaking here and there, a mezzanine level in the old church would work well.*

Her mind was still firmly in New York when Martin returned, handed her a cup of tea and jolted her out of her thoughts. From the moment she first met him, his stylish clothes and expensive aftershave had reminded her of the men she had dated in Manhattan. He had attracted her with his endless energy, the smile she could always hear in his voice and the sparkle in his eyes. And he was always good fun. But when he smiled at her now, the hint of sadness was still there, and her heart went out to him.

'Actually Olivia, do you mind if we don't talk about Libby this evening, please? She's been a great friend to me, and it's all still a bit too raw. I'm beginning to understand how you must have felt when George died, and I'm sorry I wasn't able to do more to help you.'

Another wave of sympathy swept through her.

'I completely understand.' She paused. 'Although there is something I need to clear up about the night Libby died.'

Martin wiped his hand across his eyes. 'I'm sorry, but I can't. I'd rather talk about something completely different and tell you what I learned yesterday at my meeting in Exeter. I think you'll find it really useful for building up the Goods Shed business . . .' And he launched into an entertaining account of the networking event he had attended for business mentors and coaches in the southwest that soon had Olivia smiling and forgetting her worries.

'And I thought of you, Olivia, because there was this guy who gave all these amazing facts and figures about how the southwest, and Cornwall in particular, is now leading the way for creative and eco-entrepreneurs.' He took a careful sip of his water. 'And I reckon it will be useful to have some up-to-the-minute and substantiated facts to use in future marketing. And for the members to include in their business plans and investment proposals.'

'Sounds good. Did you take our brochures and leaflets

to this event?'

'I did. The phones will ring off their hooks.'

'And will you get work from it?'

'Of course. These are exceptional events for networking and finding out about the latest investment trends and so on. George saw the writing on the wall as far as banks were becoming so risk-averse and was always keen to encourage me to seek out alternative sources of funding.'

Olivia smiled at a memory of her godfather telling her how excited he was to get Martin on board.

'He always put the members first,' Olivia observed. 'And so must we.' She shifted in her seat as a more troublesome question of her own was still forming in the recesses of her mind.

Martin was still talking. '. . . George was very savvy for a man of his age. Being so ahead of the game with his green initiatives has really paid off. And now we've got more green entrepreneurs as members, investors will be flocking to be a part of it.'

'Let's hope so.'

Martin smiled. 'Without a doubt. Investors are very keen to cash in on the green initiative. It makes them look good and feel good about themselves. A win-win situation, you might say.' He cut off, looked at his watch and let out a small gasp of surprise.

'Look at the time! That's what happens when you get me talking about business. We'd better be getting to the pub.' He stood up, but Olivia put a hand on his arm, her face suddenly tense.

'I do need to ask you something, Martin.'

'Fire away.' He sat back down.

'It's about when you said you stayed with me at Tresillian.'

His cheeks went pink. 'That's a bit of a curveball to throw into the conversation.'

'Er, there's no easy way of saying this, but I don't really remember much about that night at all.'

'You had drunk quite a lot.'

'I really didn't think so, but my headache suggested otherwise . . . I just wanted to make sure that nothing else had happened. So did we . . .?'

'Did we what? Sleep together?' He was teasing her now. 'Yes, we did. All night. And I can tell you all about your small and rather tasteful tattoo at the top of your right thigh.'

A rush of heat swept upwards through her body and suffused her face. And it suddenly mattered very much to Olivia to find out the truth.

'Did we have sex?' Her voice was sharper than she intended, and Martin subsided immediately, hurt written all over his face.

'No, we didn't. I can't believe you think I would take advantage of anyone in that state, let alone a friend.'

This time the rush was of relief, and she was immediately contrite, but before she had time to apologise, there was a brisk tapping of feet up the wood and chrome staircase, and a business-like rap on the door. Alice popped her head round the doorway, her small, bright eyes full of concern.

'I'm not sure you'll want to know this before the weekend, Olivia, but I really think it is my duty to bring it to your attention.'

Olivia felt the familiar fingers of fear squeezing her stomach.

'What's happened, Alice?'

Alice hopped from foot to foot.

'Well, a few more members have resigned. Several have informed me they won't be returning.'

'How many?'

'Um, about six.'

'About six?' Olivia's voice was sharp.

'Um, well eight, actually.' Alice winced. 'But they only had the lowest membership package and used us on a pay-as-you-go basis, so they didn't contribute hugely to our income.'

'Have you had any enquiries from Martin's networking event in Exeter yesterday?' Olivia could hear the desperation in her voice.

Alice's hopping intensified.

'No. Not as yet,' she hastily amended. 'Perhaps they're leaving it until after the weekend?'

'Haven't we got a waiting list for all the different levels of membership?' Martin asked.

'We have. And I've contacted all the relevant ones, but none of them will commit at the moment. The adverse publicity isn't helping.' She remained standing where she was.

'What else, Alice?' Olivia was becoming an expert at interpreting Alice's body language.

'I'm afraid two of your private practice appointments next week have also cancelled. They both said they'd been appraised of the situation here and they felt they had no option but to sever all ties with us and go elsewhere.'

'What?' Olivia's voice faltered.

'I'm sorry. I did my best to dissuade them, but they were intractable.' Alice looked as though she was about to cry. 'I don't know if it's just a coincidence or directly related to Libby's murd— I mean death, but I think we need to take action quickly to get our numbers back up.'

Olivia sank her head into her hands.

'So,' Alice rallied, 'I've already drafted something for the website and our social media feeds. We need to appeal to all the home-based businesses in Cornwall and plug our networking and collaboration side of things. As well as the eco benefits of co-working. Forensics should be finished, and the crime scene cleared by Monday, so I thought we could offer some drop-in sessions for non-members to get them in and experience life at the Goods Shed. Things like start-up advice, book-keeping, and business planning. Then when they have experienced all the facilities and services we offer, we can offer them special membership rates for the first three months.'

Olivia gave herself a mental shake and nodded, heartened by Alice's loyalty and determination.

'Thanks. What would I do without you? I'll clear some space in my dairy for Monday.'

'That sounds great, Alice. Count me in for the business advice. No charge. And whatever else I can do to help.' Martin rose from the sofa and guided a blushing Alice towards the door, his arm resting lightly on her back.

'Now you go home to your very lucky husband and have a wonderful weekend. I'll lock up here and then take Olivia to the pub. She looks like she needs a stiff drink.'

***

As it was raining when they left the Goods Shed, Martin suggested they drove the short distance to the village pub in his car. A low, smooth, and shiny BMW, as far removed from Olivia's inherited Land Rover, or Mollie's Fiat 500 that she sometimes shared with Cassie, as it was possible to get. His car always reminded her of the Lincoln Town Cars that Joey used in New York, the leather interior all spotless, soft, and clean smelling. Nothing like the damp dog aroma that usually filled her own vehicle. And like Joey, Martin was a city person at heart. She looked down at her muddy, country boots spoiling his carpets and winced.

Just as they pulled up at the pub carpark there was a knock on the passenger window, and Olivia opened it to reveal a very damp and bedraggled Jago Trevithick. His ancient, waxed jacket looked an unworthy opponent of the night's weather as he stood there, shoulders hunched against the worsening rain. Her heart sank.

Martin leant across. 'Fancy a drink, Jago?'

Jago looked directly at Olivia. 'No, thanks. Alice said she thought I might catch you here.'

A prickle of alarm ran down Olivia's spine. 'Is everything alright?'

Jago's face was unreadable. 'I've had a call from Edgar. He's called an Extraordinary Meeting of the trustees on Monday morning, to discuss the ramifications of Libby's murder on the future of the Station Trust. So, no. Everything is far from alright.'

CHAPTER TEN

Monday morning arrived with a continuation of the rain that had blighted the entire weekend and the whole village was wet. Fitting weather for what lay ahead, Jago reflected as he battled his way, head down against the strong westerly winds, along the walkway from the Signal Box to the Goods Shed. The clouds formed a dense canopy of grey over the creek and the gulls swooped wildly on the wind, squealing like frustrated children. He felt frustrated himself. The tone of Edgar's message had set alarm bells ringing and he knew he had to keep his wits about him this morning.

Alice met him at the door, looking suitably sombre.

'Good morning, Mr Trevithick. I've prepared the conference room. May I get you a coffee?'

He flashed her a brief smile. 'Wonderful, Alice, thanks.' He didn't really want a drink but couldn't face listening to Alice's opinions on the meeting ahead.

'Am I the first here, Alice?' He called to her disappearing back.

'As always, Mr Trevithick. I'm afraid Rosie's had to send her apologies. She and Bill are fetching their new electric mini coach from the garage in Launceston where they've had its livery done. They couldn't delay it apparently, but she sent her best wishes and said she'd catch up with you later.' Her trilling voice carried through the empty workspace.

The Brunel Room was at the end of the Goods Shed, nearest the reception area, where huge chrome letters spelling the words 'Work . . . Create . . . Collaborate . . .' adorned one wall and 'Planet . . . People . . . Profits . . .' the wall opposite. Olivia had designed the room as a multi-functional space. It could be divided into three smaller meeting rooms or opened out into a larger area. Alice had prepared it for a formal meeting, Jago noted, as he entered the room. The long, highly polished boardroom table, made from recycled railway sleepers, was arranged for eight people, with high-backed chairs, leather desk pads and water glasses all neatly arranged at each place, presumably to include Alice as the clerk, as there was no longer the full complement of trustees.

As Jago waited, his eyes drifted over the walls adorned with railway memorabilia, homage to George's beloved golden age of steam. Jago admired the collection of shining brass nameplates with gold lettering and rims representing the five different classes of GWR steam locomotives. The Goods Shed used the same classes to represent the different categories of membership available, from the most basic 'Manor class', through 'Grange', 'Hall' and 'Castle' to the highest: 'King class'. Only Jago knew the time and effort George had invested from the 1960s until his death, into sourcing and restoring these nameplates and the pleasure he had derived from doing so. The walls also displayed many of the original Penbartha station signs in the classic GWR colours of cream and dark brown and other pieces of valuable railway memorabilia that had been abandoned along with the station buildings.

'Good morning, Jago.'

One by one the trustees arrived and quietly took their

places at the long table. Jago admired the way George had appointed creative and green entrepreneurs to his board of trustees rather than the usual worthies who focused on reports and accounts and had nothing else to contribute. And the board meetings under George's chairmanship had been as vibrant and dynamic as the atmosphere in the Goods Shed itself. Jago smiled wryly as he remembered George telling him that he wanted meetings to feel like a gathering of friends at the local pub rather than distant relatives meeting at a wake. But today there was none of the usual light-hearted chatter and laughter. The atmosphere in the slowly filling room was funereal.

Last to arrive were Olivia and Martin. Even from where Jago sat, he could feel the air prickling between them, and from the look on Olivia's face he guessed they'd had words. That sparked his curiosity. Perhaps the honeymoon period was over? He watched them part company at the door. Olivia strode to her place at the opposite end of the table to Edgar, and Martin sat midway along the table, between Alice and Paula, his head down.

Jago looked round at the diminished group of trustees. Everyone seemed subdued, nervous even. But no one stood out as any more anxious than anyone else. Apart from Olivia. She sat upright and tense, trying to hide her emotions and doing a fairly good job, but the tight set of her jaw gave her away. She wore her hair loose, curls falling round her face, obscuring her expression. A convenient veil to hide behind, he decided.

'Good morning, everyone.' Edgar cleared his throat and regarded his fellow trustees over the top of his glasses. 'And thank you for convening at such short notice.'

They all nodded. The distant sounds of chatter that could be heard through the closed doors, contrasted heavily with the quiet in the conference room. Edgar fidgeted with his papers, his bony arthritic fingers and hands mottled with age spots, trembling slightly. He scratched at his bald head and then glanced up, looking every year of his age.

'I'm sorry we have to meet under such sad circumstances, so soon after George's own death, and I have already written a letter of condolence to Miss Walsh's family. As you are all aware, Olivia had the extreme misfortune of discovering Libby, and this has been the most awful shock to her, and us.'

There was an immediate murmur of sympathy from the table, and Jago noticed several supportive smiles being sent in Olivia's direction.

'I have assured Detective Inspector Trenow and his colleagues that we will cooperate in any way we can with the investigation.' Edgar looked down at his notes as though he would find the answers that they were all looking for there. 'And I would like to ask you all to examine your memories thoroughly and see if you remember anything, however small, that might help the police with their enquiries.'

Jago looked across the table again. The expressions on the assembled faces showed a combination of sadness and concern. Could he detect guilt anywhere? His gaze rested on Olivia for a moment. Her eyes filled briefly with unshed tears before she dashed them away with her fingers, but she remained silent. He thought back to previous board meetings where she'd always spoken with enthusiasm and determination, a smile on her face which never suggested she was feeling anything but confident.

Edgar fidgeted with his papers some more.

'And it pains me greatly that I also have to bring to your attention that the situation we find ourselves in and the attendant bad publicity is proving harmful to our reputation and has thrown a few things into sharp focus.'

A shocked silence filled the room this time. Nobody spoke and everybody avoided looking at each other. Olivia was nervous, Jago thought, she was trying to hide it, and doing a fairly good job, but the tight set of her jaw gave her away.

Martin stepped in, impatience clear in his voice. 'Can you just get to the point please, Edgar? The message you sent us was rather ambiguous.'

'I have had it brought to my attention that things haven't been going very well in the Goods Shed for quite some time now,' Edgar began hesitantly.

Jago noticed how Olivia's startled expression settled on Alice, but the clerk held her gaze.

'Could you expand on that please, Edgar?'

Jago detected a tremble in Olivia's voice.

'Well, there has been a significant drop in member numbers,' Edgar read from his notes.

'Only in the Manor class,' Olivia interjected. 'And, as that is our lowest class of membership, it brings in the least income. All other classes are increasing slowly.' She was obviously trying to sound upbeat and positive for the other trustees, but Jago wasn't fooled.

'Which is what we would expect at this stage.' Paula Roscoe, the board's resident social enterprise skills advisor and an eco-entrepreneur who ran a Beach School, spoke confidently. 'I think some of us,' and her gaze fell on Jess Hopkins, a young public relations and green marketing consultant with short, spiky orange hair, heavy eye makeup and a tiny stud glinting in her nose, 'are expecting to run before we can walk.'

'So, you're not overly concerned on the membership front then, Paula?'

'Not particularly. And Alice has some excellent ideas for increasing our profile.' She repeated the ideas Alice had put to Olivia on Friday evening. 'And I think we should go with them. Perhaps you could help more, Jess, as that's your area of expertise?'

The sweet way in which she spoke to the other woman failed to hide the implied criticism.

Dark colour flooded Jess's cheeks. 'Perhaps I could suggest that you concentrate on your own area of expertise and leave mine to me, Paula. I understand that several members are not abiding by your ethical and eco purchasing policy and are blatantly buying supplies from cheaper options. May I ask what you are doing to address that issue, as it flies in the face of our commitment to sustainability and the social enterprise ideology?'

Jago hadn't been aware of any animosity between these two women at previous meetings and decided he needed to pay more attention.

Paula smiled calmly, her usual elegant and calm demeanour as unflustered as her sleek silver bob which fell perfectly to her chin.

'I am fully aware of the situation to which you are referring, Jess. As is Olivia.'

Olivia's face was a mask of professionalism as she nodded.

Paula continued, her low, soft Cornish accent soothing.

'And we are taking action to re-educate our members and provide them with an up-to-date list of other local social enterprises who can supply sustainable stationery and so on at reasonable cost. I think you will find that the prime offenders are the very members who have recently resigned. They were never really committed to the Goods Shed. More playing at being in business, perhaps? And friends of yours, I do believe?'

As Jess opened her mouth to retaliate, Martin interrupted.

'You said a few things had happened, Edgar. What other developments are there?'

'Yes, Martin. Thank you.' Edgar eventually located the necessary piece of paper. 'I have received a letter from the SocialTech funding charity which, thanks to Paula here, had approved a grant for us of twenty thousand pounds for the installation of the super-fast broadband, Wi-Fi, and other digital technology in the café, for local community purposes.' He removed his reading glasses and looked at Olivia through pale, watery eyes. 'They have withdrawn their offer.'

Jago was stunned. That was a huge blow to their plans.

'What?' Once again, Paula was the first to respond. 'They can't have done! They were totally behind this project. Committed to the social impact the café will make on the community. And its eco credentials'

'Have they given a reason?' Jago asked.

'They are not obliged to.'

'Really?' Jago raised an eyebrow. Any pity he had previously felt for Edgar over the death of his old friend was rapidly evaporating. He had never particularly cared for solicitors. He'd come across too many in his time.

'I am not at liberty to divulge that information.'

'For God's sake!' Paula was as taken aback as most others around the table. 'That's preposterous. Not to mention unprofessional. And it could ruin everything!'

Jago cast a glance at Olivia who was still silent and looking straight ahead.

'So, what financial impact will this have on the café?' Martin asked Callum Armstrong, treasurer to the board.

'Well, at this late stage it means that if we can't find an alternative source of funding immediately, our only choice is to fund the tech investment ourselves. But unfortunately, we are already struggling to keep up with the repayment schedule for the renovation of the Goods Shed building and the start-up costs at the same time as paying for the café development.' He thought for a moment. 'As far as I can see, there is only one way forward.' He riffled through the papers in front of him and handed out copies of the most recent accounts. 'This is where we stand right now. As you know, my chief interest is the bottom line. If we agree a temporary hiatus to the repayment instalments for the Goods Shed and channel that money into the café fund, we should be able to manage it. Just.' He pushed his horn-rimmed glasses up his nose and looked round the table, his gaze coming to rest on Olivia. 'And it's the only way forward if we want to stay true to George's vision.'

'Okay. Let's do it.' Olivia sat up, straightened her shoulders, and smiled weakly at Callum.

The accountant paused for a moment and fiddled with his papers before he looked up again. 'I'm afraid the decision is not solely up to you, Olivia. Under the terms of the Trust, the whole board must formally agree to the proposal.'

Olivia's shoulders slumped, and she swallowed hard before speaking. 'Okay, may I propose that we agree to call a nine month pause to the repayment schedule? By then the café will have been up and running for six months and should be generating decent profits of its own.' She spoke firmly, trying to sound confident.

But Jago noticed the knuckles of her clenched fists were white. 'And I think we should all support Olivia in this proposal. Let's not underestimate the creation of social value we have already seen with the Goods Shed, which will only increase with the opening of the café and the community space for the village,' Paula added. 'That will be immeasurable in terms of financial profit.'

'If I may just say something here.' Jago felt their eyes on him. 'I accept that we have to apply commercial strategies to our business activities to make this entire enterprise a success. But I suggest that we don't forget the wishes of the person behind all this. George was ethically minded and motivated by a strong social and environmental mission. And he created this concept for the long-term benefit of the local community and the environment, rather than to make money quickly.' He paused. 'And we're already adding to the community, even at this early stage. George made it quite clear at all our meetings that any profits were to go towards our fundamental social and environmental aims, and at no point,' and at this, Jago's gaze scanned the board members one by one, noticing the fleeting expression of utter sadness that clouded Olivia's face, 'should these aims be superseded by the desire for commercial gain.'

'Hear, hear!' Paula recovered first. 'Well said, Jago. And I think we should all keep that in mind.'

Edgar coughed. 'But I'm not confident there will be any profits.'

'Give it time, Edgar!' Olivia snapped. 'I was reading Callum's reports the other day and our current figures are meeting the forecast. What's the rush?'

'Excuse me, young lady.' Edgar was offended. 'I may be old, but I understand business. Your godfather respected that.'

Olivia flushed and immediately let her hair fall across her face and it hid whatever emotion was displayed there. From the set of her shoulders, Jago suspected it was more likely to be anger than shame.

'Now, now, Edgar.' Martin jumped to Olivia's defence. 'I'm sure Olivia wasn't suggesting that you don't know what you are talking about. She's just feeling under a lot of stress at the moment, and I think we should all cut her some slack.'

Callum ran both hands through his brown, thinning hair, leant back in his chair and sighed.

'Look,' he spoke quietly, 'let me do some juggling with the figures and see what I can come up with.' He placed the lid back on his fountain pen. 'I'm confident that if we hold fire on our repayments on the Goods Shed start-up costs, we should be able to fund the tech side ourselves.'

'We haven't agreed that yet,' Jess pointed out. 'And what if the figures don't work out?'

'Well, can I be given the time to have a look, please?' Even the usually jovial accountant sounded impatient. 'Let me do a proper analysis of the figures and come up with a way forward.'

Jess cleared her throat. 'Before we agree to anything, may I remind the board of Libby's concerns about continuing with the development of the café to such a high specification retrofit-wise?' Her opinionated tone was beginning to grate on Jago's nerves. 'Haven't they been justified in the light of the recent membership issues and the obvious change of heart by the SocialTech company? Surely, we're just throwing good money after bad?'

'I think we all remember Libby's concerns,' Paula commented. 'But I would like to remind the board that supporting the local economy and protecting the environment is fundamental to our mission.'

Olivia leant forward with a determined tilt of her chin that Jago hadn't seen for a while.

'Thanks, Paula. Okay. We're all busy people, and I'm sure we all have lots of other things to do today. May I suggest that we let Callum work on his proposal to delay the repayment schedule on the Goods Shed and then re-channel that money into the development of the café?'

'And we will put it to a vote next time.' Edgar shifted in his seat. 'But there is one other matter we need to discuss in more detail before we make any major decisions.'

'And what's that?' Olivia turned her gaze to the old man.

'We haven't addressed the adverse publicity that the Goods Shed has been attracting in the aftermath of recent events.' Edgar spoke slowly.

Ah, thought Jago, *at long last*.

'What sort of adverse publicity?' Olivia's voice was edgy.

'Just wake up and smell the coffee, Olivia!' Jess was sharp. 'Someone has murdered a trustee. Membership is declining. And how long will it be before other members leave as well? It's hardly a selling point being connected to a place where there's been a murder, is it?' She held her hand up to prevent any interruption.

'And the café has been the victim of arson. There are rumours going round that the fire may have been an insurance job. And Callum's financial report reinforces that money is tight.' Her voice rose. 'And it's hardly a secret that once you realised that Libby wasn't in agreement with your plans for the café, you threatened her.' She paused for a moment. 'So, just because the police have made no arrests yet, it doesn't mean that some people aren't putting two and two together.'

Wow! Jess didn't pull her punches. 'I must urge you to think before you speak, Jess.' Jago's voice was sharp. 'Those are very serious allegations.'

'It's what everyone is thinking, but no one dares to say!'

'Really?' Olivia's voice wobbled, and she tucked her curls quickly behind her ears before gazing round the table. 'Not even on the Goods Shed App chatroom?'

Jago watched as the eyes of most of the trustees met her gaze immediately and firmly. But not all.

Edgar cleared his throat again. 'Olivia, my dear.' She visibly bristled at the old man's tone. 'Please don't take this the wrong way, but I have an important duty to discharge. I think I am right in saying that the cloud of suspicion and uncertainty that is hanging over us is attracting adverse publicity. And it is a matter of great concern to all the trustees gathered here today.' He paused for a moment and drank from his water glass.

'What are you trying to say, Edgar?' Martin spoke up, glancing anxiously in Olivia's direction. 'I hope you're not suggesting that Olivia is behind any of these events. I know there's a lot of speculation and gossip going about. But I can tell you categorically that although the police are still asking lots of questions, they haven't got sufficient evidence to link anyone to the murder, as yet.'

Jago cringed and wondered if this was Martin's clumsy attempt to get back into Olivia's good books. If so, he doubted it had worked. Edgar carried on, his face creasing deeper and deeper into a frown.

'We are all aware of the police's lack of progress and people are naturally drawing their own conclusions, despite Martin's assertions to the contrary. But as I've just said, we can't afford to have this suspicion tainting our work here. We must be mindful that the Goods Shed is vital to the members and to the wider community. And,' Edgar paused and swallowed hard, 'Olivia, if you are still under suspicion when we next meet, and we decide that your presence here is too much of a distraction and detracts from what we do, I will take no pleasure in my role as Chair of this Trust to hold a vote of no confidence in you as trustee and require you to resign with immediate effect.'

A shocked silence filled the room. Even Jago was taken aback at this sudden turn of events. He looked around at his fellow trustees while he considered what to say. Alice looked as though she was about to burst into tears. Everybody else stared down at the desk pads in front of them. All except Olivia. Her cheeks suffused with colour as she put her hand over her mouth as if to stop herself speaking. Then she scrabbled at the collar of her white shirt and clutched at the stone hung around her neck on its leather cord. Jago noticed that the smooth shiny obsidian gemstone with the amber flecks matched the colour of her mahogany eyes as they stared ahead, blinking rapidly.

Jago chose his words carefully. 'I think we need to look into this further, Edgar, before we take such a step. To make sure we're doing things properly and there will be no comeback against us.'

He glanced at Olivia's face. The full realisation of Edgar's words had sunk in. She turned anxious eyes on him, and Jago glimpsed a vulnerability he hadn't seen before. She opened and closed her mouth a few times before speaking and when she did, the tremor in her voice was unmistakable.

'So, when is this vote of no confidence taking place?'

Edgar avoided looking at Olivia.

'I think we need to see how events develop. Particularly regarding the police investigation. Then we can make a more informed decision whether we even consider putting the proposal of changing the repayment schedule to the vote. And I would like to make it clear that what we have discussed today is for trustees' ears only.' He glanced at all of them in turn then. 'Alice, if you can make sure all remaining trustees will be present so we are quorate, we will reconvene a week today. At two p.m. And put it to the vote then.'

CHAPTER ELEVEN

'A vote of no confidence? In me! When it is I who has given up everything to come back and sort this place out for George. How can Edgar even think I'm doing this for my sake, rather than everyone else's?' Angry tears trickled down Olivia's face as she followed Martin into his office and stood in front of him, fists clenched by her sides.

'I'm so sorry, Olivia. I don't know what got into Edgar. I'm sure it won't come to that. The police are bound to have come up with something by this time next week.' He hovered by his desk. 'Look, just tell me what I can do to help, and I'll do it.'

Olivia marched across to his cream leather sofa and sat upright in one corner, her shoulders rigid.

'Help? I think you've already done more than enough by kindly telling all the trustees I'm effectively the police's prime suspect and it's only a matter of time before they have enough evidence to arrest me for a murder I definitely did not commit.' She banged her feet onto the glass coffee table and glared at him.

'I'm sorry about that. I was taken completely by surprise by the turn of events in there, just as you were.'

She leant forward, frowning. 'Yet! You said yet. That suggests that they will, eventually. How did that make me look to the trustees? It's no wonder Edgar is considering calling for a vote of no confidence.'

He held up his hands in a sign of peace. 'I've said I'm sorry. What else can I do?'

'Nothing. I think you've done quite enough, thank you. That meeting was a complete disaster.'

'You're over-reacting Olivia. It wasn't that bad.'

She blew her curls out of her face, her lips pursed in concentration.

'Edgar's always been so supportive. I guessed he might have some concerns, that's understandable, but I honestly thought he'd be on my side.' She rubbed at her nose.

A look of concern crossed Martin's face. 'It wasn't that bad, Olivia. Try not to worry. You know it's not all down to Edgar; everyone will get their say. You're just tired. And emotional.'

'Emotional? I'll tell you why I'm emotional. George chose me to carry this on in his name. Me, not you or Edgar or Jago bloody Trevithick. And no one else will have the emotional investment that I have – and I can't bear the thought of it all just withering away!' Her voice rose.

Martin shrugged helplessly and brushed his floppy hair back from his forehead with his fingers. 'Calm down Olivia, please . . .'

'Have you any idea what basically being exposed as the prime suspect in a murder investigation in front of your colleagues does to you? Especially when people you thought you could trust are ready to suspect you as well. It's sending me bat-crap crazy!' Something clicked in her brain. 'And speaking of which, how on earth does Edgar know that there's a cloud of suspicion hanging over me?' She made the speech marks with her fingers. 'He said that even before you shared the news of my impending conviction.'

Martin shook his head. 'Gossip, I guess. You know what people are like round here.'

'As far as I'm aware,' Olivia pointed out, 'the only people who know about my conversation with DI Trenow are me and you.'

His look of concern grew. 'Are you sure you didn't say anything to Cassie? You know how she likes to gossip.'

'Give me some credit! That's exactly why I didn't say anything to Cassie.'

Martin thought for a moment. 'What about Jago? He seemed very sure of himself at the meeting and had a lot to say—'

'No!' Olivia cut him off. 'That man hasn't got a very high opinion of me at the best of times. Why on earth would I tell him anything? He just wants to make sure Edgar's got all his bases covered before he gets rid of me.'

Martin went over to the coffee percolator and poured two cups. With his back to Olivia, he spoke quietly, 'I've heard that he and DI Trenow are old buddies. From school or something.'

'Really? Are you suggesting Trenow told him?' Her face grew hot again. She could just imagine them having a right old laugh at her expense.

Martin's eyes held hers as he turned back to her. 'It makes sense. Trenow could easily have mentioned it to Jago. And Jago could have told Edgar, and then cooked this up with him.'

'It's certainly a possibility, but it doesn't explain who told the SocialTech Fund about the problems with the Goods Shed and the café.'

Martin placed the coffee on the table and sat back down, stretching his arms behind his head. 'Well, the list of people who knew about the fire is endless.'

'Is it?' Olivia narrowed her eyes.

'Look at all the people who were there: Rocky, Willow, Fraser, Kitten, Jago. Not to mention all the members of the Goods Shed who saw what was going on. When I got back from that networking event in Exeter there was no end of

118

people waiting to fill me in on all the excitement.'

'Why would they say something so negative about an organisation that is helping them out, and sabotage their own future?'

'Well, that goes for all of us.' Martin declared. 'Which would suggest the fire was nothing to do with anyone involved in the Goods Shed, wouldn't it?'

'Unless someone has more to gain from our failure than they do from our success.' Olivia tapped her fingers against her top lip as she thought out loud.

'That's enough.' Olivia could hear the despair in his voice. 'You're going around in circles.'

Martin's mobile beeped on the coffee table. He snatched it up, muttering something under his breath and holding up one finger to her as he listened. 'I have to take this,' he said to her, and gestured that he would go outside.

Olivia nodded as he left the office. She drank her coffee, letting her gaze wander, refusing to let her mind dwell on the consequences of Edgar's words. Martin's office reflected his personality. Smart, efficient, and professional. It was the ultimate in innovative design, all pale wood, glass, and chrome with discreet filing and absolutely no clutter. Two magnificent, large ornamental fig plants stood either side of the window, their slender, dark green leaves well-known for their air-cleansing properties and supplied by one of the Goods Shed's newest green businesses. Martin was a firm believer in supporting his clients, and he liked this latest trend in interior landscaping. Besides a slim laptop, sitting exactly parallel to the edge of the desk, there was only a pristine leather blotter pad that held an immaculate leather portfolio case, and a Mont Blanc fountain pen and mechanical pencil in a neat line. She thought of her own open-plan, busy and slightly chaotic workplace in New York, and felt a sudden surge of longing to be back there.

'Sorry about that; needy client.' Martin came back into

the room and interrupted her thoughts.

Olivia looked at him for a moment and then switched back to their previous conversation.

'What about Jess?'

Martin sat down next to her and drank his coffee. 'What about her?'

'Why do you think she was being so antagonistic towards me? She's always been fine until now.'

Martin took a deep breath. 'Don't take this the wrong way, Olivia, but I think you need to cut other people some slack as well. Everyone is worried about their livelihood and their future, and they may not think you have the same worries.'

Realisation dawned. 'Because I don't really belong here? Because I have a career in New York?'

Martin looked awkward. 'Perhaps.'

'Are you telling me that people like Jess believe what Libby said about me selling up?'

Martin patted her hand gently. 'Are you telling me it's never crossed your mind?'

Olivia paused, remembering Kitten's warning words. 'Between you and me, I can't say I haven't thought about leaving the Goods Shed in someone else's capable hands, if I could find the right person.'

'When does Joey want you to decide about the promotion?'

'Easter. When the café is due to open.' Her voice was small.

'And that all depends on the finance.' He pulled a face. 'I don't suppose you've got access to that kind of cash?'

'What? By next Tuesday? Of course I haven't.'

'And I suppose all George's money is still going through probate?'

'Yes, it is.' Olivia swallowed. 'But if I did have the money, I'd give it to the café fund, just so the renovation can carry on. Regardless of whether I'm still allowed to be involved or not.'

'Really?'

'It's what George would have wanted.' Olivia spoke firmly. 'I know that.'

'I think that may be hypothetical now, I'm afraid.' Martin's voice was sombre. 'It's not looking good, is it?'

The knot in Olivia's stomach twisted tighter and she bent forward to ease the pain. She felt Martin's hand on her back for a moment and tensed.

'I'm sorry, Olivia, but I'm just going to come out and say this, if I may?' She didn't respond, and he carried on. 'Perhaps you'll find it easier if the decision is made for you?'

She refused to cooperate. 'How do you mean?'

'Well, if this does go to a vote of no confidence, you could just go back to New York without feeling guilty.'

'I'm still not with you.'

'From where I'm standing, it doesn't look as though you are planning to stay in Penbartha long-term. You haven't even moved into the master bedroom at Tresillian yet, from what I remember of the other night, and George's things are all around the house still. It's almost as if you're kidding yourself that he's just popped into the village and will be back any minute. Then you can return to New York and pretend none of this has happened.'

She squeezed her eyelids together tightly to stop the tears that burnt behind them, glad that Martin couldn't see how near to the truth he was.

'I'm sorry if I'm upsetting you, Olivia,' he spoke softly. 'But there's nothing to be ashamed of wanting to go back to a place where you're not reminded of George and Mollie all the time, like you are here. The house, the garden, the dogs ... Perhaps you could—'

'Stop it!' Olivia didn't let him get to the end of his sentence. 'Please!' She raised her head, her face flushed and tearstained. 'I've got to clear my name and get this all sorted for the sake of the members, the villagers and the trustees. Besides which, I'm not sure Trenow will even let me leave Cornwall at the moment, never mind the country.'

'Well, he doesn't seem to be getting very far with his investigations.' He shook his head in despair. 'And I'm worried about how all this is affecting you. First George, then Libby, then the fire. You're already fraying at the edges. What else will it take before you snap, altogether? Perhaps it would be better for you to be out of it all.'

Olivia couldn't trust herself to speak. She forced herself off the sofa and went to help herself to a bottle of water from the fridge built into a sleek wooden unit. She walked to the window and looked out, trying to slow her breathing by concentrating on anything that wasn't New York or Penbartha. After taking a long drink, she turned back.

'Thanks for caring Martin, but abandoning the Goods Shed and the café at the moment is just not an option.'

Martin shook his head. 'George would hate what all this is doing to you. I'm sure he'd rather you were with your friends in New York, having fun.'

This time the mention of George's name hit Olivia deep in her chest, and she sat down abruptly. *It's time*, she thought, *to put the emotional stuff to one side. Don't let yourself be side-tracked by feelings.*

'I'm sorry. I didn't mean to upset you. And I want you to know that I'll do everything I can to help you.'

Olivia pulled herself together and looked at him. She'd always considered herself to be a good judge of character, and she liked Martin. When she'd first arrived back in Penbartha, she had been drawn to his endless energy and the way he could light up a room with his charm and his funny stories. He was just like the men she'd known and dated in New York: handsome, charming, entertaining, and simply didn't understand the way her mind worked.

Nevertheless, he had been a good friend to George, and now he was being the same for her. What more could she ask for?

An unbidden memory sprang to the front of her mind. 'You didn't finish telling me where you disappeared to at the weekend.'

'Clara called me just after I dropped you at Tresillian on Friday evening and we spoke for ages.' His face clouded over. 'She's the only other person who knew Libby like I did, and it was nice to chat about her and old times. But afterwards, I needed to get away from everything for a while. So, I went to a place I know on Dartmoor, where there's no phone reception or internet. I hate being reminded of her everywhere I go in Penbartha. Just like you must be with George. That's why I can relate to you thinking about going back to New York . . .' his voice trailed off.

Olivia's heart went out to Martin, who was clearly distressed, and pushed an image of her cosy New York loft apartment out of her mind. 'Do you want to talk about Libby?'

Martin turned his head away from her. 'Not really, thanks. You sometimes say that talking about George hurts more than it helps. That's how I feel about Libby at the moment. Besides, you didn't know her like Clara and I did.'

She swallowed. 'No, I didn't. But Sarah did. Perhaps you could talk to her.' A thought occurred to her. 'In fact, when I was chatting to her the other day, she suggested there may be more information about Libby's murder than the police are being told. You could suggest she talk to the police about it?'

Martin shook his head. 'Don't take too much notice of anything Sarah says. She had a massive girl-crush on Libby and would love to share the limelight with her in this.'

'Well, so far, Sarah's the only person who seems to

think I'm not guilty. Trenow's suggesting all the evidence shows I murdered her, and Edgar and Jess appear to be of the same opinion.' She waved away his protest as she thought out loud. 'Maybe I should talk to Sarah about it if you don't want to?'

'Why on earth would you do that?' Surprise was written all over Martin's face.

'Because now I'm thinking out loud, I need to find out whether there's a connection between Libby and all this crap that's going on at the café. Everything has only just started to go wrong, and we may be able to stop it getting any worse.'

Martin's frown deepened. 'Leave it to the police. I really don't think you should put yourself in a position to be accused of interfering in their investigation. You need to forget all about Sarah.'

'Don't you want to know who killed Libby?'

A dark shadow flitted across his face. 'Of course! I want the monster who murdered her brought to justice. But it won't bring her back, will it? Just like you driving yourself mad trying to fulfil George's dream won't bring him back.' He ignored her sharp intake of breath and carried on. 'I'm worried about you, Olivia. Particularly as you know my schedule is full for the next few weeks and I won't be around much.' He paused. 'Perhaps I should cancel some of my events so I can be here for you?'

She smiled at his at his concern. 'No way. They've been in your diary for ages, and they could be the answer to some of the Goods Shed's problems. I'll be fine. I might just have a quick word with Sarah though.'

'Just leave it all to the police. Please. Don't go off on a wild goose chase just to take your mind off George and the fact that he's gone. You can't afford to get obsessed with this mad idea about Libby's murder, as well as the station.'

'I am not obsessed.'

'Has it not occurred to you that whoever killed Libby

must have thought they had a good reason to do so? And how do you know he, or she, won't do it again? Please don't get involved, for my sake if not for yours. I couldn't bear the thought of anything happening to you as well.' His green eyes shone with unshed tears.

Olivia stood up and stared at him, her mind whirring. 'I'm sorry, but if this murder isn't solved soon, everything will be at risk: the Goods Shed, the café, the Engine Shed. But at least I'll have tried. I may not be able to do much about any of them until the trustees make their decision, but I can talk to Sarah and find out what she knows.' She walked towards the door. 'From where I'm standing, it doesn't look as though I have much more to lose.'

***

Olivia was unable to avoid the small crowd of Goods Shed members gathered in a light drizzle around the new, sparkling black mini coach parked at the electric charging station in the carpark. They were admiring its luxury leather interior and fabulous exterior livery work displaying the white flag of St Piran and Kernow Kompass Tours lettering along the sides and rear. Olivia stopped to chat to Rozy Fischer, one of her favourite members, who had just been appointed as a champion for the UNESCO Cornish mining world heritage site and ran a historic, cultural, and very popular eco tour guide business with her husband, Bill. As soon as she could, Olivia made her apologies and escaped.

Ten minutes later she was peering through the windows of the Bakehouse. It was full of villagers forced inside by the rain to exchange their usual greetings and gossip. They were chatting away good-naturedly to each other and not in any apparent rush to be served; their wet clothes steaming gently and causing the bay windows to run with condensation. In the booth furthest away from the window, Olivia could see Jago, listening carefully to something Willow was telling him. A sudden, brief smile broke across his features, transforming his face and reminding Olivia of a glimpse of sunshine behind clouds on a grey day. The laughter lines went some way to soften his sharp, blue eyes and strong cheekbones.

Feeling like a child not invited to the popular kid's birthday party, Olivia turned away and walked slowly back across the bridge. She hadn't realised Willow and Jago were on such good terms. He had never smiled like that in Olivia's company as far as she could remember. She wondered what they were talking about, and then Martin's words about her becoming paranoid crept into her mind to torment her. She needed to distract herself with something. She glanced at her watch. 11.30 a.m. It was too early to call any of her New York friends or clients, but she could go back to Tresillian, take the dogs out for a run, process the morning's events and then get on with some work.

Happier now she had a plan, she passed five minutes watching two kittiwakes tumbling on the wind above her, spinning in great acrobatic swoops across the sky, and was so engrossed in them that she didn't hear her name being called at first.

'Hey, Olivia! Wait up!' Sarah was hurrying across the bridge after her. 'I saw you outside the shop and guessed you didn't want to talk in front of other people. Have you thought any more about what I said?' The eagerness in her voice was unmistakable.

Olivia remembered Martin's view of Sarah's hero-worship of Libby. She frowned in apology. 'I've thought about it, but I really believe we should leave the police to do their job. I mean, what can we do that the police can't?'

Sarah scowled. 'It's been five days since Libby was murdered, and from what I hear they still have no solid suspect other than you.'

Olivia's heart sank as she recalled Edgar's words. 'Thanks for the reminder, but I'm putting my trust in Trenow.' She spoke firmly, trying to give Sarah enough faith in the detective to share her findings with him. 'He seems to have things under control.'

'How can you say that? Those coppers are useless and patronising, especially that ginger tuss. Isn't there even a tiny bit of you that would like to crack this case before they do and really put them in their place?'

Olivia took a step back. 'It's not a game, Sarah.'

'So have they mentioned her phones?' A secretive look came over Sarah's face.

'They found her phone at the Hut and are tracking the records.'

'That'll be her iPhone. What about the other one?'

Olivia's scalp prickled. 'What other one? I only ever saw her using an iPhone.'

Sarah gave her a knowing look and changed the subject. 'And what about her dairies?'

'How do you mean?'

'Well, they've got her business diary, but not her personal one.'

'Why not?' Olivia wasn't sure she wanted to hear the answer to her question.

'They didn't ask for it. I gave them the business one that they asked for.'

'Sarah! I'm sure that could be seen as obstructing the police.'

'I've got her personal one.'

Olivia closed her eyes. 'And?'

'Well, I think Libby was seeing someone. I reckon he was married, as she was so secretive about him.'

Olivia digested this news. The upcountry boyfriend, perhaps? Something else Libby had kept from her.

'What are you going to do with the other diary?'

'I've been trying to work out her weird version of

shorthand. I'm good at that sort of thing and I'm sure I can do it.'

'Will you take it to the police?' Olivia couldn't keep the hopeful tone out of her voice.

'I don't know.'

'Sarah! The police have resources, specialists, contacts, databases . . . Stuff we don't have. You don't know what you could get yourself into.'

Sarah's eyes narrowed. 'Well, at least I'm doing something positive to help find Libby's killer. Unlike you!'

'That's not fair. I just don't think—'

'Well, perhaps I'll ask Martin to help me if you won't.' Sarah turned away.

Olivia kept her voice calm. 'Martin will tell you to leave it to the police. Believe me.'

'What about Jago? I'm sure he would help.' Sarah taunted.

Olivia ran her tongue over her lips. 'I wouldn't waste your time, Sarah. Give your information to the police. Or do you want me to?'

'No,' Sarah hissed. 'But I want to ask you a question, Olivia.'

Olivia nodded. 'Go ahead.'

'What do you think George would do? If he was here? Because I know for a fact that he wouldn't be at all impressed if he could see you now. Moping around, looking like shit and caring more about some old buildings than the fact that someone's died.'

***

Olivia struggled to sleep that night. After her words with Sarah, she'd gone back to Tresillian and taken the dogs out for a run, and then Rocky had called round. They'd spent hours tweaking the budget and work schedules for the café, and Olivia could not bring herself to tell him it might all be in vain. As she tossed and turned, whirling thoughts chased each other around her aching head: Libby's murder, the money the café needed to replace the SocialTech fund, the threat of a vote of no confidence, the fact no one else would care about the station the way she did, the impact its failure would have on so many people, and Sarah's harsh words all buzzed in circles round her head like a swarm of angry wasps.

Olivia didn't know what woke her, but suddenly she was sitting upright in bed, listening carefully. Had she heard a noise? Had she been dreaming? She looked at her clock. It was 3 a.m. She turned her pillow over to the cooler side and tried to get comfortable again. Just as she closed her eyes, a sudden light flashed outside in the gardens at the back of the house. Flinging the duvet back, she climbed out of bed and tiptoed to the window that overlooked the gardens and creek. Zennor jumped off the bed and stood at her side, her hackles raised, and her lips pulled back from her teeth, but she remained silent. Mylor carried on snoring. The light stopped flashing and after a few moments Olivia wondered if she had imagined it, or even if it was a light from one of the bigger boats moored further out in the creek. Icy prickles crept up her spine until they edged into her scalp and her entire face felt itchy. A sudden tremendous crash and shattering of glass filled the air beneath her.

Both dogs started barking furiously as they rushed out of the bedroom. Olivia ran after them, down both flights of stairs, the carpet thick under her bare feet, across the cold flagstone hall and into the kitchen, pausing only to snatch the car keys from the hall table. She held them, sticking out from the side of her fist, as she hurried after them, calling them back. She flipped the switch on the wall to flood the room with light.

There was a jagged hole in the side window of the orangery and an inch of thick shattered glass spread across the floor. Shooing the dogs away from the glass, she picked her way carefully across the rug to the cause of the damage. A large creek boulder, worn flat by the waves, lay on the floor, face-up, with the words: STOP INTERFERING painted across it, the letters dripping red, like fresh blood.

CHAPTER TWELVE

'It wasn't blood though, it was red paint,' Olivia told Cassie as they walked along the beach with the dogs. 'Realistic looking blood-red paint.'

Olivia had refused to make a fuss or interrupt anyone else's night. Instead, she'd bolted the door from the kitchen into the rest of the house and gone back to bed, clutching the dogs to her and waited for dawn's pink fingers to creep up the creek, across the silent gardens and around the house. Eventually, at about half-past six, the sunlight slicing through the shutters and dancing across the polished floorboards, along with the loud calling of the gulls, told Olivia that it was a reasonable time to call Rocky and ask him to fix the window.

He had arrived, like the cavalry, dishevelled and half-asleep and after gathering her into a bear hug, quickly morphed into Mr Fix-It. Within an hour there was a steady trickle of people: police, glaziers, and carpenters all traipsing in and doing their bit. Eventually Cassie must have sensed the jittery vibes bouncing off Olivia in waves due to an excess of caffeine and a lack of sleep. She fetched walking boots and dog leads and bundled them all into Mollie's car, leaving Rocky with strict instructions to look after the house and deal with everything.

They drove the twelve miles to the north coast in silence, along the twisty lanes they both knew so well, and Cassie parked up in their usual place at the foot of the sand dunes that edged the beach. With no need for words, the two women and dogs set off across grass that was tough underfoot, seasoned by the blistering sun in the summer and the harsh winter storms which swept mercilessly over this part of Cornwall. Once on the beach, their feet scrunched through the shifting mounds of stones and pebbles until they reached the firm, wet sand left uncovered by the retreating tide. Only then were they able to set off along the two-mile walk along the beach to the next cove, accessible at low tide.

The dogs took off on a high-speed run, chasing each other in circles, taking it in turns to lead and follow, bounding across the sand, stretched out with all four legs off the ground and then cutting across each other to make a tight turn and change leaders. Eventually they both slowed down, tongues lolling out with joy, and waited for their second wind to arrive.

Olivia stared out at the blue of sea and sky blended into one, with just a few wisps of cloud floating lazily overhead that were mirrored in the occasional white crests on the larger waves and was glad they had come to the beach. It was one of the dogs' favourite places to run and she needed the breathing space. And some time to slow her racing heart and thoughts. Cassie was an ideal walking companion at times like this, as she never tried to force conversation. On the downside, she wasn't always discreet; and there was no way Olivia was going to tell her about the threatened vote of no confidence. She glanced through her curls at Cassie, beside her now, striding along between her and the water's edge, valiantly trying to keep up with her.

Waders fed along the glistening shoreline ahead of them. Herring gulls swooped and scavenged. The retreating tide had revealed large, smooth boulders, slippery and slimy with lengths of seaweed and bladder wrack. In between, lay deep pools, teeming with delicate fronds of pink and green seaweed, tiny crabs and shrimps. Olivia smiled as she remembered the hours that she had spent rock-pooling as a child, with Mollie at her side pointing out the miniature creatures that lived there. Mylor appeared from behind a large rock and chased all the birds along the shoreline, who quickly took off in unison. Goofy, smiling and soaked, he then bounded up to Olivia and Cassie and proudly shook himself in front of them. showering them with water and sand. They shrieked and then laughed at his antics.

'Daft dog!' Olivia bent down to pat him.

Their silence broken; Olivia told her about the writing on the rock.

'It had the desired effect whatever the medium used,' Cassie observed wryly. 'It frightened you, didn't it?'

The breeze off the sea flung Olivia's curls in front of her face. She breathed in deeply, savouring the salty tang on her lips.

'Yes.' The wind whipped her reply away, but then she turned to face Cassie and nodded. 'Although I dispute that I was interfering. All I've done is talk, briefly, to Sarah about Libby.'

'And what has the dishy DI Trenow got to say about that?'

Olivia frowned. 'Apparently, he's coming to Tresillian later, so I'll find out then. And to be honest, Cassie, I haven't even noticed if he's dishy or not. I think your hormones may be in overdrive.'

Cassie laughed good-naturedly. 'It's probably the menopause. Kitten's always telling me I should look for a man nearer my own age.' She sobered quickly. 'What did Sarah have to say for herself?'

'Not a lot.' Olivia indicated that she wanted to carry on

walking. She had decided not to share Sarah's theories with anyone just yet, and that included Cassie, which would be easier if they didn't have eye contact. 'But as she's told me to my face that she doesn't believe I had anything to do with Libby's murder, I thought she might have some ideas about what happened that night.' Olivia did not expand on her thought processes.

'And did she?'

'No.' Olivia started walking again, bending now and then to throw a stick into the water for Mylor, who was chasing the breaking waves and barking at the spray. Zennor contented herself with savaging the occasional mound of drying brown seaweed washed up by the tide.

'Well, here's another idea to throw into the mix.' Cassie spoke quietly. 'Have you considered that perhaps Sarah and Libby argued about something? They worked together and perhaps Libby upset Sarah, either intentionally or unintentionally. So Sarah just picked up the nearest thing to hand – the letter opener – and stabbed her with it as an instinctive, self-protection thing? It may well have been sheer luck, or bad luck for Libby, that the blade went in at just the right place to kill her.'

Olivia frowned. 'I don't think Sarah's got it in her. She was totally in awe of Libby.' She threw another stick for Mylor. 'Even Martin said that.'

'He may be right. But when you think about it, Sarah is the most likely suspect. She had the easiest access to the Hut. She knew Libby used that fancy letter opener, and, as she worked with her, possibly had a motive. Even if it was in self-defence or hot-blood or whatever.'

'So why haven't the police come to the same conclusion? Last time Trenow spoke to me he said that there was enough forensic evidence to put me at the scene of the crime.' Olivia picked up a flat pebble and skimmed it furiously out across the sea, thinking about Sarah's information. There was no way she was telling Cassie about that.

'So why would Sarah ask me for help if she's the murderer?' She hurled another pebble after it. 'That doesn't make sense.'

'Perhaps not. But it might make the police believe you've got something to hide if you go off investigating some hare-brained idea of Sarah's. And you don't want to be accused of interfering in their case, especially after last night.'

'Martin said that too.' Olivia stopped in front of Cassie and then looked her straight in the eye. 'Have you been talking to him?'

Cassie bent to throw a stick into the sea for Mylor and avoided looking at Olivia, who decided her paranoia was getting worse.

'He's concerned about you. He's a kind, caring man.'

They walked in silence to the end of the beach where they sat down, their backs against sun-warmed rocks out of the wind, and Cassie opened the flask of strong tea she had brought with her. The Cornish cure for all ills. They lifted their faces to the sun and enjoyed the feeling of warmth as they sipped their tea in silence; the dogs chewing happily on the carrots Cassie had brought. In front of them, the waves rolled onto the beach and covered the sand in long sweeps. Droplets of spray caught the sun like diamonds, and for a moment, Olivia just listened to the sounds of the sea sucking at the sand and hissing, as it breathed in and out in front of them. She was brought abruptly back to earth with Cassie's next words.

'Are you sure you're not obsessing over all this business with Libby to take your mind off your grief over George's death and the problems at the Goods Shed?'

Once again, Cassie's words were horribly familiar, and Olivia twisted round to look at her, at the same time pushing her sunglasses firmly up her nose to hide any emotion her own face might betray.

'I am not obsessed. Libby was murdered. Which is awful enough in itself, but to be accused of it is, is . . .' She brushed away Cassie's protestations. 'I might not be equipped to investigate a murder, but I can try to find out if there's any link between Libby and what's been going on with the Trust. At the moment, if I do nothing, the café project is at risk, and if, God forbid, I'm charged with Libby's murder, we could lose the whole thing. And if I do my darndest to get the café up and running, it will be harder for the trustees to give up on it.' Edgar's threat of a vote of no confidence rushed into her mind and she pushed it away. 'I have to fight for it, Cass, can't you see that?' She gulped. 'It's what George and Mollie entrusted me to do. I can't let them down.'

A tear trickled down Cassie's cheek. 'But they would have hated to see you like this, Olivia.' She turned to her friend. 'Don't ever tell Kitten I've said this, but perhaps you should consider going back to New York. Life would be easier for you there, back with all your friends. Although renovating all the station buildings was George's dream, I know he wouldn't want you to put yourself through all this just for him. Believe me.'

Acutely aware of the crack of misery deep within her heart at the thought of failing her godfather, Olivia stared out over the water, where white-capped waves were forming out at sea, and she soon could not distinguish between her tears and the sea spray whipping into her face.

'It's not just a dream. It's his vision, a carefully thought out and meticulously planned beacon of hope which I fully support. Can't you see that?' She decided she didn't want to continue this conversation and stood up. 'We'd better head back. Look out there.'

Cassie studied the sky and nodded knowledgeably. 'The clouds are banking up quickly, but we should get back before the rain comes in. We need Mollie more than ever.

She could predict the weather with her witchy ways better than any satellite.'

They started walking back. 'It's at times like this that I miss Mollie the most. She always knew the right thing to do.' Olivia paused. 'I wish she could tell me what to do now.'

Cassie glanced at the clouds and gestured to Olivia to carry on walking. 'You're a thirty-three-year-old woman. Mollie wouldn't tell you what to do. She'd tell you to listen to your instinct and work it out that way.'

Olivia sighed. 'You're right. She was forever telling me to do that.'

'And have you?'

'Obviously not. Or I wouldn't be in the mess I am.'

Cassie squeezed her hand comfortingly. 'If Mollie was here, she'd tell you to stop being so hard on yourself. And to learn to trust your inner voice again. It's like training a muscle and it won't happen overnight. You need to practice.'

They finished their walk along the sand in silence, accompanied by the calling of gulls and the occasional excited bark of the dogs. By the time they reached the car, Olivia's curls were sticky with sea spray. Cassie hugged her.

'Don't try to sort all this by yourself, Olivia. Let someone help you.'

Olivia took one last, deep lungful of crisp, salty air that was now blowing straight off the sea and nodded. Inside, her conflicting thoughts were shredding her mind apart with one question. If she couldn't even trust herself at the moment, how on earth could she trust anyone else?

***

Olivia was sitting at the long table in the orangery, scribbling away in a notebook, when she looked up to see the tired face of DI Trenow appearing at the window. She hurriedly closed her notebook and shoved it under the Wheal Senara plans before opening the door for him.

'No Burridge?'

The detective grimaced. 'No, I found him some important filing, but I'm running out. My office has never been so orderly. I think I'll have to move him on to photocopying soon.'

Despite her best efforts, Olivia couldn't help smiling at his lugubrious expression. 'Can I get you a drink?'

'Coffee, please. Do you mind if I sit down for a moment?' He sounded weary.

'Help yourself.' She waved him toward the sofas and went to make the coffee. She watched him as she ground the beans. He didn't look as though he had slept for days. His usually clean-shaven face had at least two days' worth of growth, and his shirt was crumpled.

As she put Trenow's coffee tray down in front of him, she sat on the opposite sofa and cleared her throat. 'I don't really know why I'm asking you this question, but are you feeling okay, Inspector?' She waved towards the plate of Cassie's biscuits which she'd placed on the vintage railway trunk that served as a coffee table. He grabbed two and ate them in quick succession before draining his coffee cup and refilling it from the cafetière on the tray. Then he sat back and fixed his gaze on her.

'Just a bit sleep deprived. And hungry.' He ran his hands over his face and up through his dark hair. 'But thanks for asking.' He swallowed another biscuit.

'Can I fix you something else to eat? Toast and honey?'

His eyes brightened, but then he shook his head. 'Let's get back to business. How are you after your little mishap last night?'

'Mishap?' Olivia said. 'Mishap? That suggests I had something to do with it.'

Trenow held his hands up in a gesture of surrender.

'Sorry. Poor choice of words. I suppose I was trying to downplay it. So you weren't too scared.'

She picked up a heart-shaped pebble from the wooden bowl on the coffee table full of similar-shaped stones she had collected over the years. No trip to the beach was complete without finding a stone in the shape of a heart.

'Sorry.' He apologised again. 'Were you scared?'

She smoothed her fingers over the pebble. 'A little.'

'And had you been? Interfering?

'No. I had two brief conversations with Sarah Santos about Libby. Does that constitute interference?'

'Some people might think it does.' His brown gaze held hers and then he pulled out his notebook and flicked through it.

'Look, Olivia, I want to be honest with you, and I hope you're being honest with me. One of the members of the Goods Shed was found murdered on your premises six days ago, after you had been witnessed arguing with her and threatening her.' He held up his hand to stop Olivia's interruption and she subsided, reluctantly. 'You found her murdered body, but in addition to the contact evidence that one might reasonably expect to find in that situation, we're now in possession of hard forensic evidence that puts you at the scene at the time of the murder.' Again, he held up his hand to forestall her interruption.

Olivia's stomach lurched, and her voice wasn't steady. 'Can you tell me what that evidence is?'

'We found a pair of your reading glasses in the Hut.' Her hand went instinctively to the top of her head where a pair nestled in her still salty hair. 'As was an earring containing your DNA, as identified from a sample we took here. Your fingerprints and DNA were on the wine bottle and glass found at the Weighbridge Hut. Plus, we lifted some of your hairs from the jumper she was wearing when she died.'

Olivia dropped her head into her hands, taking it all in with an ever-sinking heart. When she glanced up, she met

Trenow's gaze. She pulled herself together and straightened her back before she spoke.

'That can all be explained, though, can't it? I'm always leaving my glasses lying around; I could have lost the earring any time, and the hairs on her jumper could have got there at the meeting or earlier that day. Isn't it all too convenient? Too coincidental? I might not know much about committing the perfect crime, but I know about not leaving incriminating evidence behind.' Another thought struck her. 'What about the letter opener? Are my prints on that?'

'No.' The corner of Trenow's mouth curved up a little, acknowledging that she had made a valid point. 'Although some may suggest that you had the foresight to remove your prints from that but overlooked the other items in your desperation to get away.'

'So there were no prints on the letter opener? Not even Libby's?' Her voice faltered at the thought of anyone wiping the handle of a weapon that was still stuck in its victim. 'I didn't do it. How many times do I have to say that before someone believes me?'

He leant forward. 'We have to follow the evidence where it leads. That's how we work. I have to consider you as a major suspect and will continue to do so until I've had the results of the other tests that are being carried out.' He didn't take his eyes off her face. 'Whether I think you're a killer remains to be seen. After all, you've got a strong alibi. Which is a major factor in your favour right now.'

Olivia turned her sudden gulp into a cough and let her hair fall across her face. Then she busied herself putting the stone back where it belonged and changed the subject.

'So, if for one moment you just suspend belief and accept that I didn't kill Libby, then why do you think someone is going to all this trouble to make it look like I did?'

Trenow folded his arms across his chest and held her

gaze. 'It wouldn't be the first time that someone has tried to play mind games with the police and deliberately set someone up for a murder they didn't commit. And then they get some kind of weird kick out of watching us run around like headless chickens, looking like we're incompetent.'

Olivia remained silent.

'But we usually find that murdering someone can lead to all sorts of irrational behaviour.' He fixed her with a look. 'That's when they slip up and get caught.'

She wrapped her arms around herself in a swift, defensive movement.

'You don't think last night's incident is a double bluff, do you? That I did it to deflect suspicion? Oh, God.' Her voice rose. 'I really am becoming paranoid.'

Trenow shook his head. 'No. To my mind, it looks as though whoever was behind last night's escapade is trying to frighten you.'

Olivia opened her mouth, but no words came out and she sat there looking helplessly at the detective.

'Or is someone trying to help you out by deflecting police interest in another direction? Trying to gain favour with you?'

'I don't think I like either of those options.' She hugged her knees even more tightly to her chest.

He leant forward again. 'I think you need to be careful about the people around you.'

Hot tears burnt at her eyelids, and she brushed them away in a gesture of angry despair. 'Everyone is telling me something different. I'm looking at everyone with suspicion. Don't you think I'm trying to figure out who would benefit if I left? At the moment I can't think of anyone who would. All their businesses and livelihoods are dependent on the success of the Goods Shed and the station's renovation. I can't bear to think I may have hurt someone enough for them to do all these crazy things.'

'It may not be personal,' he observed.

'Well, it feels personal, I can tell you!' Olivia stood up and began pacing the floor. 'So who can I trust? You? Cassie? Kitten? Willow and Fraser? Martin? Rocky? Jago bloody Trevithick? Who I would love to be my number one susp—'

She was mid-flow when Trenow's mobile pinged with a text alert. He pulled it out of his pocket, scowled, and then thrust it roughly back and stood up.

'I have to go, Olivia. Burridge has just reminded me that I have to be somewhere else.' He shrugged his suit jacket back on. 'I'm sure you can trust Rocky.' As he pulled open the door, he stepped back, 'And you can definitely trust Jago Trevithick. He and I go back a long way.'

CHAPTER THIRTEEN

'Thanks, Jago. You've no idea how much time you've saved me.' Rocky eased his shoulders back and stretched his arms above his head, wincing, and then stood back to survey their work. They had scrubbed all the woodwork and walls in the café clean of the smoke and soot, and undercoated them, ready for a new topcoat. The lingering smell of smoke was all but gone.

Jago pushed down on the paint tin lid and stretched his own arms, wiggling his fingers against the cramp that was setting in. 'I realised you would be behind on your schedule when you didn't turn up this morning. Your apprentices were panicking a bit, so I decided I'd better pitch in.'

'Sorry about that. I've just got the panelling to do now, but some of the guys from the village have said they'll come along tomorrow and help.' He ran a paint-splattered hand over his face and through the black curls. 'I was late because I had to rush to Tresillian. Olive was having a bit of a crisis.'

'What's happened now?' Jago's ears pricked up.

Rocky's black eyes scrutinised the other man's face for a moment and then he sighed. 'Look, I don't understand any of the stuff going on. Olive's definitely becoming paranoid, not wanting to trust anyone, and I'm feeling the same. I know she has an issue with you for some reason, but I don't, and I need to talk to someone. My sixth sense is telling me I can trust you. If I can't, and I find you've betrayed us, I will personally break both your legs. Got it?'

Jago looked at Rocky's well-defined muscles straining at the seams of his T-shirt and had no trouble in believing he would keep his word. 'Got it.'

Rocky recounted Olivia's tale of the events of the previous night at Tresillian, voicing his concern about the effect it was having on her.

Jago was more interested in the facts of what had happened than its consequences and found himself lining up question after question in his head, but then bit them all back and tuned back into what Rocky was saying.

'... I know Olive better than anyone else here, probably. And Tresillian has been her safe harbour for all these years but seeing her there this morning I'm not so sure she believes that anymore.'

'Is she that spooked?' Jago asked.

'Yes. The house is like a fortress. The gates are locked for the first time in living memory and all the shutters are closed. She won't even answer the landline.' Rocky sank down onto a pile of wood panelling. 'She's proper jumpy and I'm worried about her, Jago; she's closing herself off from people and that's never a good sign.' Rocky looked as though he was about to say something else but stopped himself.

'Will she let anyone stay at Tresillian with her?' Jago handed Rocky a bottle of water and drank from his own.

'Of course not! This is bloody stubborn Olivia we're talking about. Says if she's managed on her own in New York for all these years, she can do the same here. But I don't know how long she can keep it up for.'

Jago chose his words carefully. 'And you're absolutely convinced there is no way Olivia could be behind all this?'

Rocky glared. 'Absolutely not. I've already warned you, Jago . . .'

'I know, I know.' Jago rushed to placate him, feeling the angry vibes radiating off him. 'Just hear me out, please. I'd like your take on things.'

The younger man grunted.

'You've heard the rumours about the evidence the police have got now?'

'Not proper evidence though, is it?'

Jago bowed his head in agreement and moved on. 'Would you accept that Olivia could be seen as having a motive?'

Rocky glowered even more, obviously uncomfortable. 'How do you mean?'

'Well, from what I've heard, she was pretty much humiliated in front of a lot of people at the Goods Shed.'

Rocky shook his dark head. 'You're off beam. Way off beam. That's not the way Oliva thinks.'

'But what about all the other things? The fire, the troubles at the Bakehouse and the Goods Shed. Now this attack on Tresillian? Olivia's got to be the obvious common denominator.'

'I don't know what to think, Jago. I'm a simple guy. A builder, not a detective. All I know is Penbartha has become a different place in a matter of days. And folk don't like it.'

'In which case you'd think people would want things sorted. And yet they're not cooperating with the police.' Jago didn't even try to hide his exasperation.

Rocky chuckled grimly. 'We have a history of sticking together. In the old days it was hiding smugglers and wreckers from the excisemen. Nowadays it's not answering detectives' questions.'

***

After shrugging themselves out of their overalls, Rocky locked the café and as the two men wandered along the walkway, they nodded to a few local dog walkers whom they recognised, a couple of cyclists, and some more serious walking types equipped with walking poles and gaiters, plastic map pouches hanging around their necks.

Just as they reached the Signal Box, Jago suddenly nudged Rocky. 'What's he up to?'

A man in his thirties, with dirty blond, tousled hair and designer stubble, strutted down the walkway towards them, with an enormous camera slung over his shoulder. Everything about him screamed he wasn't local; the tightly fitting black leather jacket, white T-shirt, skinny jeans and pointed black leather ankle boots. He unhitched his camera and set it up on the walkway.

'I'll do the talking. Hide your hands,' Jago hissed, as they reached him, both men shoving their paint-spattered hands deep into their pockets.

'Good afternoon.' Jago's accent was neutral as he nodded to the camera, all traces of any Cornish burr vanished. 'Holiday snaps?'

The photographer laughed. 'You havin' a laugh? This ain't my idea of a holiday destination, mate. Barbados is more my scene. Mebbe Ibiza for a mini break. Know what I mean?' His cockney accent jarred against the clear air.

'Yes, the weather can be unpredictable down here at this time of year, apparently.'

The photographer looked quizzically at them for a moment. 'You local?'

Jago ignored the look of panic that flashed across Rocky's face. 'We're just here to see the bloke at the Signal Box, but he's not here yet.'

The photographer seemed to relax. 'Typical if you ask me. I reckon the Cornish idea of 'dreckly' means the day after mañana.' He laughed at his own joke.

Aware of Rocky prickling beside him, Jago changed the

subject. 'So, what are the photos for?'

The photographer glanced around in an almost comic book fashion, to make sure no one else was listening.

'I've had to come back and take some better snaps of the area.' He waved his arms towards the creek. 'Got the timings wrong last time and completely forgot about the bleedin tide. The last ones just showed all that mud, rotting hulks of old boats and tatty old ropes covered in green slimy stuff.' His lip curled as he spoke. 'Today I got some houses in the village looking nice and the water full of brightly coloured boats. Couldn't have used those first bleedin ones to sell anyfin to anyone from London.'

'So, what's for sale?' Jago asked.

The photographer glanced around again, looked Jago and Rocky up and down, and appeared to dismiss them as harmless. 'Well, between us, there's a big property company in London interested in buying this site for redevelopment. Architects, graphic designers, and all sorts are involved. Producing fancy, glossy brochures.' He patted his camera. 'My forté.'

Jago's gaze swept the Goods Shed and the station in all their restored beauty, and a vision of the only architect he knew popped into his mind. And then he thought of her ashen face at the trustees' meeting the day before and the anguish it betrayed. Was she that good an actress?

'What are they building? Houses?'

The photographer ran his hand carefully through his gelled hair and then patted it back into place.

'Nah mate. Upmarket retirement villages are where the money is these days.'

Jago blinked, momentarily lost for words. 'Really?'

'Sure. Everyfin'll be bulldozed and replaced with fancy single-story cottages and apartments. All mod-cons, lots of glass, security gates, health spa, swimming pool, you name it.' He paused for a moment. 'I s'ppose they might save that

147

old building.' He nodded towards the freshly painted station building. 'It would be good to have somefin the old wrinklies could reminisce in together and talk about steam trains. My mate's one of the company directors, and they say they'll provide some kind of community space. Always goes down well with the planners, as a bit of a sweetener. That and a nod to all that eco claptrap.'

Jago could practically see the smoke coming out of Rocky's ears and nudged him. 'Sounds fabulous.' His face remained inscrutable. 'Who's the target audience? Locals?'

The younger man sniggered. 'You kiddin'? Not at the prices they want to charge! Nah; it'll be an exclusive development for filthy rich pensioners from London and places like that. It's a massive market, mate.' He frowned. 'Though I can't think of anyfin worse than living in a god-forsaken place like this.'

Jago nodded, trying to ignore Rocky's increasingly irate looks.

'How long was the site up for sale?' he asked nonchalantly. 'I usually follow the property markets down here, because an old aunt always brought me here when I was a kid, but I don't remember seeing anything about this place.'

'Oh, they ain't bought it yet.' He told them breezily. 'But that's a formality. Money speaks louder than anyfin else in this game. If my mate gets everyfin lined up first, agreeing a price with the landowner will be a cinch. You're probably looking at five mill an acre here at least. Who'd say no to that?'

Who indeed? wondered Jago. Didn't everyone have their price? Especially someone who was thinking about going back to New York, a place renowned for its high cost of living. 'What about planning permission?'

A closed look crept over the photographer's face. 'My mate's got contacts. It's easy to get local councils on your side in this sort of place, if you know what I'm saying. You just bang on about the economic benefits a development like this would bring to the area, exaggerate its eco credentials and bob's your uncle! Plus, a few of the richer local oldies might move in and free up the houses for the next generation. That's the thing planners like, my mate says.'

'What about local objections and stuff like that? I don't get the feeling, from what my aunt has told me,' Jago added quickly, 'that the people around here are that keen on change.'

'These bleedin country bumpkins never are.' He looked around surreptitiously again. 'But according to my mate, anyone with enough money can get around all the rules and do what they like, eventually. The planners just give up.'

Rocky spluttered and hurriedly turned it into a cough. Jago decided to quit while he was ahead and before Rocky exploded. He looked pointedly over his shoulder at the Signal Box. 'We'd better check on our meeting.' Jago nodded to the photographer. 'But before we go, is there any way I can get more details about this place? It sounds like it might be just the ticket for that old aunt I mentioned. She's got more money than she knows what to do with.'

'Sounds like our kind of person.' He felt around in his pocket and produced two business cards.

'That's me.' He handed Jago a black and white glossy card. 'And this is my mate. There ain't a website or nothin' yet. It's all being done in London at invitation-only seminars. Just give him a bell, say you've met me, and he'll send you an invite. You live in London, did you say?'

'Some of the time, yes.' Without thinking, Jago reached out a paint-spattered hand and took the cards.

Scott Baker, as identified by his business card, looked at them quizzically.

'We've been painting model trains.' Jago improvised quickly. 'The guy we're supposed to be meeting is a railway geek and has found some special editions for us. My friend here,' he nodded at Rocky's mutinous face, 'doesn't get out very much, so I promised him a treat.'

Scott Baker laughed and nodded. 'Whatever floats your boat, mate! Now don't forget to get in touch. Your old auntie will be in for a real treat.'

***

'I'll float his bleedin boat,' Rocky mimicked, once they were in the safety of the Signal Box, 'straight down the creek at high tide. And I'll make sure there are so many bloody holes in the bottom that he won't get far.'

'I don't think tea will quite do it for either of us.' Jago retrieved a bottle of malt whisky from the bottom drawer of his desk. 'Scotch?'

'Make it at least a double.' Rocky sank down onto the chesterfield sofa and buried his head in his hands. 'What the hell is Olivia going to say when she finds out about this? And Kitten?' His voice disappeared into a wail, and he knocked his drink back in one gulp.

Jago took a risk. 'Do you think Olivia knows about this?'

'What!' Jago thought Rocky was about to explode. 'No way. Not in a million years. It goes against everything we all stand for.' He held his glass out for a refill. Jago obliged and then sat back and waited.

Rocky's eyes closed for a moment, and when he opened them, they were glittering dangerously.

'Trust me, Jago. Olive knows nothing about this. There is not enough money in the world to persuade her to sell this site. It would kill her to have to part with it. Plus, she totally believes in what we are all doing here, for the environment and the community. She would never countenance the demolition of these buildings.' He closed his eyes briefly again.

'What if Olivia feels she has no choice because of

everything else that's going on?'

'No,' Rocky said without hesitation. 'She would find a way.'

His loyalty impressed Jago. He also liked Rocky and trusted his judgement. He obviously knew Olivia better than anyone else in Penbartha did, even though the person Rocky talked of so fondly differed from the one Jago had encountered so far. But now he was beginning to realise just how devastated she must have been by the turn of events at the trustees' meeting. Would she have been if she knew about these plans?

There was one more question he needed to ask. 'Do you think she'll go back to New York?'

This time Rocky thought for a moment. 'It was Libby who said she was going back, not Olivia. We haven't talked about it. But even if she did, she wouldn't sell up here.' His voice was firm. 'She'd find a way to keep it all going somehow. You don't know her like I do. She's loyal and faithful and she loved George and Mollie more than anyone else in the world. And besides, Kitten would never let her,' He took a gulp of his scotch. 'Oh, God, I can just see Kitten chaining herself to the buildings to stop the bulldozers getting through, prepared to die in the attempt to save the place.' He held out his empty tumbler for another refill. 'How the hell are we going to tell them?'

CHAPTER FOURTEEN

'Alice, what on earth is all this secrecy about?' Olivia wasn't in the mood to play games so early in the morning. She felt dreadful after another sleepless night. Her body ached, her head throbbed, and she was exhausted. But she was afraid to sleep. The nightmares about finding Libby's body and being arrested had now been joined by ones about what would happen to the Penbartha Station Trust and all its buildings if she was forced to resign.

'Mr Armstrong wanted me to arrange a meeting with you before anyone else gets in.' Alice looked pointedly at her watch. 'He's already in his office. I'll bring some coffee up.'

Olivia forced herself up the stairs with Zennor and Mylor at her heels, while Alice bustled off in the opposite direction. As she reached Callum's door she stopped and took a deep breath. *Stay calm, Olivia, stay calm.* Straightening her shoulders and brushing the tendrils of hair from her face that were already escaping from the loose knot, she lifted her chin and knocked.

'Come in!' Callum's cheerful voice replied, in invitation.

Olivia stood in the doorway, open-mouthed. She assumed it was Callum she could barely see above the mountains of buff-coloured files and paperwork on the main desk. His in-tray had collapsed under the pressure put on it and stacks of empty copier-paper boxes looked as though they had vomited invoices and grubby-looking receipts all over the floor. Framed certificates proclaiming his many and varied qualifications, along with some casual shots of his wife and three teenage children fought for space on the wall; a huge chart, colour-coded for March and April, was blocked out in different bright colours for different clients. Amongst all the piles, Olivia spotted a sick-looking pot plant with yellowing, droopy leaves and sympathised with it.

'Morning Olivia. End of the tax year. Give me a couple of weeks and this office will be as tidy as Martin's.' Callum's affable face appeared from behind his desktop computer, and Olivia wondered how many forests were sacrificed to meet the demands of accounting regulations every year, even in this digital age. Kitten would be incandescent about it.

'Don't they say an empty desk is the sign of an empty mind?' A low, resonant voice sounded from the other end of the office, and Olivia spun round in disbelief. *What the hell is he doing here?*

Jago Trevithick looked up from the spreadsheets he was examining and nodded at Olivia. 'Morning.'

Zennor gave a little yap of 'hello', skittered across the floor to Jago, and sat at his feet.

'Good morning.' With all her senses on high alert, Olivia edged carefully around the piles that consumed the floor without causing any major avalanches and sat down as far away from Jago as possible. Mylor followed.

'I'll get it, Alice. Thank you,' Callum called out to a knock on the door. He nimbly picked his way to the door, rescued the tray from Alice and shut it again before she could pass comment on the state of his office.

'Shall I be mother?' Without waiting for an answer, Callum swiftly poured three cups of coffee and handed round milk and a plate of fruit and Bakehouse pastries.

The two men munched on their croissants and Mylor, deciding that the biggest crumbs would come from Callum's end of the room, made his way to him, knocking over a few precariously piled files on his way.

Olivia drank her coffee silently, running through all the reasons why Jago could possibly be there until she became aware of someone's eyes upon her. She raised her head and met his deep blue, inscrutable gaze. Feeling as though he was reading her mind, she looked quickly away and turned to Callum with a nervous smile. 'Can we get down to business, please? I'm not sure what this meeting is about, and I've got a lot on this morning.'

'Fine. Sorry for all the hush-hush treatment, Olivia, but Jago and I were both rather alarmed by the turn of events at the meeting on Monday and wanted to treat this on a need-to-know basis, if you get my drift.' Callum pushed his glasses up his nose and beamed at her.

Olivia's wary expression said it all, and Jago stepped in.

'What Callum is trying to say,' he began brusquely, 'is that we may be able to help you come up with the cash that's needed for the café, without the need to vary the original repayment schedule for the Goods Shed.'

Olivia felt an unfamiliar bubble of hope somewhere deep within her and she turned eager eyes to Callum.

'So the trustees won't have to agree to a delay in the repayments and we can go ahead with the café? That's amazing!' Tears pricked at Olivia's eyelids at this unexpected, good news, but she brushed them away with her fingers and got back to business. 'I reckon the trustees will be far less likely to give up on the café, or the Trust as a whole, if the financial burden of getting it up and running is taken off their shoulders. Callum's forecasts show that the café will support itself, once it's open.'

'Hopefully.' Jago's solemn tone brought her back down to earth. 'What we're proposing should release sufficient capital to fund the rest of the renovation work to the café and fitting it out with Wi-Fi and so on. It should also help with the acquisition of the extra equipment we need. But isn't in the budget.'

Olivia tried to push down the sheer relief she was feeling and force herself to be calm and practical. 'May I ask where the money is coming from?'

He cleared his throat and avoided her eyes, giving nothing away. 'All you, or anyone else needs to know, is that as partners in our railway memorabilia business, George and I had a formal partnership agreement that in the event of his death, certain assets would pass to me to create what he liked to call a rainy-day fund. To use with your agreement.'

Olivia swallowed. 'He did?'

'And these assets include a significant number of items that George rescued, quite legitimately from Paddington Station when he was Chief Engineer there at the time of the Beeching Report and the nationalisation of the railways.'

She nodded. She had grown up on stories from George's time there.

'Well, to cut a long story short, George rescued loads of things that would have been just thrown in a skip or burnt. All quite legitimately. He also rescued hundreds of posters, paintings and even original artwork for the posters, which is rare. And they're all stored safely in London in archive conditions, so they are as good as new.' Olivia nodded at him through narrowed eyes, still not letting herself exhale fully.

'The posters alone may be the answer to your needs. And, under our partnership agreement I can now sell them to raise the cash needed for the café.'

Callum leaned forward, dropping crumbs to the delight of Mylor, his eyes shining. 'The important thing, Olivia, is that we won't have to part with many of them, maybe only about fifty, to more than cover the money that's been withdrawn by the SocialTech fund, and for the cash needed to complete the refurb works.'

'And they're not subject to probate or inheritance tax or anything else that makes them impossible to get at?' Olivia still couldn't believe it was that easy.

Callum shook his head. 'Just regular tax, which I've included in my calculations.' He thrust a spreadsheet under her nose and pointed at the columns she needed to read first. 'And Jago and I are hopeful that if we can raise the money we need this way, and with your blessing, it will show the trustees you're fully committed to the entire project.'

Callum nodded to the spreadsheet in her hands and excused himself from the room for a moment. Mylor gave up on his quest for food and lay down by Olivia's feet.

Olivia scrutinised the numbers, her lips pursed, and then leaned back in her chair. Jago was busy scribbling figures in the margins of his own spreadsheet. He leaned across the table and poured more coffee into their cups and then sat back in his chair, crossed his long legs at the ankles and folded his arms. Then he turned his intense blue gaze on her.

'You've gone very quiet, Olivia.' His deep voice brought her to her senses, and she sat up straight, ever cautious.

'What's the catch?'

'Callum will tell you, there's no catch.' His gaze didn't falter.

She bit her lip. 'Isn't there always a catch?'

He shrugged. 'Not always.'

Olivia met his gaze firmly. 'So why do you think George would want me to agree to this?'

Jago pushed a hand through his short, silver hair in an impatient gesture until it was standing up in spikes. 'As much as it grieves me to say this, I agree with George that you're the best person to move forward with the renovation of the station building for this job and growing the Goods Shed. You've got the necessary vision and enthusiasm and ability.'

Olivia was shocked into silence by his compliment, even if it was backhanded. She waited for the caveat.

Jago moved around the table and sat opposite her. 'But you do realise that this doesn't mean that Edgar will necessarily call a halt to the vote of no confidence? That they are two completely different issues?'

Wow, he didn't pull his punches. The same shiver of anxiety that had kept Olivia awake at night rippled through her again and she closed her eyes for a moment. When she opened them, he was watching her closely.

'I'm aware of that thank you. But it doesn't alter the fact that I want to help the café renovation to go ahead. I want to show the trustees that I fully support everything we're doing here. Why do you ask?'

'I just wondered if you'd still be so keen on agreeing to this proposal if you realised your future here as a trustee was still at stake. The money raised from the sale of those assets would otherwise have come to you eventually.'

Icy rage flooded Olivia's veins and tingled all the way down her arms to her fingertips.

'Of course I would! This isn't about me. It's about everything George stood for, and I believe in. Do you really think so little of me?' Her voice rose.

Jago's jaw tightened and he crossed his arms. 'Olivia, what I think of you and what you think of me is really of secondary importance to everything else at the moment. I just need to be sure that you know what you're agreeing to.'

'Well, I do,' she snapped, and glared at him. *Really, had the man no compassion? If he thought he was helping, he was way off-beam.*

The atmosphere between them hummed with hostility. Jago sighed, got up and walked to the window. She flinched as he walked past her, instinctively moving away from him.

He turned round. 'You really don't trust me, do you?'

Heat flooded Olivia's face and she bent down to pat Mylor, who had pressed himself against her legs. 'Let's just say I'm having some trust issues at the moment.' She didn't look up.

'I can understand that, with everything that's going on. But I made certain promises to your godfather that I intend to keep. George had complete faith in you,' his voice softened, 'but he understood human nature better than most people and was aware that if everything wasn't completely set up and running with the Trust before he died, you may have a few issues to face.'

'Did he know he was going to die?' Olivia blurted out the question she had been wanting to ask for ages.

'I don't think so.' Jago's voice was firm. 'He was full of plans. I just think he wanted to make everything as uncomplicated for you as he could.'

Olivia forced her eyes shut against the tears that were burning there. She couldn't cope with thoughts of her godfather's death at the moment.

'Your godfather was very good to me, and I want to honour the promises I made to him. Realising the cash that we need in this way should at least help with the café.'

With her eyes still firmly closed, Olivia allowed the reassuring authority in his voice to convince her she was about to agree to the right thing. It wasn't for her, she reminded herself, but for the community. She opened her eyes and met Jago's gaze directly.

'Thank you. I understand what you're saying, and I agree to your proposal.' She reached out and shook his proffered hand. It was warm and dry and comforting.

'You're welcome.'

The door opened, and an anxious-looking Callum reappeared, followed closely by a man Olivia instantly recognised.

'I'm so sorry, Olivia.' Callum's voice wasn't quite steady. 'This is . . .' he turned to the man behind him, who stepped forward and took over. Mylor scrambled to his feet, his hackles rising, a deep growl in his throat.

'DS Burridge, Miss Wells. I've come to return the minutes of the trustees' meeting held before Miss Walsh died. There's now a copy on file, so you can have the originals back.'

Mylor's growl intensified as the detective moved closer towards her.

'I've warned you about this dog before. You need to keep him under control.'

'Mylor's fine. A bit protective perhaps, but he's under control.' Jago sat back down, twiddling two paperclips.

Burridge didn't look convinced but cleared his throat and carried on. 'If I could just talk to Miss Wells alone, please?'

Callum exchanged brief glances with Jago, who gave a slight nod of this head and left with a friendly pat on Olivia's arm. Jago remained where he was.

'And you, sir?'

Jago slowly raised his head to look at the detective. 'I don't think so, detective sergeant. I think Miss Wells would like me to stay and listen to what you have to say. And, if my understanding of the law is correct, I believe she is allowed to have someone present.' His relaxed but commanding tone obviously took Burridge by surprise.

'Well, this is all very irregular.' He reddened. 'But I am prepared to make an exception in this inst—'

Olivia intercepted a look from Jago which stopped Burridge mid-flow.

'Would you like Mr Trevithick to stay?' Burridge asked her.

'Yes, please.' The words came out instinctively. She knew she needed help now, and although she had no idea what help Jago could be, he was better than no one. Burridge remained standing, apparently enjoying looking down on his audience.

'Miss Wells, I am aware of all the developments in this case. And while my colleague may think he has all the experience I lack, as far as I can see, he's just putting off the inevitable.'

'Which is?' Her voice was a whisper; her legs began to shake.

Burridge consulted his notebook. 'To arrest you on suspicion of your suspected involvement in the commission of a criminal offence, i.e.,' he snapped his notebook closed and turned a triumphant face to Olivia, 'the murder of Miss Elisabeth Walsh.'

The room started to spin, and Olivia clutched the desk in front of her. This was it. She was going to prison and all their plans would turn to dust.

'And?' Jago's deep and utterly smooth voice pierced her fog.

'And what?' Burridge scowled.

Jago stood up slowly and moved round the table until he was right by Olivia's side. She was acutely aware of his presence and felt nothing but reassurance. He was considerably taller than the detective, who now had to look up at him.

'Detective Sergeant Burridge, as you will know, under Section 25 of the Police and Criminal Act 1984, a lawful arrest by a police officer requires two elements, both of which must be satisfied.' He held up his hand to stop Burridge's blustering interruption. 'And I quote: one, "a person's involvement, suspected involvement or attempted involvement in the commission of a criminal offence" and two,' his sharp gaze was directed at the detective, 'that "there are reasonable grounds for believing that the person's arrest is necessary".'

'I believe it is necessary.'

'Do you, detective sergeant? May I ask on what grounds?'

The detective fumbled through his notebook again.

'Perhaps I can help you with that.' Jago slid his hands into his jeans pockets and strolled to the window, before turning and speaking smoothly and firmly. 'Under Section 24 of PACE, you need to consider whether a person's arrest for an offence is necessary and proportionate. Such considerations include whether the police are already in possession of their name and address, which I believe you are; whether they are likely to cause physical injury to themselves or anyone else, which I would suggest Miss Wells is not, and various other conditions which I can assure you are not relevant in this case. I can recite the remaining six subsections if you're having trouble recalling them, sergeant, but I would like to remind you that Miss Wells has been happy to assist with your inquiries to date and will continue to do so. Won't you, Olivia?'

Olivia switched her gaze between the two men, a little spark of hope flickering in the bottom of her stomach. She just about managed to nod.

'Perhaps Miss Wells would like to call for proper legal representation?' Burridge blustered. *No doubt*, Olivia thought, *he had Jago labelled as a harmless railway geek, with a fondness for detective fiction.* Suddenly, she wasn't so sure.

'That won't be necessary. I will represent Miss Wells, won't I, Olivia?' He turned to her with a reassuring smile and an overwhelming sense of authority, before settling an icy gaze on Burridge.

'If you would like to make a note of this for your records, detective, my full name and title is James Trevithick QC.'

CHAPTER FIFTEEN

'I am so sorry about all this, Olivia.' Trenow looked mortified. 'Please believe me when I say I had no idea the little idiot would act way above his pay grade and try to arrest you. I was tied up at the lab with the post-mortem results for Libby. Rest assured; Burridge will be directing traffic at Land's End or something for the foreseeable future if I have anything to do with it.'

Jago watched Olivia closely. Any relief she had shown earlier when walking away from the Goods Shed, a free woman, now seemed to have completely disappeared. Her dark eyes were bigger than ever in her pale, pinched face, and without her sweater he could see how her shirt hung over her jutting collar bones. The physical toll that recent events had taken was clear. She appeared relaxed, sitting on the sofa in the orangery at Tresillian, feet tucked up beneath her and Zennor on her lap. But Jago wasn't fooled for a minute. He could practically feel the air vibrating around her. She eventually broke the silence.

'Am I allowed to know what the post-mortem showed?'

Trenow sat with his head in his hands for a few moments before rubbing his eyes and clearing his throat.

'Look, both of you, what I'm about to say is completely off the record and it must stay between us. If it ever gets back to my superiors, there will be hell to pay.'

Both Jago and Olivia nodded, and Trenow slowly withdrew his pocketbook and began reading.

'The PM confirmed that Libby died as a result of a penetrating wound to the abdomen caused by the letter opener. As the instrument was long and sharp, it required only a relatively light pressure to penetrate her clothes and the skin, etc. And such a needle-like tipped instrument would create little or no external blood loss, but it penetrated major blood vessels and the liver and spleen. As a result, the internal haemorrhage into the abdominal cavity would have been profuse and would have led to immobility, loss of consciousness and death, quite quickly.'

Olivia closed her eyes and lowered her head.

'There was no evidence of defence injuries on her hands, or arms. No bruises, scratches or contusions. They found nothing under her fingernails, so it doesn't look like there was any struggle at all.'

'Suggesting that she knew her attacker,' Jago commented.

'And that she wasn't expecting trouble. That Libby trusted the person who was with her in the studio, right up to the point of attack, when she had been taken by surprise. There was no sign of sexual interference either.' Trenow paused for a moment and lowered his notebook. 'All of which suggests the attacker was a friend.'

Olivia's face drained of colour.

Jago didn't flinch. 'And yet statistics show that ninety per cent of violent crime against women is carried out by men they know intimately.'

Trenow moved on quickly. 'The results from tests carried out on the stomach contents showed that she had been drinking white wine.'

'She only ever drank white wine,' Olivia said, wincing.

'Really?' Jago sat forward on his chair, frowning.

'Sure. She always made a big thing about only drinking French and Italian whites. She didn't approve of my preference for New World reds at all.' A memory flashed through her mind. 'There were two bottles on the side, weren't there? Both red? Did they both have my fingerprints on them?'

'One of them did. The other was clear.' Trenow confirmed, exchanging glances with Jago. 'And the glass with your prints contained the remains of red wine, although to a much-reduced extent, suggesting that someone had rinsed it out with water. The other glass contained white wine and had Libby's fingerprints on it. But there was no sign of a bottle of white wine anywhere on the premises, or in the immediate locality.'

There was a long silence while Trenow consulted his pocketbook. He opened his mouth, and then closed it again.

Jago met his gaze for a long moment. 'Let's face it, Ross. You've got no evidence to connect Olivia to Libby's death from the post-mortem, and the evidence found at the crime scene is only circumstantial, at best.' His voice was firm. 'I presume you've considered the possibility, and some might say likelihood, that all that so-called evidence was planted there to incriminate Olivia?'

Trenow nodded. 'I have, yes. And what they've done so far is all sloppy. Which gives me slight hope that they might just slip-up soon and make a mistake.'

'That's a possibility. But what concerns me is that some less experienced and less cynical detectives might just take the evidence that's given to them at face value. As your colleague demonstrated this morning and then didn't even get his attempt at an arrest right.'

Trenow sighed. 'Give me a break, Jago, please. I'm juggling pressure from above and below to arrest you. What you did today is not exactly going to endear either of you to the rest of the team, and my Senior Officer is having kittens about it.'

'Excuse me for pointing out the error of your sergeant's ways,' Jago interrupted coolly. 'Just think of the paperwork it saved you in the long-term, as you would have had to release Olivia. Not to mention the threat of a miscarriage of justice . . .' His voice hardened.

'Er, excuse me, I *am* here.'

Jago switched his gaze to Olivia.

'May I ask a question?'

'Fire away.'

She turned her dark eyes on Trenow, her hand clutching her pendant. 'You're being very open with your information, suddenly, Inspector.' She swallowed. 'Is that because you and Jago are old pals?'

Jago looked at her in surprise. *How did she know that?*

Trenow jumped in before he could speak.

'As I told you, Olivia, I trust Jago. And I'm beginning to believe you might be of vital importance to this investigation, and therefore, of more use to me if we're on the same side.'

Olivia's eyes widened.

'But I need your word that anything the three of us discuss won't go any further.'

Jago glanced quickly at Olivia, and she nodded.

'And we must keep the results of the PM strictly between us.'

'Okay, okay, but I'm not sure what I'm supposed to add to this when you still have no idea who the murderer is, even with your gazillions of resources.' There was no mistaking the frustration in Olivia's tone.

Trenow's mobile buzzed and he sighed. 'I must get on. I need to smooth some ruffled feathers back at the unit.' He stood up. 'Keep your head down, Olivia, but your eyes and ears open.'

'I'll try.'

Only Jago could see the expression on her face, and he

suppressed a small smile.

Trenow turned briefly, as he walked through the door, his face creased with tiredness and strain. 'I've never known a case like this. There is practically zero intelligence out there. Nobody is saying anything.'

Oh yes, they are, Jago thought. *You just need to ask the right questions. Of the right people. Unlikely people.*

***

Olivia sank back against the cushions of the sofa. 'I can't believe there's someone out there who is so desperate to get me away from here that they are prepared to murder someone I thought was a friend and then do their damnedest to frame me for it. And now the police are split between wanting to arrest me and wanting me to help them find who did it.' A sob caught in her throat before she swallowed it down. 'It's ridiculous!'

'If it's any help, and I don't suppose it is. I agree with you.' Jago's mind was working hard.

'You do?' There was a note of hope in her voice.

'But I'm afraid it doesn't matter whether I believe you. Or even whether Trenow does. He'll be under immense pressure from his superiors, who will reckon there's sufficient evidence to put a case to the CPS and have you formally charged.'

'Even though he accepts there are good reasons for the so-called evidence being where it is?'

Jago sighed, thought about being disingenuous with her but decided to be honest. 'I know that. And you know that. Even Trenow knows that. But the case will be taken out of his hands, and it wouldn't be unheard of for the police not to disclose evidence that might help the accused. Believe me, I've seen it happen.'

Her eyes widened, and her hands began to shake again.

'But you've got an alibi, and that's a strong defence, and

one which they can't dismiss.' His blue eyes stared straight at her, watching for her reaction.

A dark flush travelled up Olivia's cheeks, and she closed her eyes. Then she struggled to her feet, dislodging a protesting Zennor, and walked out of the room, leaving Jago to his thoughts.

He became aware of an unfamiliar stirring deep within him he hadn't felt for a long time: a desire to see justice done. And done properly. He'd dismissed the feeling straight after Libby's murder, put it down to old habits dying hard, but he had prosecuted enough murder cases in his time to know how the police worked – for good and bad.

Years of prosecuting and defending murder cases had inured Jago to the pleas of so-called innocent people being charged with, and convicted of, murder. He could honestly say, hand on heart, that all the people he had successfully prosecuted were guilty. At least they used to be. Now, he knew all about the police believing they had charged the right person and hiding evidence that might help the accused. He knew about the non-disclosure of vital witness statements and other evidence. And he was aware of the cutbacks in legal aid, leading to an increasingly poor quality of defence barristers, making glaring errors, spending less time in pre-trial conferences with their clients, and the lack of resources in the CPS. In fact, he knew more about what went on in the UK legal system, supposedly envied across the globe, than he wanted to.

But it wasn't just the police that posed a threat to Olivia now. It was also her fellow trustees. A dainty foot pawed at his leg, and he looked down at Zennor, who was sitting in front of him, her head cocked on one side. He observed the little dog gravely and sighed. 'Oh, okay then.'

The sound of cupboard doors being banged told Jago that Olivia was in the kitchen. When he began fearing for the hinges, he moved across and watched as she pulled things out of cupboards, yanked the Aga plate cover up and banged the kettle down so hard that water flew out of its spout and bubbled and hissed across the surface.

'Are you okay?'

She spun round, eyes blazing. 'Obviously not! I'm caught up in a complete nightmare. Everything's falling apart. And I have absolutely no control over it.'

'You could always take control.' Jago spoke to her back.

'How?'

He remained silent, and Olivia eventually turned and held his gaze with a curious mixture of defeat and defiance.

'The sale of the posters may not take long if I can find the right buyer. But you've only got until Monday for the police to find a viable alternative as a suspect, or the worst-case scenario is the trustees will kick you off the board. Unless you find them first.'

Olivia spun round, her eyes wide and her mouth open. 'I'm sorry?'

'I can help you.' A part of Jago couldn't believe he was suggesting anything that would bring them into more contact with each other. Helping her sort out the finance for the café was one thing, getting involved in a criminal investigation was a whole different ball game.

'We? Us?' The horror was clear in her voice. 'What? As in you and me?'

Jago remained calm. 'I've always been a sucker for the underdog, and this whole thing appeals to my sense of justice.'

Olivia stared at him, floundering. 'I don't know if I can . . . I'm completely out of my depth, Jago. I'm an architect for God's sake, not a detective or a private eye. If they even exist in the real world. I'm used to dealing with buildings, not people. I don't have the skills, the resources, or the contacts. I wouldn't have a clue where to start.' She walked to the window, gazing out over the gardens to the creek, where a solitary male curlew made its way along the shore, dipping its long, slender down-curved bill into the mud, foraging for lungworms and small shellfish.

'You also deal with people, Olivia, every day of the week. Not only here, but in your architecture practice, I'm sure. Clients, planning officers, conservation officers and building inspectors. And builders. I've seen the way you are with members of the Goods Shed. How they open up to you. And there will be people out there who would talk to you in a way they wouldn't talk to the police.'

He caught her pointed look that revealed she was checking his words for any slight or insult and tried to smile. 'I can bring my own skills as a barrister to the table. I have different experiences from yours and we can organise our efforts in a logical, rational way, and hopefully come up with a plan.'

'Whereas you assume I base all my theories on intuition and instinct?' Olivia's tone was sharp, but not as sharp as he had expected. He moved to stand beside her, watching the curlew's mate join him at the creek side, and caught a waft of something sweetly fragrant: fresh notes of green herbs and jasmine with a lingering perfume of rose petals.

'There's nothing wrong with instinct and intuition,' he said. 'But they are most useful when combined with reason and logic, I've found. And when we engage our brains rather than our emotions. The police may well have their badges and warrants and authority, but we have the information we can glean from local gossip. And we can do this by using our combined talents for analysis, rational thought and intuition rather than detective work.'

Her dark eyes scrutinised him so intently he didn't dare look away. He wished he could read her mind and know what battles she was fighting with herself. He took a deep breath and looked down at her, suddenly aware of how slim she was beside him. But whatever she lacked, physically, she made up for in spirit.

'I realise you have no reason to trust me at the moment, Olivia, and that I haven't been entirely honest with you about what I used to do for a living. But this isn't about me. And from where I'm standing you've got the most to lose if the police don't find the real killer.'

Olivia moved away slowly and finally turned to face him. 'You're right. Can we talk about it somewhere else? Anywhere but here?'

***

Jago drove them to Falmouth in his Land Rover. If Olivia was surprised by his untidy and muddy vehicle, she kept her comments to herself, but he noticed the careful way she placed her feet in the passenger seat's footwell, avoiding the detritus that had gathered there, and the way her nose quivered slightly as it caught the damp dog aroma that was ever-present. They chatted about inconsequential topics on the way, and Jago could feel her mood lifting as they drove further away from Penbartha. It continued as a waitress showed them to a window table. Jago realised he was finding her good company. They lapsed into silence as they chose their meals and then gazed at the views of nearby Pendennis Castle and out to the Lizard Peninsular. Under the grey and blowy March skies, a group of dog owners walked together, chatting and enjoying the freedom of the beach before the local council enforced the dog ban at Easter.

It was only when they had finished their lunch that Jago felt brave enough to broach the subject that had been bothering him for a while. 'So if we're going to work together, there's something I need to ask you about.'

Olivia's shutters came down immediately; she shifted position on her chair so her body was facing away from him and concentrated for a moment on chewing a piece of cucumber.

'Okay.'

'When I first met you, I said something which put us on the wrong footing. I'd like to know what I said to make you dislike me so much.'

'I blamed you, I guess, for George's death.' For once, Olivia's emotions were written all over her face.

Jago's mouth fell open. 'I can assure you—'

'Not like that,' she cut him off. 'I resented you for being the last person he spoke to, spent time with. You said you didn't notice anything was wrong.'

He flinched. 'I've thought about that evening a great deal. Racked my brains to see if I missed the signs. I blamed myself for a while, too. I'm sorry.'

She nodded and looked away. 'It wasn't your fault. I've asked enough questions, done my research. There wouldn't have been any signs. It would all have happened after you left.' Tears filled the dark eyes, making the flecks of gold glitter and reflect in the pendant she'd once again clutched in her hand. 'I let my anger with you fill some of the void that grief had left behind. I wanted to blame someone.'

Jago was suddenly eager to explain himself. 'I was trying to help, by telling you about that evening and how happy he was. But my gesture backfired. I'm sorry.'

She took a deep breath. 'I'm sorry I behaved that way towards you.'

'Accepted.' He brushed it away and changed the subject. 'Now, may I tell you something about Mollie?'

She wiped her eyes and pulled her hair back into a messy bun with an elastic band she unhooked from her wrist. 'Okay. As long as it won't make me cry again.'

Jago watched three dogs chasing their balls into the sea, then looked up and caught her glancing at him from under her curls. He carried on.

'A while ago, something made me question everything

in my life.' He swallowed. 'And, serendipitously, I met Mollie just at the right time. And she was the wisest woman I've ever met.'

Olivia tried to smile, but Jago could see the sadness in her face and her obvious love for her unusual godmother.

'I already knew George, and he invited me to stay with them at Tresillian while I took some time out to consider my options. And Mollie helped me with some decisions I'd been thinking of making for a long time. They showed me round the Goods Shed and something clicked in my brain. I was slightly worried that the members might all be lentil eating, sandal wearing tree huggers,' he noticed her smile and carried on, 'but I couldn't have been further from the truth. They were all genuine ecopreneurs and creative types with green values who were combining their business activities with environmental awareness. These people had worked out what would make them happy and were all united in their dream to build this special business community, where people practice what they preach. It was all so very different from the working environment at the London bar and it appealed to a part of me I hadn't listened to for a long time.' Jago smiled then; a lopsided, self-deprecating smile that crinkled into the lines at the corners of his eyes. 'So when they asked me to help them, in whatever way I could, I just knew instinctively, it was the right thing to do.'

Olivia's dark eyes slid round to his face and held his gaze. 'Mollie was very keen on listening to her inner instinct, and I know what you mean. I've grown up with their slightly alternative views of the world and our need to find our place in it. They'd definitely both found theirs here. That's why I feel so strongly about Penbartha Station Trust. I want to see their vision fulfilled.'

'I get that.' He drained his beer. 'And that's why I'm here, a trustee, and why I'm offering to help.'

'Okay.' This time when she met his gaze.

Jago could feel a subtle shift in her internal battle over whether she could trust him.

Olivia's hand closed round her pendant. 'I don't like the idea of viewing everyone I know in Penbartha as a potential suspect.'

'I understand, and I think we need to be a little more focused in our investigation.'

'How do you mean?'

'You said earlier that it felt like someone was desperate to get you away from here. Do you still feel that way?'

Olivia thought for a moment. 'I guess so. All these problems started when I came home and made it clear that I wanted to see things through at the Trust.'

Jago ran a hand through his hair and scratched at the back of his head. 'And do you have any idea who would want to set you up for a murder?'

She bristled again, and he cursed himself for his clumsy question.

'Are you asking me if I have any enemies? I'm not like you; I don't mix with criminals . . . if I upset a client, they just engage another architect, not hunt me down.'

He let her comment pass. 'So, if this isn't about you personally, do you agree that it's to do with the Trust?'

'Possibly. But who? Everyone here is so committed to the place.'

A vision of Scott Baker's face floated through Jago's mind, and he took a deep breath. 'Right Olivia. We need to talk, share our ideas, and decide on a course of action.'

'Can we walk on the beach? I think better when I'm moving.'

CHAPTER SIXTEEN

'Look, Olivia,' Jago concluded, after recounting the entirety of the exchange with Baker. 'I thought long and hard whether to tell you about meeting this guy . . .'

They walked along the beach in silence, leaving a trail of footprints behind them in the wet sand.

Olivia concentrated on breathing in time with the waves breaking rhythmically on the shore, trying to control all the loose, vague connected facts that were whizzing around her head and constantly changing shape like the inside of a child's kaleidoscope. 'Thank you for telling me.' She spoke quietly. 'D'you reckon that someone who wanted to put the frighteners on me to persuade me to sell the land could have put the rock through my window and set fire to the café? To make me so frightened that I would accept the first offer that came along? Wouldn't that make sense in light of what that photographer said about someone wanting to buy the land?'

A shadow of a smile had crossed Jago's face. 'And would that ploy work?'

Olivia thought for a moment and then shook her head and started walking again. 'Not in the long-term, no.'

'Exactly. Anyone who knew you at all would realise that

you aren't that easily intimidated, which could suggest it may be someone who doesn't know you that well.'

She saw him looking at her out of the side of his eye and refused to react. 'So, what is it they accused you of interfering in?'

'I took it to mean that they knew I was considering talking to Sarah.'

The look of confusion on Jago's face led to Olivia telling him all about her conversations with Sarah and what she had confided about Libby.

He was impressed. 'This is exactly what I meant about people being willing to talk to you, but not to the police.'

Olivia was horrified. 'Do you think I should question Sarah?'

'No. Questioning people is Trenow's job. Just talk to her, when you get the chance, see what she has to say. Keep it casual.'

They reached the Land Rover as rain began to fall gently. Olivia subsided against it, groaning.

'This is driving me crazy, Jago. The endless questions and the blind alleyways and all the going round in circles. I feel like someone has hijacked my life and I'm holding my breath all the time, just waiting for the next dreadful thing to happen.'

As the words had left her mouth, she regretted them. She had not intended to confide her feelings in anyone, least of all Jago Trevithick. He turned his blue gaze on her, and she was hit by the sudden energy radiating off him. He seemed sharper and more focused.

'You said earlier that you'd let me help you.'

'I know. I'm just not used to asking for help.'

'You didn't ask. I offered.' An impatient sigh escaped his lips.

She turned away. 'I can't be seen as weak. Especially not here. Not now.'

'Sometimes, you have to let other people in, Olivia.'

'Like you did with Mollie? Coming back to Cornwall,' she managed a smile, 'escaping London?'

He got into the Land Rover. 'That was different. I'll tell you about it sometime.'

Olivia pulled open the passenger door and climbed in, took a deep breath and looked out to sea for a sign, the smallest sign of what she should do. She could either carry on as she was and get nowhere, or she could reach out and accept the help that was being offered. As she looked over the sea, the most beautiful rainbow appeared, a perfect arc in all its technicolour glory. That was her sign. She turned to Jago, who was about to start the engine. 'Thank you.'

***

During their drive back to Tresillian, they agreed that Jago would go to London to arrange the sale of the railway posters for the best price he could get and make contact with the would-be developers of Penbartha station site. Later, over mugs of strong tea in the orangery, Olivia had pulled out the notebook she had been working in, listing all the potential suspects for Libby's murder and their possible motives and opportunities. Jago had taken it from her and flicked through it, his interest growing with each page.

'What's so amusing?' Olivia had demanded.

Jago pointed at each of the pages as he turned them slowly. 'Do you even realise that you've drawn a sketch of each of your potential suspects, rather than just writing down their names? And pictured their motives and so on?'

Olivia had pulled the book from him, frowning. 'That's how I think best. In pictures. Don't you?'

He had shaken his head, suppressing a genuine laugh. 'No. I'm a lawyer. I prefer words. But your drawings are very good. I can tell exactly who they are. And see your thought processes behind what you have come up with.'

'That sounds very patronising.'

'Sorry.' He hurried to explain. 'It wasn't meant to be. I suppose I'm envious. Perhaps this is what we need to do. Think outside the box.'

Olivia's ears pricked up. 'How do you mean?'

'We need to approach this from a different angle. The police will be covering all the obvious stuff: lovers, ex-lovers, business contacts and so on. Perhaps finding out who's behind this redevelopment, will lead us back to the person who killed Libby.'

Olivia shifted uncomfortably. 'I think I'd prefer them to be two separate issues. No development opportunity could justify murder.'

Jago let that pass. 'Talk me through your thoughts on it all. Please?'

They worked through it systematically, Jago with his reason and logic, and Olivia with her instinct and intuition. Pages of notes, mind maps and diagrams covered the table until Jago turned the last page to see an incredibly detailed pencil drawing of himself. He examined it for a while, and then looked up at Olivia. For the first time since she had known him, Jago was uncertain.

'So what do I think of you?' She challenged him.

He looked down at the picture and then back at her. 'Do I always look that cross?'

Olivia couldn't stop her chuckle escaping. 'You should try smiling sometime,' she suggested. 'It burns more calories, apparently. As well as making you more approachable.'

'And there was me thinking architects only dealt with structure and practicality,' he observed drily. Then he stretched and stood up, explaining that he needed an early night before his drive to London the next morning. He stopped on the way out of the door and turned back. 'I'll focus on the proposed development while I'm in London. Can you carry on looking for connections with anyone here?' He smiled then. A lop-sided, self-deprecating smile that crinkled into the lines at the corners of his eyes. 'Goodnight.'

'Goodnight, Jago.' A sudden lightness filled her chest; a sensation she hadn't felt for a very long time.

***

With a welcome burst of energy Olivia sprinted up the steep incline, seeking the perverse pleasure of the tugging at her leg muscles and the burning in her lungs. She knew the pain would be worth it for the view she would enjoy at the top, where the sea stretched out for miles in front of her. She reached her target, a lichen-speckled wooden bench bearing a brass plaque in memory of 'Stanley Hazel', who had so loved his years of evacuation in Penbartha that he had returned there as an adult and made it his permanent home. She collapsed on to it, panting, and watched a single sailing boat rounding a red buoy at the head of the creek, its white sail billowing as it caught the wind and picked up speed.

Olivia turned her face up; light clouds scudded across a slowly clearing sky. She could just about feel the sun's gentle rays breaking through. Contrary to the weather forecast and the pinky fingers of sunlight that had painted the early morning sky, it looked like it would be a fine day. As Zennor and Mylor bounded through the long grasses and wild pink campions that covered the headland, Olivia breathed in huge gulps of fresh, salty air until she could feel that the sea and the scenery had worked their usual magic and soothed her soul.

By lunchtime she was feeling a rare sensation: hunger. She had been into the Goods Shed to go through the new membership plans with Alice and to catch up on some of her mounting piles of administration when the thought of Fraser's new bread got too much for her and she headed for the Bakehouse.

'Good afternoon,' Fraser's cheerful greeting welcomed her. 'Take a seat and I'll give Willow a shout. She's just out the back.'

Olivia slipped into the empty booth, noting that Sarah was gesticulating to her from behind the counter. She nodded hello.

'Hi, Olivia.' Willow kissed her cheek and took the seat opposite her. 'How are you holding up?'

'I'm coping, thanks.'

'And I'm sure you'd be better if the police were having more success.' Fraser planted a kiss on her cheek. 'Are you here for lunch?'

Olivia's stomach growled as the smell of delicious bread filled her nostrils.

'Please. I'm actually hungry today. Must be the sunshine.' She intercepted the exchange of glances between husband and wife. Now she was viewing everyone as suspects, even the simplest things took on ominous implications. 'Have you any of your beautiful cheese and red onion bread?'

'We sure do. Do you want me to rustle you up a ploughman's lunch with it?'

Olivia rolled her eyes theatrically. 'Oh, would I ever Fraser? Thanks so much.'

'Willow? Same for you?'

'Just a small one, thanks. I'm not that hungry.' The resigned tone made Olivia look at her friend for a long moment. Her face was showing all the signs of someone else who was not sleeping. She waited until Fraser had gone off to prepare their lunches and Sarah was busy serving customers, before she stretched out her hand to cover Willow's. 'What's up, Willow?'

Tears sprang to the other woman's eyes, and she pulled her black and white checked baker's cap off her hair and twisted it round and round in her hands unit her knuckles were white. 'You've got enough problems of your own at the moment. You don't need to listen to mine.' She wouldn't look at Olivia, who leaned forward and gently prised the cap from her friend's hands.

'You've listened to me enough times.'

'This is different.' She eventually raised tired blue eyes, her lovely Nordic face uncharacteristically hard and tense.

'How is it different?'

Willow looked around the bakery, opened her mouth and then closed it again. 'Let's sit outside at the back. It's just about warm enough in the sun.'

'Sure.' Olivia hefted her bag onto her shoulder. 'Lead the way.'

The two women chatted inconsequentially as they ate their lunch, enjoying the sensation of the spring sun on their faces. Eventually, Olivia set down her knife and fork. 'Come on, Willow. Out with it. What's worrying you?'

Willow looked around again, making sure no one was in earshot. 'It's all this business with Libby and the problems we're having with customers and suppliers.'

'Are you still having trouble?' Olivia interrupted, immediately concerned.

'Not since that time you were here last week. That's what's worrying me. Slightly.'

Olivia raised a quizzical eyebrow. 'It's worrying you?'

Willow's eyes slid away and then back to her friend. 'Don't you think it's a bit of a coincidence?'

'Are you saying that you think Libby was behind all your problems?'

'Well, perhaps not all of them. But a lot of them.'

Olivia thought back to her notebook and her page dedicated to Willow and the strange things she had hinted at about Libby and Fraser.

Willow sighed. 'I'm beginning to think so. And Fraser's still acting really strangely.'

An unsettling feeling sliced through Olivia. 'You don't

think Fraser had anything to do with Libby's murder, do you?' Her voice wasn't steady.

Willow sank her head into her hands. 'I don't know, Olivia. What does it say about me that I can even suspect my husband of murder?' Her voice rose into a wail and Olivia looked round quickly, hoping that no one could overhear their bizarre conversation.

'You must have your reasons.' She took hold of her hand. 'Tell me.'

Willow straightened her shoulders. 'From the moment Libby came on the scene she was flirting with Fraser. Really openly, always popping in, making excuses to see him, pulling him aside and excluding me from their conversations. Coming on to him.'

'Are you sure? I know Libby could be a bit full-on sometimes, but . . .' Her voice trailed off as she remembered Sarah's theory about Libby's secret, married lover.

'Fraser just laughed it off to begin with, but then he started acting a bit oddly. Disappearing off to unspecific customers or suppliers with no follow-up action, or obvious results.' Tears welled up in the blue eyes again.

Olivia squeezed her hand. 'I'm sure it was just a coincidence.'

Willow's face hardened. 'I'm not as forgiving a person as you are. Not anymore.'

Looking at the long, pale face in front of her, Olivia saw a stranger for the first time and an uncomfortable sensation ran down her spine. She swallowed.

'Willow. You are one of the nicest, softest, most generous people I have ever met. You're under an enormous amount of pressure getting this business off the ground. I understand that. You should cut yourself some slack. And Fraser,' she added as an afterthought.

'Good old Fraser.'

Olivia recoiled at the bitterness in Willow's tone as she

shredded the paper napkin on her plate.

'We didn't tell you the real reason we left Edinburgh, did we?'

Olivia closed her eyes.

'Good old Fraser was having an affair. With a secretary at work. Such a cliché.' Her voice was now a monotone. 'Of course, I found out, courtesy of a very concerned friend who didn't like to see me being cheated on. I gave him a second chance on condition we got out of Edinburgh and started a new life.'

'I see.'

'Do you? Do you really see? We risked everything to come here, invested all our savings in those special bakery courses and then buying and fitting out this place. It was supposed to be the answer to all our problems. But despite working our backsides off, we're still struggling to make it a success. Fraser knows that he only has one chance with me. That he'll never get another one. What if he was so desperate to get rid of Libby and all the problems that she caused that he murdered her?'

Olivia's mind flicked back through everything she knew about the murder scene, the evidence, and how everything had been set up to point to her. Would Fraser have done that? Had he had access to her reading glasses, earrings, fingerprints on a wine bottle? With a sense of deep unease, the memory of an evening at the flat above the Bakehouse just a couple of nights before Libby's murder flashed into Olivia's mind. She had spent an enjoyable evening drinking wine with Willow and Fraser.

Usually, Olivia's instinctive reaction to a situation like this was to run and hide and let someone else sort it all out. But the few hours spent with the pragmatic barrister the day before had taught her to take a deep breath and stay calm. She patted Willow's hand.

'I'm sure there's another, much more straightforward explanation for all that's happened. You're not even sure that there was anything really going on between Fraser and Libby, are you?'

A sudden movement at the kitchen door caught her eye and Sarah appeared, her small body tense and her eyes bright.

Willow saw Sarah at the same time and pulled herself together in a dramatic transformation from sobbing wife to furious employer. 'This is nothing to do with you, Sarah. How dare you eavesdrop on someone's private conversation!'

Sarah stepped backwards; her face flushed. 'I'm sorry, Willow,' she protested. 'I had no idea.'

'Stop right there,' Willow snapped. 'I don't know how much of our conversation you overheard but I'm warning you now, forget everything you think you heard and repeat none of it. Ever. Do you get that?'

'Yes.' Sarah nodded and walked back into the kitchen, flashing a triumphant look in Olivia's direction.

'Oh God, Olivia.' Willow turned frightened eyes to her friend. 'Now what have I done?'

CHAPTER SEVENTEEN

'Evening, Rocky, Olivia.' The pub landlord, dressed in his customary uniform of jeans and blue and white striped T-shirt, greeted them warmly as they walked into the pub garden, and he came outside to collect empty glasses. 'Your first round's on the house; us locals have got to show solidarity.'

Olivia was touched. 'That's so kind, Jack. Thank you.' She swallowed. 'And I'm sorry if the police are bothering you at all.'

'Don't you worry, lass. No one who matters has complained.' He clinked the glasses together. 'You've done wonders for this village. That Goods Shed has given us a whole new lease of life. My profits are definitely up!'

Olivia swallowed. More people to let down.

He leaned forward. 'I've had some people in, not locals mind, pretending to share condolences, but really they're just being bloody nosy, and hoping I'll give them a juicy bit of gossip.' He sighed. 'It's one of the biggest drawbacks of village life if you ask me.'

Olivia smiled as they left him chatting to the smokers. Non-locals always assumed that Jack had been a fixture in the pub for decades and he rarely let on that he had, in fact, retired to the village ten years before after a thirty-year career in the West Midlands Police force.

Inside, the pub was heaving. The low beams, flagstone floors and smell of woodsmoke from the open fireplaces, regardless of the time of year, along with the menu of delicious home-cooked food made it particularly welcome on this chilly March evening. At the bar a group of fishermen were lamenting their poor catch of the morning and another group were discussing rugby. Two tables pushed together in the window were overflowing with several members and tenants from the Goods Shed. Olivia didn't think it was her imagination that she was an object of curiosity as she weaved her way past various tables. She was acutely aware of the looks and smiles of support and wondered how long that would continue if she had to resign from the board of trustees.

She made her way to the back of the pub where Kitten was waving her arms about, bangles and bracelets clashing noisily. She was wearing her usual, eclectic combination of vintage clothes and necklaces. Only her hair was more subdued than usual with the blonde outweighing the pink for once.

As soon as Olivia squeezed into the bench seat next to her, Kitten immediately launched into a detailed update on the café. Olivia zoned out. She really didn't want to be here. Her mood had plummeted since her lunch with Willow, and she wanted to be back at home, to think about what Willow had told her and how it fitted in with Sarah's theory. She'd even tried calling Jago and talking it through with him, but his phone had gone to voicemail, and she hadn't left a message. The last thing she felt like doing was putting on a brave face and pretending everything was going to plan in front of her two best friends whose livelihoods largely depended on the success of the redevelopment. But Rocky had thwarted all Olivia's attempts to stay at Tresillian rather than accompany him to the pub for his weekly night out. In the end he had resorted to good old-fashioned blackmail, and she had capitulated.

'So, what do you two think of The Waiting Rooms as a name?' Kitten asked excitedly, as Rocky eventually fought his way back to the table and handed over two glasses of red wine.

He took a long, thirsty swig of his beer before exchanging a teasing glance with Olivia. 'What are the alternatives again?' he asked mildly.

Kitten tutted and divested herself of the top two layers of her clothes to reveal a T-shirt that proclaimed: 'Choose Eco Not Ego'.

'Only the obvious ones. The Station Café, The Junction Café, The Whistle Stop Café, but I thought we could use that last one for a pop-up venue. Or for an outside kiosk for ice cream and take-outs in the busier months.'

'The Waiting Rooms has more of a genteel sound to it,' Olivia observed. 'It's more the feel we are going for I would think. The others sound a bit like greasy spoons.'

'You are such a snob, Olive.' Rocky laughed. 'There's nothing wrong with greasy spoons.' He rubbed his stomach. 'They're vastly underrated.'

Kitten poked her forefinger into his stomach, which was hard and flat and full of muscle. 'You need to think of your cholesterol levels, Mr Berryman. You're no good to me if you drop dead of a heart attack at thirty-five.'

He grimaced. 'I'll try to wait until I've finished the entire list of jobs you've got lined up for me before I do anything as selfish as have a heart attack.'

'You better had. I'm warning you, Rocky.'

Olivia listened to the banter, a smile on her face. 'I think The Waiting Rooms is a great name.'

'Really?' Kitten's silver dolphin earrings swung energetically. 'Can I arrange the artwork we agreed on for the signage and so on?'

'As long as they do the authentic GWR colours and font,

then sure.' She forced a smile on to her face as she raised her glass. 'Shall we drink to it?'

'To The Waiting Rooms!' They all chorused and clinked glasses.

'May I join in the celebrations?'

All three heads turned to see Martin pulling up a stool between Olivia and Kitten and placing his pint glass carefully on a beer mat.

'I'm so sorry, Olivia. I can't believe I haven't seen you since Monday, but I've been in back-to-back meetings all over the southwest ever since. Business is just crazy!'

Olivia waved away his apology, thinking back over the past four days and her rollercoaster of emotions, revelations, and discoveries. Was it any wonder she had barely given Martin any thought at all, other than when his routine texts reminded her of his existence?

'No worries, I've been busy too. There are just so many people out there wanting to upgrade their houses to make them more energy efficient. And this man,' she shot a look in Rocky's direction, 'just keeps finding me clients.'

Martin glanced at Rocky and smiled. 'I'm happy you've been able to take your mind off the police investigation. Any developments?'

Olivia took a large gulp of her wine. 'It's all gone quiet on that front, thank God. The police must still be following up on all their leads.'

He nodded morosely 'Glad to hear it. I just hope they find the killer soon. Poor Libby. I still can't believe she won't come bursting through the door.' He took another sip of his pint as the mood fell around the table. Then he looked up at them. 'What are we celebrating?'

Kitten blushed. 'We're celebrating finally agreeing on a name for the station café. Is that a bit insensitive?'

Martin shook his head. 'Life goes on. And I think it's good to be positive.' He looked at Olivia. 'Especially after the meeting last Monday.'

187

Olivia shook her head at Martin quickly.

'Oh, I'm sure everything will be sorted out fairly quickly and The Waiting Room café will open as planned on Easter Saturday.'

'With a very grand opening,' Kitten interjected.

'Excellent news!' Martin turned to Kitten and raised his pint in congratulations. 'So what's left to do?'

Kitten looked delighted by his interest. 'Just odds and ends, really. Jago has been a genuine star and given Rocky a lot of help these last few days.'

That was news to Olivia, and she turned to Rocky. 'Has he?'

Rocky shifted in his seat. 'Yes, he has.'

'That's good of him,' Martin commented mildly. 'It's nice to know everyone's pulling together. George obviously chose his trustees well.' His eyes scanned the busy pub. 'Is Jago in here tonight?'

'I think he mentioned going to London for the weekend,' Rocky swallowed the end of his pint.

'My old stomping ground. It's ages since I was up there, and I miss it.'

Olivia turned to him in surprise. 'Do you? I'm not sure I do.'

Martin played with his beer mat and smiled at her. 'I can't believe you don't ever miss the hustle and bustle of living in a city. After all your years in London and New York?'

'I do miss New York,' Olivia protested, aware of Kitten's gaze. 'Sometimes more than other places.'

'Well, I've been to both,' Rocky volunteered glumly, 'and hated them equally. Couldn't wait to get home.' He sent an apologetic glance to Olivia, who had been his hostess in both cities. She smiled fondly at him, remembering that, without the creek on one side of him and green fields on the other, he had been like a fish out of water the whole time.

'So have I,' Kitten, another of Olivia's houseguests, rushed in. 'And I loved them both. But I couldn't live in either of them. Too much pollution and selfishness,' she declared, and was about to launch into one of her lengthy explanations when Rocky pointed out one of her friends and steered her across the pub to say hello.

Martin shook his head at their backs, amused by their open devotion to Penbartha and then turned back to Olivia, a more serious look on his face. 'Olivia, I must say you deserve a prize for resilience.'

Her pulse quickened. 'How do you mean?'

'I really admire the way you can put on a brave face and pretend everything's okay at the Trust.'

'Shh!' She glared. 'You heard what Edgar said about keeping it between us. I'm still hoping everything will be alright.'

Martin sighed. 'Well, that's partly why I was looking for you. I was hoping to be around this weekend and spend some time with you and talk through your options for the meeting.' He paused and examined her face for a moment. 'But unfortunately, I've been called away. One of the principal speakers at an access-to-finance event in Bristol has been taken ill, so they've asked me to step in.'

Olivia forced herself to smile. 'That's a bit of an honour, isn't it? Don't forget to spread the word about the Goods Shed.'

Martin scanned the pub and then turned back to her, his voice low. 'I wanted to be with you because I'm worried that everything that's going on might have compromised your judgement. A little bird told me—'

'Excuse me?' Her eyes widened.

'I was looking for you earlier at Tresillian to let you know about the weekend, and when I couldn't find you, I popped into the Coach House. I was surprised to hear that Jago's car was there for quite a while the other day. Last week, you couldn't stand the guy.'

Olivia inwardly cursed Cassie. 'It was just something to do with the memorabilia business. Nothing important.'

Martin sat back. 'Don't you think it's odd that he didn't bother with you at all when you first came back? And now he's all over you like a rash.'

Her pulse quickened. 'Hardly. As I said, it was just a small business matter.'

Martin turned his brightest smile on her. 'Of course. Ignore me. I'm just being paranoid. After everything that's happened lately; I think George would want me to be looking out for you.'

Long, icy fingers of concern began creeping around Olivia's insides. Martin had unintentionally planted a small, poisonous seed of doubt she couldn't ignore. Everything he'd said about Jago was true.

Without waiting for her reply, he drained his pint and stood up. 'And now I must be off. I might not be back until Monday morning, as there's some kind of wrap-up on Sunday evening, but don't worry, I'll definitely be at the meeting to support you.' He leaned down to kiss her cheek and then waved to Rocky and Kitten across the pub.

'Thanks. Have a good weekend.'

The tight knot in her chest squeezed a little more as she watched Martin speak to various people on his way out. Kitten and Rocky re-joined her.

Glancing at Olivia's face, Rocky lifted his empty glass in Kitten's direction. 'It looks as though Olivia could do with another glass. Your round, KittiKat, I believe.'

***

'So, are you and Martin a thing?' Kitten placed the tray of drinks down on their table.

Olivia rushed to the rescue of the fat cream candle that sat in the middle of the scrubbed wooden table, before she knocked it flying.

'Absolutely not,' Olivia replied firmly. 'You know that me and relationships aren't a good mix. Friendship is so much better.'

'Are you saying you won't have a relationship ever again?' Kitten persisted. 'Just because you've had a few unpleasant experiences?'

'Well, that bloke Felix or Phoenix or whatever his name was you were seeing before Mollie died was a complete and utter knob, if you ask me,' Rocky spoke up, frowning.

'Let's just say he was never going to be my happy ever after.' She didn't mention that after Felix, she had decided she never wanted one.

He caught her eye and covered her hand with his. 'Thank God for that. But you seem to go for the sort that you could never settle down with.'

Kitten jumped in. 'Rocky's right. You deliberately choose men who are either emotionally or geographically unavailable.'

Olivia wriggled in her seat. Kitten was uncomfortably close to the mark. She had a proven track record of moving on as soon as she felt she was getting too close to someone, or they to her.

'Kitten, stop trying to wind Olive up,' Rocky intervened, his tone uncharacteristically sharp.

To Olivia's amazement, Kitten apologised. 'I'm sorry, Olive.'

'That's okay. I need to concentrate on the Trust, and I don't want any distractions or complications.'

'Don't you think you deserve some happiness?'

Olivia intercepted the look that passed between her two friends and a lightbulb went off in her head. 'Is that your clumsy way of telling me you two are a thing now?' She kept her tone light-hearted.

Kitten's face flushed a dark crimson and Rocky's cheeks went pink. 'Are you okay with it, Olive?'

She studied the face of the man she had known all her

life, her oldest and closest friend. His strong features were a contrast of dark and light. Black eyes, black curly hair and heavy eyebrows. He was nearly always in need of a shave but his even, white teeth and the light shining from his eyes stopped him from looking altogether like a pirate.

'Olive?'

She felt a mixture of emotions. She couldn't imagine her life without Rocky as her best friend. A selfish part of her wanted him to stay single so he would always be there for her, but a bigger part wanted him to find love and happiness.

'This won't change our friendship, Olive. We've been best mates for too long for that.' A crooked smile crossed his face. 'And you know all my secrets.'

Olivia couldn't help but laugh at his worried expression. 'Too right I do. And don't think I won't use them if I have to.' She smiled. 'I'm really delighted for you both. Honestly.' Her voice faltered on the last word, and she bent her head to hide the tears that were filling her eyes.

One big, calloused and rough hand and one small, pale one found both of hers and squeezed. Olivia thanked God for her friends. Rocky raised his pint.

'To the three of us!'

'To us!' They all clinked glasses, smiles firmly and genuinely back on their faces.

Olivia's resolve hardened. If Rocky and Kitten were going to get their happy ever after, she needed to get to the bottom of everything that was going on.

CHAPTER EIGHTEEN

Bad weather rolled in on Saturday morning and stayed all Sunday. Strong westerlies brought rain lashing against the windows and gushing down the drainpipes; the wind rattled the fronds of the palm trees and the waves crashed relentlessly against the quay at the end of the garden. By Monday morning Olivia's body was twitching for another long, therapeutic run. She pulled on her running kit, leaving the snoozing dogs behind for once, and slipped out of the boot room door, into the garden. Sharp, icy raindrops pelted down on her from a dark and angry sky. Even darker clouds were gathering over the distant sea, beyond the creek, where angry white horses galloped across the waves. There was no sign of the rain passing over soon and, unlike the birds who had all headed inland for shelter, Olivia decided to get on with it. She needed hard, physical activity; another long steep run until the pain was almost unbearable and her mind couldn't think about anything but her breathing and her pace.

Once she reached the summit of the coastal path, she slowed to a walk. Her mind wandered to her runs in New York, where every morning her nostrils had been assaulted by clashing smells: exhaust fumes from taxis, buses fighting with cigarette smoke from commuters, overcooked pretzels and nuts on street food carts, mingling with decaying garbage piled on the kerbside. Each set of smells told her exactly where she was on her route, and she felt another pang of longing for Manhattan. She allowed herself to forget the constant dodging of commuters; the tourists moving at a snail's pace and stopping every thirty seconds to gaze up at another New York landmark; the crazy, entitled cyclists zooming past. Minor irritations apart, her life was so much simpler in New York.

***

By noon, the heavy downpour of the early hours had eased off to a drizzle and the blackest of the clouds had moved away, though the sea mist still clung to the banks of the creek. She made her way downstairs and met Rocky at the back door, clad in his work clothes and waving his mobile around.

'Jago's just called.' He followed her into the kitchen, looking hopefully at the kettle.

'Did he say if he'd be back in time for the meeting?' She tried, but failed, to keep the concern out of her voice.

'Calm down, Olive. Everything's fine. He had to sign something at 9 a.m. and is driving straight down. He said he doesn't want you to worry.'

Olivia pushed two slices of wholemeal bread roughly into the toaster and rammed them down.

'That's all right then.' She spoke through gritted teeth.

Rocky made a pot of tea, found mugs and milk, and carried them all over to the table.

'Why didn't you tell me about the funding problems for the café?'

She buttered the toast and added marmalade. 'I didn't want to worry you unnecessarily. You've worked so hard.'

'And you haven't?'

She put the plate on the table and sat down. 'That's different.'

'How is it? This place means more to you than everyone else put together.' Rocky's voice rose in exasperation.

Olivia glared. 'Jago had no right to tell you. It was supposed to be confidential.'

'He wanted me to come and tell you in person. So you knew before the meeting.'

She refused to meet his eyes. 'He could have called me him—'

Rocky cut her off. 'He tried. You didn't pick up. You have to believe Jago wants to help.'

'I'm sorry.' She touched his work-roughened hand briefly. 'I know I'm behaving like a total whackadoodle. There's just so much riding on this funding. For so many people.' Not to mention the vote of no confidence, that Rocky obviously didn't know about.

Rocky chewed on his toast. 'Forget everyone else for a moment, Olive. What do you want to do?'

Her eyes widened. 'What on earth do you mean?'

'I meant what I said. What do you, Olivia Rozenwyn Wells, want to do?'

The ghost of a smile flitted across her face at the sound of her full name, but it was soon replaced with a deeply creased brow. 'I want Libby's murderer brought to justice.'

'That's a given. What else?'

'I want what George and Mollie wanted. For me to fulfil their legacy and realise their vision.'

'Have you ever thought that you're their legacy? And not the Station Trust?'

She contemplated his words, running her forefinger around the rim of her mug. 'I really don't know.'

Rocky squeezed her hand. 'Well, I know. And you're doing fine, Olive. Trust me.'

'I do trust you, Rocky. And I am trying to trust Jago, honestly. But it's difficult, and this legacy feels more of a burden than a gift at the moment. George and Mollie's ideas for the Trust were so clear and so honourable, and I was as committed to it as they were. Now, I'm not sure I can do it anymore.' She shut her eyes tightly.

He caught hold of her hand again. 'Do you want to know what I think?'

'Yes, please!' She couldn't keep the surprise out of her voice. Rocky never volunteered his opinion. She usually had to prise it out of him.

'I think you need to stop trying to please everyone else all the time and think long and hard about what it is you truly want. Perhaps it's time to pursue your own dreams. I know you think you want to go back to New York, but I believe you belong here, Olive.' His black eyes held hers. 'This is where your home is, your friends and the closest thing to a family you've got. Perhaps the risk of having it all taken away from you is what it takes to make you realise that? And rather than running away from everything that has happened in the past, you just need to face things head-on. Now, more than ever.'

She gazed around the kitchen, taking everything in. The house she and her godparents had redesigned and developed together over the years with love and care and great thought and out to the rain-scarred gardens which held such happy memories. She smiled weakly.

'I'm not sure this is about me, and what I want. Not yet. But you're right. I do need to face things head-on. This is about more than bricks and mortar. It's about what they stand for. It's where I've always been loved and wanted. Tresillian and Penbartha station are in my soul.' She took a deep breath. 'I don't think there's much I can do about Libby's murder, no matter what Jago or Sarah say. And I might well go back to New York. But before I can do that, I will do everything in my power to save Penbartha station and everything it stands for.'

***

By 1.30 p.m. there was still no sign of Jago, and Olivia's resolve faltered. She was pacing up and down the unfinished floor of the café, getting in Rocky's way, clenching and releasing her fists repeatedly; using every ounce of self-control to resist her urge to scream. She ignored all Rocky's pleas for her to calm down and his reassurances that Jago would be there. When she could bear it no longer, she marched onto the platform and listened to the sound of the gulls circling over the creek. She stood staring down the walkway at the trees, already turning green, the wildflowers blooming in the damp, mild weather. Blackbirds and robins were busy making their nests and repeatedly visiting the feeding stations Alice had positioned on the small terrace outside the Goods Shed. Was this the last time she would see this view while still being a trustee? The site was so perfect now, so much a part of George and Mollie and now a part of Rocky, Kitten and herself, that the thought of losing it all horrified her so much her chest squeezed with pain at the thought of letting it all go.

She left it as near to two o'clock as she could before forcing her shoulders back and walking into the boardroom, eager to avoid any uncomfortable conversations or accusing looks. Everyone was there except Jago. Olivia knew all the trustees, to varying extents. She had celebrated their successes, helped with their problems, sympathised with their losses. But the mood today was low and, as she slid into her seat, no one would meet her eye. Only Martin was trying to be cheerful and make conversation, complaining about the traffic on the A30 because of an accident that was causing huge tailbacks.

'Well, that's as maybe.' Edgar sounded stressed. 'I'm prepared to wait for Alice to bring the tea and coffee through, but then we must start.'

'I would like to suggest we wait for Jago?' Callum asked uneasily. 'Because—'

'We can't wait around for trustees who put other business ahead of the Trust,' Edgar interrupted him crossly. 'We are quorate without Mr Trevithick, so we can go ahead with the vote.'

Olivia's heart sank.

'I'm afraid I need us to start on time.' Martin looked anxiously at the clock. 'I have a client meeting after this. And it could turn into an exciting lead for the Goods Shed.'

'Tea and coffee,' Alice trilled, bright-eyed, as she bustled in under the weight of a very full tray. She took a long time placing a cup and saucer in front of each trustee and served them all individually. Jess began tapping her pen against her teeth.

'I'll just distribute the paperwork and then we can start,' Alice said briskly, as she straightened up and looked out of the window.

'Excellent timing.' She beamed round the table. 'Mr Trevithick has just driven up.'

Olivia's white knuckles gripped the table. Only Callum seemed to have noticed anything amiss. Then Jago was striding through the door, loudly declaring his apologies for being two minutes late.

'Apologies accepted, Jago.' Edgar sounded like he was speaking through clenched teeth. 'We were just about to start.'

It was only when Jago took his usual seat to the right of Edgar, accepting a brown envelope from Alice, that Olivia dared look at him. He looked smart, she grudgingly admitted; in a well-cut suit and pale blue shirt; his tie impeccably knotted and silver cufflinks just peeping out beneath his suit sleeves. She had never seen him in a suit before and noticed that it made him seem even more serious and sharper. A force to be reckoned with. Not a flicker of emotion crossed his face as their eyes met. He just looked straight at her and passed a thick white envelope to Callum.

'Can we get started, please?' Jess asked, looking at her watch. 'Some of us have our own businesses to run.'

'Indeed.' Edgar shuffled his papers. 'Well, as this is an Extraordinary Meeting, there are only two items on the agenda. Whether we sanction a temporary cessation in the repayment schedule for the Goods Shed refurbishment costs to release finance for the completion of the station café and the installation of the necessary digital technology etc.' He looked over his glasses. 'And of course, we need to discuss the possibility of calling for a vote of no confidence . . .' He sipped his coffee.

Alice cleared her throat. 'May I speak, Mr Moore? As clerk to this board?'

'If you must, Alice. But please be brief.'

Alice reddened. 'As clerk, and even though this is an Extraordinary General Meeting, it is still my duty to ask all present to declare any pecuniary interests that may affect the decisions we make.'

Everyone sighed, and several trustees began tapping their pens against their papers.

'Oh, for heaven's sake, Alice, can we just get on with it?' Jess snapped.

'Alice has a valid point. We need to make sure we follow procedure as we're discussing such a serious matter. *And* have a paper trail to prove it.' Jago's deep voice spoke up. 'What do we have to sign, Alice?'

Olivia looked at him sharply, but he wouldn't meet her gaze.

Alice passed round several forms. 'If you could all read these, complete them as necessary and then sign, I would be very grateful.'

'Surely Olivia is the only one with a direct pecuniary interest in this place? As the beneficiary?' Jess asked crossly, as she scanned her sheet of paper.

'It's not just about direct interests. It also includes any indirect business or financial interests we may have,' Alice explained, as if she was talking to a slightly slow child. 'It's so we are transparent and accountable in all our business dealings. Perhaps you could explain it better, Mr Moore. As a local parish councillor, you must come across this all the time?'

If Olivia hadn't been watching carefully, she wouldn't have seen the way Alice practically collapsed with relief into her chair, her carefully rehearsed speech delivered. Her duty done. Nor would she have seen the colour drain from Edgar's face as Alice's precise words sank in. Everyone else was examining the forms in front of them and, presumably, their consciences. Martin was the first to sign his with a scratchy flourish and sent it back down the table to Alice.

The words on the form swam in front of Olivia's eyes, despite her reading glasses. She raised her head and looked round the table with a pounding heart. What was this all about? If this meant what she thought it did, she wouldn't have any power to fight. She tried to speak, but her throat was tight, and she struggled to get her words out. She took a gulp of her tea and pushed her glasses up into her curls. 'As I have a direct financial interest in the assets of the trust, I assume I have to abstain from the vote about the repayments?'

'I'm not sure that's legally necessary,' Jago spoke before Edgar could. 'As long as you have declared your interest, and it's all open and transparent, you still have a vote.'

Olivia's head swivelled round. All the trustees' eyes were on Jago, but he spoke with complete and utter authority, and no one dared to contradict him.

'Do you agree, Edgar, as the Trust's solicitor?' Jago deferred to the older man, who simply nodded.

Still holding her breath, Olivia looked at him through

narrowed eyes as Edgar moved on.

Callum coughed. 'Before we get to the main resolution, may I just say that I have come into possession of a legal document that means we no longer need to vote on the cessation of the repayment schedule for the refurbishment costs on the Goods Shed.' He held up several sheets of paper. 'I have just received official notification that the funds to fill the gap for the station works have been provided by Olivia via a third party. So, as trustees, we can continue with the repayments as per the original schedule.' He beamed.

Olivia let out the breath she had been holding with a whoosh.

'Can she do that?' Jess enquired shortly, her cheeks bright pink with annoyance.

'Absolutely. If it's all above board and legal, who are we to disagree?' Callum spoke with authority. An audible sigh of relief rippled round the room.

'I wish I had that sort of money to just throw away on a whim,' Jess muttered. 'Little princess.'

Martin beamed. 'That's fantastic!' He turned to Edgar. 'I take it that means I can get off to my client now?'

'Wait a minute!' Jess exclaimed. 'I thought we were supposed to be discussing whether Olivia is more of a liability than an asset to the Penbartha Station Trust.'

'There has been an increase in interest in membership,' Paula jumped in and carried on speaking before Jess could interrupt her. 'Which has converted into several new members . . .'

'And things have calmed down considerably in the Goods Shed, now the police have finally moved off the site,' Alice spoke up.

'Libby's murder is yesterday's news, I'm afraid.' Rozy smiled awkwardly. 'No one's even talking about it anymore.'

'And yet the police haven't got any further in their

investigation.' Jess got unsteadily to her feet and scowled around the table. 'Which suggests to me they already know who did it, and yet you lot are just going to sit here with a murderer amongst you and let her wriggle off the hook!'

'I found her, Jess. I did not kill her,' Olivia spoke firmly. 'I'm not the sort of person who resorts to physical violence to settle an argument. And from what I knew of Libby, neither was she.'

Jess snorted and sat down heavily in her chair. 'Well, you obviously didn't know her as well as you thought you did, as she spilled all your secrets and said all those things about you.' She glared round the room, her eyes almost glazed. 'Let's face it everyone, Olivia has motive, and as the police haven't been able to come up with anyone else to take over her current position as number one suspect, I strongly suggest we call a vote of no confidence in her as a trustee.'

Olivia froze. This was it. She tried to ease the panic that was grabbing at her throat by swallowing hard. Her eyes flew round the room and settled on Edgar. He looked rattled, removed his glasses and cleaned them slowly with his greying handkerchief, before opening his mouth to speak.

'That's not possible,' Jago's calm, deep voice spoke first.

Now everyone looked confused and focused on the only person in the room who still looked calm and in control.

Jago extracted a piece of paper from the envelope Alice had given him. 'This is the Trust's governing document, and it does not provide for removing a trustee by a vote of no confidence, if that trustee also happens to be a beneficiary.'

Jess was the first to recover. 'I might have guessed,' she spat the words across the table. 'So you get away with this as well. Does anything ever stick to you, Olivia?'

Olivia was stunned into silence by Jago's revelation.

'Don't you think the fact that Olivia is prepared to finance the works herself, shows that she's acting in the best interests of the Trust?' Callum spoke with some force and then smiled at Olivia. 'I think we should give her a chance.'

Murmurings of agreement spread amongst the trustees, and Olivia felt like the ceramic ball in a pinball machine, being ricocheted between bumpers and targets, completely under the control of others.

Eventually, Edgar spoke. 'I can see no reason not to continue as we are. On the proviso that we keep everything under review.' He coughed again and Olivia glanced at him. His face was ashen and there were beads of sweat on his upper lip. He seemed crushed, much less of a force than before. 'However, considering all that has been said here today about probity and so on, I have decided to abstain from all future votes.'

His old, watery eyes scanned the table. 'Not that there are any pecuniary interests I need to declare you must understand, but George was my friend and I've thought a great deal about these matters over the weekend. I now believe that my loyalty to our friendship makes my involvement in votes pertaining to the future of this Trust inappropriate. I am sure you will all understand.'

Olivia drew in a breath and stared. Then she looked at her fellow trustees one by one. Their faces were unreadable, apart from fury on Jess's, sympathetic smiles on those of Paula, Martin and Callum, and a look of pure relief on Alice's.

Jess glared at everyone. 'You could still just do the right thing and resign, Olivia.'

Olivia stiffened and then met Jess's wild gaze unflinchingly. 'Why?'

Jess blinked. 'Because, even if you're not a murderer, you're still an eco-cheat, like Libby said.'

Olivia could feel her face heating up. 'I'm sorry?'

'Well,' Jess's eyes travelled the room. 'Just think about it. The members here are doing their best for the environment and reducing their carbon footprints and you completely undo all their good works by flying backwards and forwards across the Atlantic.' Her voice rose again. 'Everyone knows that it's impossible to live a sustainable life while continuing to travel by air. You're nothing but a hypocrite!'

Olivia held her hands tightly in her lap to stop them trembling.

'I'm prepared to own that hypocrisy, Jess.' Her voice was not quite steady. 'And I feel bad about it, but I'm doing my best. Isn't that all we can ask of ourselves?'

'Of course, it is,' Rozy spoke up. 'And it doesn't help to start flight-shaming anyone. I think we all accept that Olivia didn't exactly choose the position she's found herself in.'

'Really?' Jess's voice got louder. 'And do you think our children and their children will forgive our generation for what we've done to the planet? Because I don't. And just because people like Olivia can afford to greenwash their consciences by planting a few trees every time they fly off somewhere; the problem doesn't go away. It's just made worse.'

Shame, anger and guilt bubbled up inside Olivia. 'For your information, I give to a renewable energy scheme in Chile, but this isn't the time or the place for this discussion.'

'Oh, really? Perhaps you'd rather meet me later, alone. Like you did Libby?'

'That's enough!' Jago's voice cut through the shocked silence. 'I think you need to calm down, Jess.' He turned to Olivia. 'You, too.'

Jess threw her pen down on the table and stood up. 'I need to get back to work, after having my time completely wasted. Some of us actually have to work for a living, you know.' She flounced out.

Martin rose to his feet and smiled weakly round the table.

'I'm sorry, folks, but I must meet this client. If I can get him on board, we'll have new members flocking in. Edgar,' he turned to the old solicitor, 'I'd like a word on some legal matters. Shall I call you?'

Edgar nodded and then turned to Alice. 'Could I have some water, please?'

***

Olivia's body was twitching for another hard run after the charged meeting, but instead she followed Jago to the Signal Box. Any relief she had felt at the meeting's outcome had been overshadowed by humiliation caused by Jess's words and confusion generated by Jago's. She stood in front of him, hands on hips, her dark eyes flashing sparks. 'What the hell was all that about?'

Jago carried on unknotting his tie and pulled it off. Then he undid his top button and eased the collar from his neck, before removing his cufflinks and rolling up his sleeves. 'I was trying to help.'

Olivia shook her head in disbelief. 'I've been to hell and back this weekend.' Her voice rose. 'You could have given me the heads-up about the governing document before you went to London. Then I wouldn't have had to worry as much. I called you, left a voicemail.'

He dropped his cufflinks onto the desk. 'I had to be sure before I said anything. I didn't want to give you false hope.'

'Trust works both ways, Jago.'

He flinched and looked away. 'I was struggling to get a good price for the posters, so I needed a Plan B and C, just in case. I didn't close on the posters until this morning.' He sat down behind his desk. 'And I needed a copy of the governing document to prove you were off the hook. By not knowing, you didn't have to pretend anything at the meeting.'

'And all that pecuniary interest stuff?'

'It bought us more time.'

'And you spoke to Alice? Involved her?'

'She wanted to help. She made me promise to call her if there was the smallest thing she could do. So I did. And she found the governing document and did all the pecuniary interest stuff. Because she wanted to. For you.'

'For me?' Olivia blinked.

His jaw tightened; his face tired and strained.

'She adores you. Everyone in this place seems to. Apart from Jess, of course.' His eyes held hers. 'People want to help. I want to help.'

Olivia looked away, her cheeks warming.

'No need to thank me, Olivia, but I've had a long drive.' Jago stood and moved over to the door. 'Real life isn't like your buildings. You can't control everything and be certain things will end up exactly as you planned. You have to adjust your sails when the wind doesn't blow your way. Maybe it's time you realised that.' He opened the door, radiating tension, and pointed to the gemstone round her neck. 'And perhaps have a bit more faith in that, like Mollie intend—'

The sound of heavy footsteps marching up the wooden stairs stopped him mid-sentence. A morose and tense-looking DI Trenow appeared in front of them and gestured for them both to stay inside. He sank down onto the chesterfield sofa. After a few moments, he lifted his head. 'There's no easy way to say this. Sarah Santos's mother has just rung in to report her as missing. And from the extra information she's given us, we are treating this extremely seriously.'

CHAPTER NINETEEN

Jago was sitting at his desk in the Signal Box, scrutinising an online catalogue for an upcoming auction, where he had his eye on a GWR twelve-inch mahogany-cased drop dial clock, but his mind was elsewhere. When Steren whined at the door, he gladly abandoned his task. A bracing walk in the fresh air would cleanse the grime of London he could still feel on his skin and his mood.

Steren sniffed in the undergrowth for all the delicious smells she knew she would find there after the rain. Jago tried briefly to decode the morning chorus of birds but was soon distracted by the unsettling thoughts that had been niggling at him since his trip to London. He knew he hadn't dealt well with Olivia at the trustees meeting, and even less so afterwards. The way her legs had buckled beneath her and the look of absolute horror and shock on her face when Trenow broke the news about Sarah's disappearance, confirmed Jago's belief, once and for all, that she had nothing to do with the recent spate of criminal activity in Penbartha.

After a night of little sleep, he'd constructed a timeline of events, slotting in what he had learned in London. After swearing off crime a good while ago, he didn't know why he was getting involved now, but his instincts had told him there was something odd about Libby's murder and things were getting more complicated very day. Now, to make matters more complicated, he was worried he may have lost any ground he had gained with Olivia, who was an intriguing and frustrating mystery in herself. Most of the women he'd known at the Bar were all polished, assured, ruthlessly ambitious career-women. Olivia was arty, creative and impulsive and an idealist who wanted to make a real difference in the world. But for the sake of the world, rather than her own self-aggrandisement. He'd seen the way her eyes moved over Penbartha station. Not in an assessing way, but as though she was trying to gather it up and protect it. She was emotional, whereas he was used to calm, objective and level-headed people. And she was frustrating because her energy pulled him towards her, but she was constantly refusing his help and pushing him away. He admired her quick mind, and even her sharp tongue. He was beginning to see the woman George had spoken of so fondly. And George, he reminded himself, was the reason he was helping Olivia. Plus, he realised, he was enjoying using parts of his brain he had allowed to lie dormant for some time.

As he turned back along the track, Steren pricked her ears up and started wagging her tail. Jago immediately recognised the upright, lithe figure striding towards him and the determined set of her chin. 'Good morning, Olivia.' He could see the exhaustion in her face, and she didn't bother with pleasantries.

'Can I get straight to the point, please, Jago, and apologise for the way I spoke to you yesterday afternoon? It was unprofessional and I was acting as thought I was ungrateful.'

He blinked, but then nodded. 'My behaviour wasn't any better. I, too, would like to apologise.'

A look of surprise crossed Olivia's face, and she took a step backwards.

They stood there awkwardly for a few moments until Jago broke the silence. 'D'you fancy going up to the Bakehouse for breakfast?' He looked at his watch as he waited for her refusal.

'Not the Bakehouse – too many people.' Olivia said. 'But I'd love a cup of tea, thank you.'

Jago hid his surprise and inclined his head towards the Signal Box. 'After you.'

***

They sat on opposite sides of his desk, and Steren snuffled in her basket, lost in her doggie dreams.

It took a few moments of polite chit-chat for Olivia to relax enough to tell him about the conversations she'd had with Sarah and Willow and her plans to meet with Sarah later that day. '. . . and now Sarah's gone missing,' Olivia finished breathlessly, her eyes clouding over.

'Another cup?' Jago moved over to the kettle as he digested the new information.

'What do you think?' She leant forward, eager for his opinion.

He took his time making the tea, thinking it all over, aware of her watchful gaze.

He sat back down. 'I'm pretty sure, from what I know of them, that neither Fraser nor Willow would be capable of killing anyone. Besides, I really don't think Fraser would have set you up to take the rap for Libby's murder. He's not that kind of guy; the pressure he would be under maintaining that façade would be immense. Believe me, I've seen it before. Most people crack sooner rather than later.'

'Surely Willow would know that, so why was she so suspicious of him?'

'Couples stop talking at times of stress.' Jago held Olivia's enquiring gaze. 'Willow and Fraser have a lot riding on their venture, remember. That they were both prepared to give up everything they had in Edinburgh for the sake of their marriage shows how important it is to them both.'

'Let's hope you're right. But if Fraser is out of the frame, we're back to square one. And I can't even bear to think about what could have happened to Sarah.'

He nodded. 'Agreed. But we don't know that anything *has* happened to Sarah. She might have taken fright and decided to lie low for a while. Let's wait for Ross to get back to us before we go jumping to any conclusions. Get some evidence.' The slight smile took the sting out of his words.

'You lawyers and evidence.' Olivia grimaced. 'What's wrong with a vivid imagination and some good old feminine intuition?'

Jago pulled a face. 'They get in the way of the facts. I enjoy dealing with facts. And logical analysis.'

'Rather than feelings? You're probably right. Look where they've got me. I promised I'd talk to Sarah over the weekend, but other stuff kept cropping up that I felt was more important, and now she's gone missing,' Olivia's voice broke.

As she reached forward to pick up her mug of tea, Jago caught a waft of the delicate scent that reminded him of a Cornish country garden. 'And I hate looking at everyone with suspicion. I know what it's like to be wrongly accused of something, and it's horrible. I don't want to do that to anyone else.'

Jago sat back, trying to make sense of the infuriating mix of frustration and admiration he felt towards her. He was almost at the point of cursing George for the responsibility he had given him, but then paused: what would his old friend do in these circumstances?

'How can Sarah going missing be your fault? There was nothing you could have done to stop it. And who knows if

Sarah's theories had any basis in fact?' He spoke quietly to her bent head. 'Look, I can only guess how you're feeling about trusting me at the moment. But—'

'I'm not good at trusting people. They let you down.'

'I won't.' It surprised him how much it meant for her to believe him. 'I know you don't know me that well, but Mollie and George did. And they accepted me.'

Olivia slowly exhaled the breath she had been holding, finished her tea and sat up straight. 'May I ask you something?'

'Sure'

She fingered her pendant. 'How did you know Mollie gave me this?'

He put down his mug and dug his hand into the pocket of his jeans. 'She gave me one too. She said it was the stone of strength.' He handed her the small oval stone, almost egg-shaped and still warm from his pocket. It was more reddish-brown in colour than Olivia's, with only a few specks on the back of it. She ran her fingers over its smooth, warm surface and then raised her incredible dark eyes with amber flecks that perfectly matched the stone hanging round her neck.

'She always told me that. Said it would help me in times of need.'

'And help you make the right decision whenever you reach a crossroads in your life,' he added.

Her intense gaze sliced right through him. 'Do you believe in it?'

'What, me? A level-headed, logical barrister?' He didn't answer her question. 'Mollie did. And that's what matters.'

'She gave me mine before I went to New York. She said it was my special stone because it matched my eyes and had the qualities I needed most.' Her eyes pinned him to the spot. 'I recognise this stone – it was the one Mollie kept. She must have had a very good reason to give it to you.'

'I think she did.' He coughed to cover his sudden awkwardness.

Olivia was still watching him, assessing him as a fellow recipient of Mollie's special stone. He held her gaze until the expression that crossed her face told him she had made a decision. She gave him back the stone and took a deep breath. 'Did she also tell you that these stones help you overcome past harmful experiences that get in the way of moving forward with your life and choosing a new path?'

'She did.' Jago swallowed, unwanted memories suddenly flooding his mind.

Olivia stood up and wandered over to the window. 'Did you know I had a brother Aidan, who died?'

'Rocky mentioned him once.'

'It was my fault he died.' She stated the fact flatly, but then her voice wobbled as she continued, and Jago wondered if she was putting her feelings into words for the first time. 'We were on a beach in Thailand with my parents and Australian grandparents for my mother's fortieth birthday. Aidan and I were messing about in the sea on our own. He was daring me to swim further and further out, and I took on every dare, as usual. Then he went out even further and got caught in a riptide.' She drew in a quick breath as if to steady her emotions. 'I went to help him. But I wasn't strong enough. I fought and fought to get through the waves. I still have nightmares about it, see him slipping under the water, the riptide dragging him down.' Her voice rose and then broke, and she focused hard on the people on the walkway beneath the Signal Box.

'How old were you?'

'I was ten. Aidan was twelve.'

'And where were the adults in all this?'

Olivia didn't lift her head. 'They were on the beach and thought we were just messing about. By the time they realised what was going on, it was too late. They got to us and pulled us out, but Aidan was already dead.' She cleared her throat. 'And my mother blamed me.'

'What?' Jago couldn't keep the incredulity out of his voice.

'I was a better, stronger swimmer than Aidan.'

'You were a child!'

Olivia turned to him, and he saw a dark spear of pain flicker in her eyes.

'After Aidan died, I had to cope with my grief alone. My mother was beside herself and she barely even noticed that I was there. I just wanted to be here, where everything was bright and warm, and people laughed and smiled. And loved me.' She sniffed. 'That's when I started running away.' She stopped suddenly, turning her face away from him again, and he knew it was because her eyes were filling with tears, and that she didn't want to cry in front of him.

'I ran away to leave all the pain and sadness behind. After a few false starts and being picked up by the police, I actually made it here, once. All by myself.'

The pride of the ten-year-old Olivia was still clear on her face, but Jago was horrified. He had come across some pretty awful cases in his time at the Bar, but this got to him in a way he didn't even begin to question.

'What about your parents?'

She shrugged. 'My mother was so caught up in her own grief, she was almost indifferent. And my father has never been very good at dealing with his emotions.'

She spoke with an acceptance that appalled Jago.

'When my mother found out she was pregnant again they asked George and Mollie to look after me until the baby was born and settled in at home. The plan, apparently, was that I would then go back, and we'd all be one big, happy family.' Her voice wavered. 'Except that never happened. That call never came, and I was happy in

Penbartha with George and Mollie. I went to school in Truro and never lived with my birth family again. They did invite me to go to Australia with them when I was twelve, but I was settled in Cornwall by then. George and Mollie became my legal guardians. And they made me feel safe.'

'Even though you were living by the water full time?'

She raised her eyes to him then. 'I enjoy being by water, but I never go in. I just can't. I haven't swum since the day Aidan died.'

'So you run instead?'

'School was a bit of a nightmare about me not swimming at first. But George explained, and they let me take up cross-country running instead. And I learned to be good at that, so they were cool with it.'

A vision of Olivia running smoothly and efficiently along the walkway every morning flashed through Jago's mind and he stared at her; this fierce, frustrating, intelligent woman, so full of attitude. On the outside at least. But underneath . . .

There was one thing he had to make clear. 'You need to believe you were not responsible for Aidan's death. You were ten years old. A child.' He crossed to where she stood and turned her from the window. He put gentle fingers under her chin and moved her face round so he could look into her eyes. 'I'm sure you did all you physically could to save him.' His eyes locked onto hers. 'It was an awful, devastating tragedy. But it was not your fault. You need to let go of that guilt.'

'But what if all that's going on at Penbartha is my punishment for Aidan's death? I got away with that, so now I have to atone for it by being accused of other murders?' The words slipped out in a whisper.

'Stop it! That's ridiculous.'

'But—'

'But nothing, Olivia.' His hands moved to her shoulders, his eyes never leaving her face. 'You were not responsible for Aidan's death, whatever you might have been telling yourself all these years. You need to forgive yourself.'

Olivia's gaze met his and held it for a long moment, before nodding and moving away.

Jago sat back behind his desk and began fiddling with a pile of papers.

Olivia drained her tea, tucked the escaped tendrils of hair behind her ears and slipped into professional mode.

'What happened in London? At the seminar?'

He cleared his throat, reminding himself how he always began his closing speeches at the end of a trial. Momentarily, he wished he was facing a jury of twelve unfamiliar faces rather than one he knew wasn't going to like what she was about to hear.

She raised her eyebrows but remained silent, biting her bottom lip.

'I went with Penny, the wife of an old colleague of mine. She's fab, late sixties, terribly glamorous and jumped at the chance to masquerade as my aged aunt for the afternoon. Especially when she discovered the free champagne. She had them eating out of her hand and falling over each other to get her to sign up.'

'To what?' Olivia cut to the chase, as he'd come to expect.

He sorted through the newspapers and catalogues jostling for space on his desk and handed her a glossy brochure.

'Take a look.'

Olivia rummaged in her bag for her reading glasses and flicked through sixteen pages of stunning photographs and artist's impressions of Penbartha, all the former railway buildings and the surrounding area. The brochure reeked of sophistication and elitism. Even more beautiful drawings, and computer-generated images showed the proposed development of specialist retirement properties and all it offered, with one and two bedroomed luxury apartments, amazing, subtropical gardens and sumptuous communal lounges and restaurants, a fitness suite and beauty salon. No expense had been spared.

Jago watched Olivia's face closely as she read through each page carefully without looking up. Eventually she closed the brochure and placed it back on the desk and looked questioningly at him.

'The first part of the presentation was full of statistics presented via PowerPoint showing the potential problems we, as a society, face.' Jago picked up some papers and flicked through them. 'I won't bore you with all the details, but basically there's not enough specialist private sector retirement housing available for the number of elderly people living in the UK.'

'And by providing retirement housing they are freeing up houses further down the chain., so meeting the country's housing needs at both ends of the ladder. Talk about a win-win situation for them!' Her lip curled.

Jago nodded. 'They really went to town on extolling the virtues of retirement living here and the positive impact on health and well-being. There were impressive statistics showing that living in these properties gives people the best of both worlds: independent living alongside community and support.'

Olivia observed him for a moment, her head on one side. 'What did Penny think?'

Jago's face split into a wide grin and he was immediately taken aback by the look on her face. Then he remembered her drawing of him. When and why had he stopped smiling?

'Penny?' He dragged himself back into the moment. 'She went along with it all. In private she confided to me she would rather die disgracefully than be surrounded by old people being subjected to 'organised fun'.'

Olivia managed a small smile. 'And did they mention the minor issue of planning permission, never mind ownership of the land?'

'They just skated over the minor issue of ownership,' Jago mused. 'And you know as well as I do that you don't have to own land to apply for planning permission on it.'

Olivia frowned and gazed round the room. Now he was getting to know her, he could see behind the calm façade and sense the upset that churned beneath it.

'Surely they don't stand any chance of getting planning permission for a site of those proportions here in Penbartha?'

Jago chose his words carefully. 'Well, the developers don't seem to foresee any major problems with that. They explained about the government's plans for retirement housing to be given enhanced planning status, so it's looking as though planning permission will be much more easily granted.'

Olivia remained silent, but he could feel the tension radiating off her. He paused for a moment. 'And of course, they were really emphasising the eco credentials of the development.'

'I beg your pardon?' Her whole body stiffened.

'How they would be developing a disused brownfield site, rather than encroaching on greenbelt land.'

Olivia rushed to the window to look down over her beloved station. 'By demolishing beautiful Victorian buildings and replacing them with hideous modern boxes? That's about the most unsustainable thing you can do.'

'They say they are replacing them with more energy efficient buildings, which are cheaper to heat and easier to maintain.'

Olivia turned to him then, her dark eyes flashing. 'But they won't be more energy efficient. That's the point. It would take over eighty years just to make up for the environmental impact of their initial construction.'

Her enthusiasm for her specialism shone out of her. Jago could just about remember feeling that passionate about the justice system and he envied her.

'This sort of development goes against everything I stand for, Jago.'

She clasped her pendant and gazed down at the buildings for a long moment, struggling with her thoughts. Then she sat back down suddenly and met Jago's eyes.

'I know I get carried away with the idea of rescuing old and unloved buildings. But Sarah was right when she said that people are more important. Do you think this development would be good for Penbartha? Better than what we're doing?'

Jago blinked and realised he might have seriously underestimated Olivia yet again. It went without saying that she had an emotional attachment to the station. What he hadn't appreciated was the sense of social responsibility she felt to do the right thing for the whole village.

'There is no way that this development could ever be better for Penbartha than the Goods Shed and the café and everything else we're doing.' Jago spoke firmly. 'Especially in the long-term. And I'm sure George would agree.'

Olivia held his gaze, her face drained and exhausted, but she shook herself and returned to the development proposals. 'Obviously, I won't ever sell, so we need to make things as difficult as possible on the planning front. What about national restrictions? Isn't Penbartha in an Area of Outstanding Natural Beauty?' Olivia leant forward again. 'In my experience that holds the most sway with planning officers to stop unwanted developments.'

'You're right, it is, but I spoke at length with a planning QC friend on Sunday and she warned me that being in an AONB is not an automatic protection anymore. If a planning committee feels there is a good reason to waive the rules, they generally can.'

Olivia rubbed at her left temple. 'What else did she say?'

Jago looked away. 'That these developers are usually

prepared for the financial outlay on legal fees for planning applications and for appeal after appeal. Unfortunately, nowadays most councils can't afford to go to litigation.'

'Great. Backhanders and brown envelopes full of used notes to help councillors make their decisions?' She went quiet for a moment. 'What about listing? That could be more of a protection for us.'

'The buildings here aren't listed, are they?'

'No, George didn't want them to be a millstone round anyone's neck. He thought by keeping them unlisted, it would offer us more flexibility with redevelopment and renovations.' She sat, pursing her lips. 'But there's nothing to stop us applying for listing now, for those buildings we've renovated.'

Jago glanced at her sideways. 'You reckon?'

'I can try. I'll get in touch with Historic England and talk to them today.'

After a long moment, she took a deep breath. 'So,' she began slowly, 'what I want to know is why these developers have gone to all this trouble and expense to propose a development on land they don't own and for which they don't have planning permission? And what,' she continued, 'is in it for these favoured older clients, that the developers will go to all the expense of hiring an events room in a swanky hotel and provide nibbles and champagne for?'

'I was coming to that,' Jago spoke quietly.

Olivia moved back to the window and leant against it, her arms stretched out behind her on the windowsill.

'From what I could gather, the majority of the clients at the seminar were people who had previously invested with associates of a company called Carless Venture Developments. Hand-picked, high-net-worth individuals keen to earn more money on their investments than the current low returns they get from the banks. Carless, promise a fifteen to twenty percent return on their investment within twelve months.'

'Almost too good to be true. And you know what they say about that.'

'Indeed,' Jago acknowledged her scepticism. 'If these clients buy an apartment off-plan they pay up to twenty-five percent less than if they wait for the development to be completed.'

'So what's the catch?'

Jago joined her at the window, and they watched a couple of dogs and their owners enjoying the fresh morning air after a few days spent cooped up indoors, away from the rain. 'I'm not sure yet. I need to see the paperwork. Check what is being sold. I suspect that they might not be selling the property, but an interest in it.'

'Which they can't if I own the land.' Her voice was firm.

Jago took hold of Olivia's upper-arms and turned her round so she had to tilt her head up to look him in the eye.

'The land is held in trust, with you as the ultimate beneficiary.'

'Isn't that the same thing?'

'Theoretically yes. You can willingly wind up the Trust if you choose to do so.'

'Never.'

'Do you know what will happen to the Trust if for any reason you are not in a position to fully exercise your role as beneficiary?' Jago hated himself for being so blunt and felt her body sag.

'If I'm in prison you mean?'

He winced at Olivia's own bluntness. 'I suppose so.'

'Or dead?'

Jago gave up trying to break it gently but held more firmly onto her arms. 'In circumstances such as those, the Trust is to be wound up and the assets pass to your father, as George's closet living relative.'

Olivia closed her eyes. 'That will be the end of everything here. He's in Adelaide and not at all interested.

He'd probably just sell to the highest bidder.'

'And that's why these developers are banking on you agreeing to sell. People usually go with the highest bidder.'

'I will never sell, Jago. I might not be able to do anything to help Libby or perhaps Sarah now, but I can protect this land for the sake of the village and for George.' Her eyes filled with tears.

'Olivia, face facts. I don't want to scare you, but whoever is behind this will want to make sure you sell this land. Willingly or not.'

The sun shining through the window highlighted each individual fleck of amber in her dark irises, made even brighter by her unshed tears.

'Are you saying these could be the people who are desperate to get me away from the project, who have been trying to scare me off?'

Jago met her gaze squarely and calmly. 'Yes. And who may also be responsible for Libby's murder and Sarah's disappearance.'

CHAPTER TWENTY

Olivia checked her online diaries for both the Goods Shed and her New York office and calculated how much time she had before she joined a conference call with Joey at 2.30 p.m. She made a brief phone call to Alice and then replied to her most urgent UK emails, all while keeping one eye on the paperwork which covered her messy desk. *It's almost as bad as Jago's*, she thought to herself with a small smile.

She contacted the regional office of Historic England to talk about listing and had an interesting and worthwhile conversation with the person in charge of applications. Then she turned to her laptop search engine and immediately fell down a series of rabbit holes in Cornwall's online planning portal, researching restrictions and exceptions.

Around eleven o'clock, she took a break and picked up some old post from a pile on her desk and took it through to the kitchen. Sighing, she counted four letters addressed to Mr George Stevenson, that she still hadn't dealt with, knowing she'd have to inform yet more unsuspecting souls of his death. Last week, she'd cancelled his library card, which should have been easy, but led to an awkward, sniffly conversation with a woman at Falmouth library, which had left them both in tears. Letters and cards still arrived, though more intermittently now she'd got almost to the bottom of her list of people to notify. She slid the kettle onto the hotplate and selected an inoffensive looking brown envelope, with a faded logo of Treliske hospital stamped on it.

'Dear Mr Stevenson,' she read aloud. 'Our records show that you missed an outpatient appointment on 17th January in the clinic of Mr Michael Fulton. As a result of this non-attendance, we are discharging you back to the care of your GP and you will need a new referral in order to be seen in this clinic in future. Missed appointments cost the Royal Cornwall Hospitals £4 million each year and . . .' Oliva cursed the tactlessness of the letter and didn't read on. Instead, she called the village surgery where the receptionist greeted her warmly.

'Hi, Olivia, it's Keren Tremain. I was so sorry to hear about Mr Stevenson. He was such a lovely man.'

Olivia was taken aback. In New York, the receptionist at her doctor's office didn't have a clue who she was.

'Er, thank you. That's why I'm calling. I've just found a letter from Treliske saying that George didn't attend an appointment in January. I must say I found it a bit insensitive. Surely, it's on their system that he died?'

'I'm so sorry Olivia. That's dreadful. Let me just take a look.' There was a lot of keyboard-tapping. 'Here we are. Oh, dear. That letter must have been automatically generated. Hold on a minute.' There was more tapping. 'It looks as though he missed his last three appointments.'

'What?' Olivia gasped. 'But that clinic checked on his aneurysm repair. The appointments were really important! I'm sure he always attended them.'

'Apparently not.' Keren was sympathetic. 'But I agree that it doesn't sound like Mr Stevenson.' There was a pause. 'Was he getting forgetful?'

'No! I don't think so . . .' she faltered as Keren's words

filtered through her brain. 'Oh, my God. If he'd attended the check-ups he might not have died when he did. He must have forgotten.'

***

With a surge of grief, Olivia whistled to the dogs and rushed through the gardens, down to the creek's edge. There, an old granite quay with a stone balustrade covered in lichen and weathered by almost two centuries of storms, stretched along the water's edge. Mollie had deliberately planted each season's most fragrant flowers around this spot, and now the beautiful fragrance of white narcissi mingled with the soothing cocktail of seawater and fresh air. Olivia sat flanked by the dogs, at her favourite childhood spot and let her tears fall, grieving for the man who had been father, grandfather and wise counsel to her. The man she hadn't noticed wasn't looking after himself properly.

Spring had arrived. Snowdrops and primroses filled the flowerbeds, catkins and unfurling green buds were on the trees and the birds were singing in beautiful harmony. The midday sun reflected off the glassy mudbanks exposed by the receding tide in the middle of the creek, where a pair of oystercatchers searched in the mud for worms with their long orange beaks. Olivia watched them for a while, still thinking of George and how things could have turned out so very differently.

Her mobile buzzed in the pocket of her fleece and jolted her out of her thoughts. She whipped it out.

'Hey, Olivia,' Martin's voice came down the line, obscured by the sound of heavy traffic in the background. 'How are you?'

'Oh, you know,' she replied carefully. 'Things seem to carry on as normal. Where are you? Somewhere busy by the sound of it.'

'I'm in Plymouth.'

'Plymouth? Why are you all the way over there?'

'Well, remember that contact I mentioned at the meeting on Monday? He's put me in touch with this amazing business school here for sustainable and creative entrepreneurs. They're looking for someone to help the participants get investment-ready by the end of the course, so I came across here straight after that meeting. And they've just offered me the role.'

'That's good.' Olivia tried to sound enthusiastic.

'They have delegates from all over the country, looking to relocate to the southwest. It could be really good news.'

'It sounds like a lot of work for you. Are you okay with that?'

There was a pause at the other end of the line. 'A steady supply of members is just what the Goods Shed needs right now, Olivia. Are you sure you're okay?'

She didn't like lying, least of all to Martin, when he was trying so hard to help. 'I'm sorry, Martin, I'm having a sad day. And Joey's putting me under pressure again, so I feel like I'm spinning plates.' She crossed her fingers.

'Well, like I said. I'll do everything I can to help you keep the Goods Shed going . . . and we can talk more when I get back . . .' The loud burst of a horn interrupted his sentence. 'Oops! must go.'

Olivia stared at her phone, heartened by thoughts of Martin being so helpful in spite of still working through his grief for Libby. George had chosen well.

'Ahoy there,' Jago's deep voice interrupted her thoughts. The dogs barked and rushed up to him, Mylor's tail wagging like a metronome on fast-speed and Zennor standing on her back legs for Jago to fuss her.

'Sorry. I was miles away.' She got up slowly from her seat where she had been protected from the stiff sea breeze, suddenly glad of her extra layers. She nodded towards the brown paper carrier bag decorated with the

Bakehouse's distinctive logo. His other hand held a slim leather briefcase. 'Lunch?'

'As promised.' He inclined his head to look at her more closely. 'Is everything okay?'

Olivia forced a smile onto her face and lied again. 'Yeah, I'm good. Let's go eat.'

***

They enjoyed a companionable lunch together at the refectory table in the orangery; the dogs curled up nearby in their baskets. Conversation flowed easily; the old tension between them had passed. Olivia's heart was lighter, she realised, since talking to Jago about Aidan. Yesterday, she had felt something shift deep within her, as though she had found the end to the huge knot that had coiled inside her for over twenty years. Had Jago's firm, calm and rational words allowed her to begin the long, slow unravelling of that guilt? *Perhaps he would be equally pragmatic about George's missed appointments? No,* she decided, *confiding in him about that can wait for another time. George would want me to concentrate on the present, not the past.*

'Right,' Jago pushed his plate away and wiped his hands with a napkin, 'shall we get down to business?'

Olivia quickly cleared away the detritus and collected her own notes and laptop from the study.

Jago looked through his notes, for once in a neat pile in front of him.

'I'll kick off, shall I? Carless Venture Developments is a newly incorporated company, with four directors, all men, whom I couldn't find any details about, despite their brochure claiming "fifty years combined experience. And they haven't filed any accounts yet".'

'So where's this company registered?'

Jago tapped his notes with his pen. 'It's a business park

somewhere in Peckham. Sounds like a serviced office.'

Olivia scrunched up her face in thought. 'So, no obvious links to Penbartha there?'

He shook his head. 'No.'

'Did you or Penny get the chance to speak to any of the other favoured clients at the seminar to find out what sort of previous investments they had made?'

'I didn't. I'm afraid I was too busy listening to what they are offering. I don't know about Penny. Although,' he paused and scratched at his thick hair with his pen, 'she was engaged in deep conversation with an irritating older man who was sitting to her right. I'll have to ask her.'

'Okay, give me the list of the directors' names and I'll check them against the councillors' names on the local councils here. See if I can establish any link that way. You can put the kettle on.'

Five minutes later she had drawn a blank. 'This is so frustrating. We're just going round in circles.'

'Did you get anywhere this morning?' Jago stretched his long legs out in front of him and bent down to scratch Mylor's head, who immediately rolled over onto his back in surrender.

'Not really.' Olivia sighed. 'Although, I'm now an expert on the very long and detailed Local Plan for Cornwall which, among a lot of other things, sets out the policies to guide all future planning decisions.'

'And?'

'I can see where Carless is getting its ammunition from. There's particular reference to the changes in population, with an increase in older residents and the associated impact on health facilities and services.'

'Which Carless claims to ease with its retirement villages?'

'Exactly. Plus, there's emphasis on sustainable development, at long bloody last. Like I said earlier, now it's trendy and profitable everyone is jumping on the bandwagon.'

'Better late than never?' Jago's admonishment was gentle, but it riled Olivia.

'Companies like Carless don't give a damn about the environmental needs of future generations or reducing energy consumption. They just want to save money and make even more money.'

'But the desired effect is the same.'

'That's not the point! You get all these companies setting up "green" businesses just to claim subsidies and gain contracts, not because they believe in what they are doing. It's pure hypocrisy.' Olivia's voice rose. 'That would be like you defending someone you really thought was guilty and just using your clever arguments to get him or her off.' She paused for a moment and frowned at him. 'You didn't do that, did you?'

'A person is innocent until proven guilty in our legal system. Barristers are paid to represent their clients and put their best argument forward. They are not paid to believe them. Or like them.' It sounded like a well-practised answer.

'So it's all about being paid for you as well, is it? Not morals, or justice?' Her dark eyes glittered.

He held up his hands calmly. 'We digress, Olivia. Let's not get side-tracked. We have more immediate concerns to address. What else did you find out?'

Olivia pulled herself together. 'The Local Plan supports the best use of brownfield sites and existing buildings, rather than infringing on greenbelt land. Which is the case here. And the aim is to have most decisions made at a local level where the interests of the local communities are best represented. There're loads of other things, but it's too depressing to go into right now.'

She waved at the pages of notes covered in her stylish handwriting, diagrams, and drawings and pressed her fingers against her temples for a moment. 'And I recognise the names of most of the local councillors, but I didn't realise Edgar sits on the Planning Committee.'

'Does he now?' Jago's eyebrow rose.

'He's also a councillor for the central sub-area for the County Council. And sits on the Planning Committee there too.'

Jago leant forward. 'And what do they deal with, if they like to devolve most decisions down to the local level?'

'Appeals and large-scale applications apparently.'

'Interesting.'

'And it does seem that if a planning application is turned down at the local level, it's invariably granted on appeal to the next level.'

'Which Edgar sits on.'

They exchanged glances. 'Yes. But I really don't think Edgar would be involved in anything iffy like this. He's always been totally committed to our sustainability goals and would never countenance the destruction of old buildings. Besides which, George thought the world of him. He'd been his solicitor for years.'

She saw Jago's expressive right eyebrow rise and waited for him to speak.

'Well, George must have had his reasons for appointing each and every one of us as trustees if we use that reasoning. I think we ought to look into Edgar's interests more if he's a potential link between the Trust and Carless though, even if it is a little tenuous at the moment.'

'I can do that. Although I'm not sure I agree with you.'

Jago closed his notebook. 'Have we time for a coffee before we get back to our own businesses?'

Olivia glanced at him in surprise. His bright blue eyes, with their dark rings of navy, reminded her of the Cornish seas which changed colour as the water got deeper and their moods altered. Now, they held a definite twinkle.

'I'll put the kettle on. And then powder my nose.'

She was halfway across the kitchen when Jago called

her back. 'Just for the record, Olivia, I mainly prosecuted.'

CHAPTER TWENTY-ONE

While Olivia was out of the room, Jago wondered again why he was still there. One moment they were working well together, bouncing ideas off each other, and he was enjoying her company, her energy, and the way her eyes sparkled when she talked about the buildings she worked on in New York. And then he would say something, or make a throwaway remark, and the spiky Olivia was back, and he felt wrongfooted again. So much for letting himself believe that he was slowly penetrating the carapace she had carefully constructed around herself. He looked down at Zennor, who had placed a dainty foot on his shoe, and reminded himself of the enormous pressure Olivia was under and resolved again to do everything in his power to make sure she was removed from the police's suspect list for good.

'And then life can get back to normal,' he told Zennor, as he picked her up. The little dog kissed his nose daintily with her bright pink tongue and Jago chuckled.

'What's so funny?' Olivia came back into the kitchen and warmed the cafetiere before making coffee and carrying it over to the table.

'You have a visitor,' Jago commented, as a familiar face appeared at the window and let himself in through the doors. 'Hi, Ross.'

'I'm glad you're both here. Kills two birds with one stone. Sorry.' Trenow sat down heavily on a chair. 'Poor choice of words. May I have a cup, please? Black. I need to stay awake.'

Jago regarded the detective while Olivia was fetching another mug. He looked exhausted, red-eyed, and stubble darkened his jaw in a very un-Trenow-like way. Even his shirt didn't look fresh on today.

'Things not going well?' He waited for an answer while Trenow drained his coffee in one gulp and held out the mug for a refill.

'You could say that.' He ran his hands across his face, rubbing his eyes and stubble. 'I can't believe I told Lara that life would be easier down here and she would see more of me. She's not happy.'

'I suppose that's the risk you take when you marry a detective,' Jago observed.

'Unfortunately.' Trenow took a deep breath and stared at them both. 'There's no simple way of saying this and I'm too knackered to break it gently. We found another body early this morning, in the undergrowth off the walkway.'

Olivia paled and her hand flew to her mouth. 'Not Sarah? Please, not Sarah?'

Trenow shook his head, but Olivia's face showed no sign of relief. Her huge, dark eyes never left the detective's face.

'Who then?' Jago broke the silence.

'We've been able to keep a lid on this one so far, as it was further up the walkway. But I will tell you.' Jago noticed that Trenow was watching Olivia closely, almost as though he was building the suspense. 'It's Jess Hopkins.'

'Oh my God. No . . .' Olivia gasped, sounding like someone had kicked her in the stomach. She collapsed onto a chair and held her head in her hands.

He went on, surprisingly, and Jago realised he was

imparting information usually kept back to test how much they knew. *Are we both suspects now?*

'The on-scene pathologist suggested she was poisoned,' Trenow read from his pocketbook, 'but they're not sure with what yet. It looks as though it was a highly toxic substance.'

Olivia raised her eyes briefly, and Jago noticed they looked sad and dull. 'Poor Jess.'

Trenow nodded. 'We're not sure of her time of death because of the rain. It looks as though the poison worked quickly, causing tremendous damage to her organs before passing out of her body. She could have been there for anything between eight and twenty-four hours. Because the rain was so bad, few dog walkers were out and about at that part of the walkway.'

'Any other leads?' Jago asked.

Trenow hesitated for a moment. 'There was no sign of sexual interference. It looks like she was killed elsewhere, and her body moved to the walkway after death.'

No one said anything.

'Oh, one other thing.' Trenow closed his notebook and shoved it back in his jacket pocket. 'She was covered in scratch marks. But they were her own fingernails that had made the marks. Almost as though she developed some kind of skin reaction to the poison and was madly scratching at it.'

Olivia swayed and Jago's arm shot out and caught her by the elbow. He pushed her head between her knees while Trenow rushed to get her some water.

Much to Jago's relief, she began protesting almost immediately, forcing herself upright and glaring at him.

'What the hell are you doing?'

'You fainted.'

She squared her shoulders and lifted her chin before looking him in the eye.

'I,' she informed him crossly, 'have never fainted in my

life and don't intend to start now. Especially not in front of you.'

'I apologise.' He held her gaze. 'So why did you slide off your chair?'

Olivia opened her mouth to reply, then shut it again immediately. Tears suddenly appeared in her eyes, and she got up from the table. Trenow handed her a glass of water and she drank from it gratefully.

'Thanks. I'm fine now.'

'Are you sure?' Trenow enquired. 'You still look a bit green.'

'I'm fine,' she repeated. 'It was what you said about the itching. And the vomiting. I think I might know what the poison was.'

Both men stared at her.

'Not long after my brother died, I was staying here for the summer and picked some pretty flowers from the garden for Mollie.' She turned away from them. 'I didn't want to pick roses or any of the usual flowers that we had around, and I remembered seeing some beautiful deep blue flowers at the far end of the garden where it's a bit boggy and marshy. A place we weren't allowed to play.' She took a deep breath. 'Anyway, I picked three or four of the stems and proudly carried them into the kitchen to present them to Mollie.' She paused, a cloud passing over her face. 'It was the only time she ever shouted at me. Because I scared her. I'd picked Monk's Hood, one of the deadliest poisons you'll ever find in a garden.'

'Why on earth was it growing in a family garden if it was so poisonous?' Trenow was astonished.

'Mollie was a specialist in herbal medicine.' Olivia reminded him. 'And we knew that part of the garden was out of bounds. I guess I thought I'd get away with it, given the circumstances. What I didn't realise was that even touching the leaves and the stem could poison me.'

'So, what happened?' Trenow asked.

Olivia pulled a face. 'Mollie made me drink something that made me sick, horribly sick. For hours. That was enough to make sure I never went near that plant again.'

'What was it called again?' Trenow got his pocketbook out.

'Monk's Hood. Its Latin name is aconite. In the States it's called Wolf's Bane because they supposedly used it on arrow tips to kill wolves. If it's swallowed by a human, in the most severe cases, it causes vomiting, dizziness and diarrhoea followed by palpitations and death. Within about an hour of swallowing it.'

'You seem to know a lot about it,' Trenow observed.

Olivia flushed. 'I was disgustingly sick because of it. I found out all I could about it,' she declared. 'And that's not the sort of thing you ever forget.'

'What else do you know?'

Olivia shrugged. 'As far as I can remember symptoms begin with intense itching and tingling. That's what reminded me.'

'Did you get that?'

She turned a rueful face to them. 'No. Mollie got to work quickly, and I was throwing up within about four minutes of picking them. Anyway, I didn't swallow any of it, just touched the stems and leaves.'

'So, is the whole plant poisonous?' Jago was intrigued.

She nodded. 'Although the root's the most powerful.'

'And presumably the most potent for medical purposes?'

'Yes. In a liniment or tincture form it's applied externally to treat neuralgia, sciatica, and rheumatism.'

'Did Mollie use it for her rheumatism?' Jago asked, remembering how the old lady had suffered.

Olivia nodded. Then swayed again. 'Oh, my God, the krowji,' she whispered. 'That's where she kept it. In the big cupboard.'

Trenow jumped to his feet. 'Would there be any still

there?'

'I don't know. Cassie might. It's always locked away within the krowji, which is also locked.'

'Can we look?'

***

Trenow left, carefully holding a heavy wooden box containing both the aconite liniment, and some dried root. Olivia sank on to the sofa in the orangery. Mylor and Zennor jumped up on either side of her and snuggled close. Jago sat opposite, alarmed that Trenow seemed too tired to fight against the constraints of the system. He was only too aware of cases where the police only investigated what suited them to build a case against a suspect that would stick. He knew that sometimes the facts which pointed away from a suspect's guilt would be ignored or not properly examined. And he had come across plenty of occasions in his legal career where evidence that exonerated a suspect had gone undisclosed. All of which had contributed to his decision to leave that part of his life in London and move to Cornwall.

Jago didn't think Trenow would charge Olivia with the murders just to help his own statistics, but he wasn't foolish enough to believe that his superiors wouldn't be putting him under pressure to get the case sorted. And now Olivia had told Trenow about Jess's confrontational attitude towards her at the last meeting, he would interview all the trustees and their statements could be used to build a case for motive against her. That went against everything Jago believed in and was a major reason he had become a criminal barrister. It hadn't just been a desire to prevent miscarriages of justice, but a need to seek justice for the victims of crime. And in his opinion, Libby, Jess and Olivia were all victims in their own ways. He felt an old, but familiar stirring deep inside that he had to do the right thing. For all of them. It was time to move things up a gear.

'I reckon that whoever did this to Jess used the aconite from Mollie's krowji to make it look as though I did it.' Olivia's voice jolted him out of his thoughts. 'Please tell me that's a crazy line of thought.'

Jago was his usual calm self. 'Let's wait for the toxicology reports before we jump to any conclusions.'

'But everyone will see that I'm the obvious link between the two murders. Both victims argued with me in public and people will think I murdered them to shut them up. And they'll find evidence that proves I'm involved in Jess's murder as well if the aconite came from the krowji. And even though I told Trenow all about it, they'll just say I'm playing more of those mind games he was on about. But I didn't do it, Jago. I didn't do it.' She turned huge, frightened eyes to him, her breathing rapid and shallow. 'I need to get out of here, I can't breathe.'

'Shush,' Jago crossed the room in seconds and pulled her awkwardly into his arms, patting her back in soothing motions. 'I know you didn't do it. Trenow knows it too, deep down. We'll sort it.'

They stood together for a moment until Jago sensed the panic rushing through her ease and felt her breathing slow and quieten.

'What do I do now?' She lifted her eyes to his.

'What do you want to do?'

'Run. As far away as possible.' Olivia spoke instinctively. 'But I guess that's not an option. I can cope with the land problems, just about, but these awful murders are . . .' the tears pooled in her eyes were in danger of falling, and Jago could see the effort she was making not to cry. He moved closer, but she pulled away, still sniffing, then forced her shoulders back.

Jago's strong fingers caught hold of her hand and squeezed it, grateful for the return of some of her old spirit.

'Trust me, please. I want to help you.'

She removed her hand carefully, and turned her sad face away from him, but not before he could see the familiar old doubts flash through her eyes.

'Thanks, Jago.' She looked back at him. 'But I can't deal with this right now. I need to let it settle for a bit.' She glanced down at her watch and groaned. 'I've got a conference call with my boss in ten minutes that I need to dial in to.'

'Is he still putting you under pressure to go back?' He followed her to the door.

She avoided the question. 'I have some clients there that only want to deal with me. And that suits me. I can almost forget that this total nightmare is happening when I'm in the middle of a New York client conference call, negotiating over details that are totally insignificant in the grand scheme of things.'

Jago smiled. 'Well, don't negotiate for too long. Try and get an early night.'

CHAPTER TWENTY-TWO

It was a weary Olivia who pulled on her running shoes and whistled to the dogs. She headed out on her regular early morning route along the creek path to the walkway, hoping she wouldn't run into Mrs Chynoweth.

The soft snap of a twig in the bushes behind her was her only warning. The hairs on the back of her neck stood up; all her senses suddenly alert and she swung round, instinctively shifting her right leg forward to balance herself and raising her arms to protect her face. A heavy, painful blow to the side of her head sent her sprawling to the ground, her cheek cracking against a boulder. She lay gasping and dazed as black spots danced above her. High-pitched, terrified squealing from Zennor forced Olivia to her knees, and she scrambled up blindly, spitting out a foul-tasting mixture of mud and blood. Through a red haze she could just make out her hooded attacker; a man, who was flailing around, trying to grab at the dogs. Mylor snapped back, his large teeth flashing, but Zennor was no match for the brute who was forcing her little body under his arm.

Olivia's heart thudded against her ribcage as she staggered towards them. As the little dog's frightened screams got louder, her mind cleared. It was one thing to hurt her, but to even attempt to harm Zennor was a step too far. She approached the man, scrubbing at her eyes with dirty hands and smearing a mass of blood, mud, and tears over her face. Adrenaline was rushing round her veins, preparing her for attack. Her assailant was having trouble getting away with the little dog squealing, wriggling, and writhing under his right arm, while Mylor was circling him manically, growling fiercely and jumping up repeatedly, teeth bared. With a furious roar, Olivia launched herself at the man's back, grabbing at his face with her nails, struggling to unbalance him. He shoved her away, but she kicked out in rage at the back of his knees. As he threw out his left arm to regain his balance, she grabbed hold of his wrist in her right hand and twisted his arm at the elbow. She slammed her entire bodyweight against his elbow joint until she felt it splinter and give way. The accompanying screams told her she had broken it.

'You mad bitch,' he screamed, dropping Zennor and cradling his badly misshapen arm. 'You've broken my fucking arm.'

'I'll break the other one if you don't leave my dogs alone and get out of here,' she spat, moving towards him again.

'Fucking lunatic woman! Have your bloody dog.' He kicked out towards the dogs and Mylor, launching his own attack, sank all his teeth into the man's upper thigh. With another howl, their attacker limped off down the walkway, heading towards the village.

Olivia fell to the ground beside Zennor, who was still bleating pathetically. As she hugged and cradled the frightened little dog to her, the whimpering increased until she realised the noise was now coming from her own mouth. Shaking, she pushed herself back up on her feet. Unable to see Mylor, she started calling his name, more and more desperately, her voice rising. Fears for her other dog took over and still clutching Zennor to her chest, she staggered along the walkway towards the station buildings, unable to control her terrified sobs.

***

Jago was enjoying his early morning cup of tea with the *Today* programme's usual presenters when Steren sat up suddenly, her head on one side. He smiled briefly at the thought of the only person who visited him at this early hour and moved over to the door. Only one set of clattering paws met his ears and a single, high, anxious-sounding bark. He threw open the door.

'Morning, Mylor, come to convert me, have you?' He peered down the stairs. 'Where's your infuriating mistress?'

The reference to the early Cornish saint was lost on the distressed dog. Mylor circled round him, looking up, barking nervously and starting back down the stairs, before running back up and repeating his actions.

'Okay, boy, okay. Now I feel like I'm in a Lassie movie. Do you want me to follow you?'

Mylor yapped anxiously and set off down the stairs and along the walkway, stopping and turning back at regular intervals to check that Jago was following him. A sudden icy grip seized Jago's chest, and he ran faster than he could remember running for a very long time, behind Mylor, until they reached a crumpled figure, curled in a ball with a whimpering dog still clutched in her arms.

'Olivia!' He dropped to his knees beside her and tentatively put a hand on her back. She was so still and cold he felt his own heart stop for a moment.

'Olivia. It's Jago. Open your eyes.' He gingerly felt her neck for a pulse and let his breath go in a tremendous rush when he felt the steady beat of her heart.

She uncurled slowly, flinching with pain. As he carefully brushed her cheek with his fingers to remove

241

some of the blood, she opened her eyes. Jago's fingers moved over her scalp with a firm, gentle touch, parting her thick curls which had come loose from the ponytail. Her hair was matted with blood, mud and grit. There was a nasty gash behind her ear, bleeding profusely. His face darkened; he fumbled in his pocket for a clean cotton handkerchief and pressed it against the wound.

'Let's get you to the Signal Box.'

She jerked her eyes open, the panic clear on her face. 'The dogs! Where are they?'

'They're fine,' he tried to soothe her. 'Look, they're here. Mylor was quite the hero.'

Both dogs pushed their noses against her, tails wagging, their own traumas forgotten. Olivia sank back, resting her head against Jago's thigh. 'He was trying to get Zennor. That was why he bashed me so hard.'

'Let's get you somewhere more comfortable and then you can tell me everything.'

'I'll walk.' She struggled away from him, but he was too strong for her.

'Let me help for once, Olivia. Stop being so bloody independent.'

***

Olivia lay on the chesterfield, still shaking. The beginnings of a huge bruise spread from her hairline down to her cheekbone, but the rest of her face was ghostly white. Jago tucked a blanket around her. He checked her pupils for signs of concussion, and satisfied that there were none, he began to make mugs of tea for them both. Even before he had finished swirling the tea bags around in the mugs, a set of heavy footsteps rushed up the stairs and a troubled looking Inspector Trenow burst into the room.

'What's happened? I didn't catch everything you were saying.'

Jago pulled a warning face. 'I'm not sure yet. She's still a bit confused. I've called the local GP, as she's refusing to go to hospital. He should be here soon.'

Trenow stood looking down at Olivia, who still had her eyes closed. He turned to Jago. 'She looks awful. Where was she hit?'

'On the back of the head, by the look of it. And hard, too. Then, when she fell, she must have bashed her cheekbone against a boulder or something.'

'What was it all about? A random attack?'

'Are you serious, Ross?' Jago spun round. 'Here in Penbartha? The guy was trying to grab Zennor.'

Trenow sat down in a chair and accepted the mug of tea Jago offered him. 'So why would anyone try to kidnap a dog?' Trenow mused out loud.

'Not just any dog,' he snapped. 'Olivia's dog. Or rather Mollie's.'

Trenow groaned. 'This just gets worse. So you think he was directly targeting Olivia?'

'Yes! I reckon it's someone's attempt to frighten her off. She hasn't exactly taken a lot of notice of the warnings so far, has she?'

'What? Most people wouldn't care that much about a dog that wasn't even theirs, would they?'

Jago grimaced. 'Which suggests that the person behind this knows exactly what Zennor means to Olivia. She and Mylor are the last living connections she has with her godparents. And I can't put into words how close they all were.' He swallowed the last of his tea. 'I hate to think what this would have done to Olivia if this guy had been successful.'

Trenow was silent for a moment, but Jago carried on, his voice dangerously calm.

'If I'm right, Ross, this could have huge implications for your case. With two murders and everything else that has been going on around here, whoever is behind all this means business. And it's getting more and more personal.' He lowered his voice, 'Olivia is obviously the common denominator. So, I don't think I'm overacting when I say she could be in serious danger. What's stopping him from coming back?'

'I think I broke his arm.' A small, shaky voice spoke from the depths of the blanket.

'You what?' The men spoke in unison as they watched her struggle to sit upright.

'I twisted his left arm and slammed into him just above the elbow joint.'

'Are you sure you broke it?' Trenow asked.

Olivia's pale face went a distinct shade of green. 'It made the most sickening crunching noise. And he screamed.'

That impressed Trenow. 'I'll bet he did. Where on earth did you learn to do that?'

'I promised George I'd learn self-defence when I moved to New York, and I found a system that combines fitness and a kind of street fighting.' She touched her head and winced. 'I've never had to use it before.'

Jago stared at her. *Will this woman ever cease to surprise me?*

Trenow got out his mobile. 'I'll get Burridge to put calls in to all the local hospitals to check if anyone turns up with a badly broken left arm. Any other injuries?'

Olivia thought for a moment. 'I think Mylor bit him hard as well. On the thigh.'

The larger dog thumped his tail proudly against the floor at the sound of his name.

'Good old Mylor.' Trenow bent and patted him. 'I doubt there will be many men in casualty departments with a broken upper arm and a nasty dog bite on their thigh.' He paused. 'I know it's a big ask, Olivia, but did you manage to get a good look at him?'

She shook her head. 'I'm sorry. But he was in dark

clothes with a black hoodie obscuring his face.'

'Did he say anything?'

She paused. 'Only when his arm broke. He swore at me.'

Jago couldn't stop the smile creeping across his face. 'Good. Did he have an accent?'

Olivia closed her eyes for a moment. 'London. I think. South London perhaps. And he smelt of weed.'

'Excellent! Thanks.' Trenow seemed eager to take back control. 'If you could let us have your clothes when you change, we'll send them off for fibre and DNA analysis. See if we can pick anything up from them.'

Olivia held out her filthy mud and blood covered hands.

Jago raised an eyebrow at her.

'I scratched him. On his face and hands, I think.' A sob caught in her throat and her voice rose. 'I was trying to make him let go of Zennor. I didn't know what he would do to her.' She sniffed and rubbed ineffectually at her face with her sleeve in a curiously childlike gesture.

'Right, I'll sort forensics,' Trenow said to Jago, as he walked to the door. 'You wait here for the doctor and let me know what he says. I'll need to get a statement when he's said she's okay to do so.'

Zennor was curled up on Olivia's lap with Mylor's shaggy head on her knee when he got back to them.

'I know I'm being pathetic, take no notice of me.'

Jago sat next to her and curled his arm around her shoulders, pulling her close. 'Don't be so hard on yourself. You've had a nasty shock.'

She stiffened but then leaned in to him.

'I've been trying so hard to keep everything together since I got back, and now it's come to this.' A tear rolled down her cheek. 'I'm not crying.' She sniffed. 'I don't do crying.'

'No.' Jago brushed her tears away with his fingers. 'I know you don't.'

He rocked her gently from side to side, stroking the

curls from her face without speaking. He just held her and stroked her back until the GP arrived.

***

'Smells good.'

Jago could tell she was trying to sound normal, but when he turned, she looked dreadful. Instead of the bright and confident Olivia he had come to know, he saw a scared woman, barefoot and makeup free in a pair of jeans and a shirt. Her face was even paler than earlier, and she had a nasty bruise, already turning from red to purple, down the left side of her face. She shook her damp dark ringlets over her cheek, but Jago eased her hair to one side to examine the damage.

'Ouch,' he winced, as he moved his hand from her forehead and let it rest against her cheek. 'You'll have a lovely black eye in the next day or two.'

Dr Kitson had checked her over and patched her up with steri-strips. A crime scene investigator had taken DNA samples from her fingernails, now scrubbed clean, and a female detective, who Olivia much preferred to Burridge, had taken her statement.

'Do you think they'll catch him?' she asked abruptly, once they'd moved to the orangery after their late lunch.

Her words shook Jago out of his own thoughts. 'The guy who attacked you? I should think so. He won't get far with those injuries. It just depends on how effective the boys in blue are.' He kept his voice neutral.

'You don't sound convinced.'

He cursed himself. She was seeking reassurance he couldn't provide. It just wasn't in his nature to talk in platitudes. He dealt in facts. 'I'm sure Trenow is doing everything he can.'

'I'm scared.' Her voice was small.

'No way.' Jago tried to make light of the situation. 'You

just broke a man's arm with your bare hands. You're one of the toughest people I know.'

'I'm not tough,' she said eventually. 'Everyone thinks I am, but I'm not. Not really.'

To Jago's surprise, she leant into him, and he wound his fingers into her curls as Olivia turned her face in to his with a look of gentle surprise.

The loud jangling of the front doorbell sent the dogs into a frenzy of activity, and Jago never found out what could have happened next.

***

A harassed-looking Trenow followed a slightly flushed Jago back into the orangery. He refused Jago's reluctant offer of a drink and sat opposite them both.

'We've located the guy who attacked you. He only made it as far as Treliske hospital and was pretty easily identified from the injuries inflicted.' He flashed a quick grin at Olivia. 'We have a uniformed officer there with him, keeping guard. He's had a tetanus for the dog bite, but he needs surgery to pin his arm, and the hospital is very busy, so he won't be going anywhere for a while.'

'Has anyone spoken to him yet?'

Trenow shook his head. 'According to the hospital, he's fabricated an entire story to explain his injuries. We'll let him suffer a bit before we try. Our man is keeping a very close on eye on him.' He looked at his watch distractedly.

'Not Burridge?' Olivia tried a small smile but winced and held her cheek.

Trenow grimaced. 'No. The traffic's still dreadful at Land's End.' He sobered quickly. 'What I really came to tell you both is that we've had the comparison of Jess's preliminary toxicology results with those from Mollie's aconite back from the experts.'

Olivia sat upright, her steady brown gaze firmly on

Trenow.

'They reckon it is fairly definite that it was aconite that was used to poison Jess, and it's also looking likely that it was the stuff from Mollie's krowji. I need to know who else had a key?'

'Only Cassie, as far as I know. She's been doing some potting up in there recently.' Olivia pulled her knees up to her chest and sat rocking back and forward.

The two men exchanged worried glances.

'Look, Olivia.' Trenow put his hand on her shoulder. 'I'm concerned now. Whoever's behind these murders is sending you a very clear message. And the attack on you today shows he's stepping up a gear and escalating things just in case you weren't getting it before. You need to take this seriously. There's still no news on Sarah. I don't want to have to investigate your death next. Part of me thinks you might be safer if I take you in for questioning.'

Jago held Olivia's gaze for a beat. 'No way! How would it be if we headed off for the weekend? Give you a couple of days to question this guy?'

Trenow scratched the back of his head and then turned to Jago. 'I understand where you're coming from and I'm putting my neck on the line here. Don't tell me where you are, but do keep the lines of communication open, just in case.' His tone was sharp. 'And then I won't have to lie to my superiors, who might not see things the same way.'

CHAPTER TWENTY-THREE

Olivia stirred for the first time since leaving Bristol, just as Jago turned on to the Euston Road, heading toward Kingsway. The traffic, now coming up to a dark and damp rush hour, was unusually heavy, even by London standards. He wondered how her headache was now. He glanced across at her, worn out and bowed down by pain and anxiety and was reassured by her ability to get some sleep during their journey. Tears had rolled down her cheeks when they left their dogs with Rocky who had promised to take them all to Jago's parent's farm near Launceston and she'd been quiet and withdrawn ever since.

Olivia moaned as her injuries made themselves felt and then sat upright, wincing as she eased the tension out of her neck and shoulders and peered out of the window at the busy London street. Black taxis and red buses crawled up the road in the opposite direction, overtaken by stressed-looking pedestrians hurrying along the crowded pavements.

She sighed heavily and leant back, watching the red and white reflections from the rear lights dance across the wet tarmac. 'It feels good to be anonymous again.'

Jago took advantage of the lull in traffic movement to

take a proper look at his passenger. The only colour on her pinched and drawn face was coming from the massive purple bruise that was spreading and blackening her cheekbone. Her dark curls tumbled over her shoulders, for once let free to do their own thing, but even they had lost their bounce.

'You can relax when we get there. You'll be completely safe, I promise. And we can catch up with Penny.'

A small, grateful smile appeared from behind the curls and Jago resisted the temptation to squeeze her hand. He couldn't take advantage of her vulnerability. Their near-kiss at Tresillian had been a mistake.

She appeared to be concentrating on the street outside as they crawled down Kingsway, looking as though her thoughts were elsewhere.

'I bet commuting in New York wasn't much more fun than it is here?'

'That crazy Manhattan stampede to and from the office was one of the things I disliked most. My Penbartha commute is much quieter.' She touched her head. 'Usually.'

Jago nodded knowingly. 'Mine too.'

His mobile phone went off and he switched it to hands-free.

'Jago. It's Rocky. Everything all right?'

'Sure. We're nearly there. Just caught up in some traffic. What about at your end?' he added quickly.

'All okay here. I told Kitten that you and Olive are meeting up with business colleagues for the weekend.'

'Did she accept that?'

'Reluctantly. She's asking a lot of questions. Which I don't know the answers to, fortunately.'

Jago glanced across at Olivia. 'I think it's best to keep it that way.'

'Righto. Take care of Olive, mate.'

'I am here, Rocky. And I'm not an invalid.' Olivia's indignation was audible. 'Are the dogs okay?'

Rocky's relieved chuckle came over the speaker. 'You sound more like your old self already, Olive. The dogs are absolutely fine. When I left, Zennor was curled up on Jago's dad's lap, having forty winks with him. Now, try and keep out of trouble and I'll see you soon. Bye.'

Jago and Olivia exchanged a look and then he turned his attention back to the rush-hour traffic.

'How come you've still got a place in London?' Olivia asked.

'There's a story behind that.' He paused. 'I've always been in chambers here and I took silk just before I was forty.' He stopped talking while he let someone pull in front of him. 'I suppose that was when things changed. I was doing more and more serious cases. More violence, more rapes and murders. I hadn't married, hadn't met anyone that I wanted to spend the rest of my life with.'

'Hard to believe,' Olivia teased, coming out of her low mood.

'Oh, I had girlfriends, but no one special. I was too busy working to make time for anything else.'

'I can relate to that.'

'Then about three years ago, I met Lucy. And it got serious. She was great. Not a lawyer, which was a plus. A medic. And we were happy. I took on a big prosecution case at Southwark Crown Court. A nasty gangland murder.'

He turned left again, down High Holborn and a few minutes later drove through a discreet stone archway leading to Gray's Inn and pulled up at the Porter's Lodge and turned off the engine.

They sat in silence for a moment, until eventually, Jago continued. 'Sometimes, in particularly violent cases, you're offered police escorts to and from court, in case anyone follows you. But I'd prosecuted worse cases, so I just shrugged it all off. Then, one night, Lucy and I were on our way home from a restaurant when two guys with knives ambushed us.'

'No!'

'They were part of the gang whose members I was prosecuting, and they wanted me off the case.'

A man in uniform approach the car and stood to the side, waiting for a signal from Jago.

He nodded but finished his story. 'They succeeded. They did a good enough job with their knives to make sure I spent the next six weeks in hospital, the first one in Intensive Care.' His voice was a low monotone, and he closed his eyes for a moment, then shook himself trying to rid himself of his thoughts.

'Lucy's medical training saved my life. She was able to stem the flow of blood enough for me to still be alive when the paramedics arrived.' Jago took the keys out of the ignition. 'Physically I healed well. But it was a slow process. I ended up here because the Inn and my Chambers felt some responsibility for my safety and security.'

Jago opened the door and signalled to the man to step forward.

'Mr Trevithick. Good to see you, sir.'

'Good evening, Tom.' Jago got out of the car and the two men shook hands warmly. Jago carefully manoeuvred Tom away from the car and exchanged a few words. As he climbed back in, he turned to Olivia.

'Everything's sorted. Let's get settled in.' He drove through the first square, past another security lodge and finally drew into a second square: the parallel world of the Inns of Court – a warren of historic courtyards made up of barristers' chambers, solicitors' offices and immaculately kept lawns, all tucked secretly behind one of London's busiest roads. As they made their way to the nearest door with their luggage, Jago received a reassuring nod from the second security guard.

'This way.' He gestured with their bags towards a lift.

Olivia was reading the names hand-painted on the panel by the front door. The first three floors housed legal premises. According to the panel two residential apartments occupied the top floor, one belonging to Sir Alistair and Lady Browne, the other was simply declared to be private.

Fishing in his pocket for keys, Jago ushered Olivia into the lift where they stood in silence until they arrived at their destination, and he opened the various locks to the un-named apartment. Simultaneously tossing his keys into a wooden bowl on the hall console table, flicking through the post the porter had handed him and turning on lights against the growing dusk outside, Jago eventually glanced back at Olivia.

'Welcome to my London pad. Let me show you round.'

The flat was surprisingly large, with high ceilings, wooden floors and simple but elegant furnishings. There was no sign of a woman's touch here. No surplus cushions, sentimental belongings, or ornamental trinkets. It was undeniably Jago's apartment. The paintings on the walls were an eclectic mixture of old county maps, and watercolours of steam engines and Cornish coastal scenes. The leather sofas in the sitting room, overlooking the square, were aged and comfortable, the kitchen modern and streamlined and the main bathroom sumptuous.

'And here's the guest room.' He threw open the door to a pretty blue and cream room, just big enough for a double bed, an oak wardrobe and chest of drawers. 'The study is next door, and my room is further around the corner by the front door. I have my own ensuite so the main bathroom's all yours.'

'Thanks. It's lovely.' She yawned. 'Sorry, I'm just so tired.'

He realised he was standing much closer to her than he needed to and moved away in the kitchen's direction.

'Look, why don't you take a bath and I'll throw some

food together. Housekeeping will have filled the fridge for me, and they usually do a decent job.'

'Sounds good.' She turned away. 'Thanks, Jago. For everything.'

'My pleasure.'

They turned back and regarded each other seriously; a silence hanging between them they were both unwilling to break. Eventually, Olivia gave him a small smile and went into her room, closing the door quietly.

***

They sat on opposite sofas, wineglasses in hand. Jago, clad in jeans and a plain white T-shirt and wearing thick socks, regarded Olivia. She sat with her bare feet tucked up beneath her, her face free of makeup and her damp, dark curls twisted into a loose knot on top of her head. In the light cast from the lamps, her bone structure looked softer. She was still pale, and the bruises were slowly turning a deeper purple, but there was more of an upward tilt to her chin, and Jago's spirits lifted with it.

'How are you feeling now?'

Olivia tilted her head to one side. 'Sore, sad, a bit confused.'

'Confused about what?'

She placed her glass carefully on the low table between them.

'Lots of things.' She paused and screwed up her face as though she was wrestling with a decision. 'Like, why you ended up in Penbartha.'

That surprised him. 'Aren't you going to ask me what happened to Lucy?'

She shrugged. 'Only if you want to tell me?'

'Well, it turned out that Lucy had been going to give me the boot the very night we were attacked. She was fed up with the hours I worked, among other things. So she kindly waited until I was well on the road to recovery before she kicked me into touch.'

'Nice.'

'I don't blame her now, looking back. I was a physical and emotional wreck for quite a while. Anyway, she's married now, living in Toronto and according to a mutual friend has just given birth to identical twin boys.'

'Well, if it's any consolation, I've always thought love is completely overrated. Friendship is far better.' Her cheeks reddened, and she hurried on. 'So, what happened after the court case?'

'I hit the gym to make up for my dismal inadequacies on the street-fighting front.'

'Ah, that explains the muscles.' Olivia observed drily, some of her old spark peeping out.

'I reckon the system you've followed is probably more effective. I'm not sure they have that in London. Or even if it's legal.'

'I could show you a few moves if you like?'

They both laughed and Olivia winced.

'I eventually went back to the Bar,' Jago continued his story. 'But my heart wasn't really in it anymore. I'd convinced myself that the world was an ugly place, and I didn't like the way I was thinking. Then I met George at an exhibition in London and we got talking. I went down to Tresillian for a weekend to meet Mollie, and she made me realise I needed time to take stock. And gave me my stone.' He smiled at the memory. 'And eventually, George offered me a share in his memorabilia business, and the rest is history.'

Olivia's smile grew. 'So you ran away to Penbartha, too?'

He considered that. 'I suppose you could say that. George and Mollie were fantastic to me. I received a hefty compensation payment, sold my flat in Farringdon and moved back to Cornwall. My parents were delighted I was back nearer home and doing something I loved again. I enjoy visiting the various dealers, trade fairs and auctions. And I can come here whenever I need to get away from things in Cornwall. I haven't officially retired from the Bar. And I can do some work as a part-time judge in the Crown Court, if I choose to, so I'm leaving my options open for a while.'

'Do you ever regret moving back to Cornwall?'

'Not really. After twenty-five years up here, I wanted to wake up to the sounds of birdsong and water again rather than police sirens and the Metropolitan Line.'

'And your life here in London?'

He shook his head. 'I was tired of prosecuting senseless murders – day after day of stabbings and I didn't feel I was making any difference at all.' He took a deep breath. 'Meeting George made me realise there are still some really good people out there who are trying to make the world a better place. And I wanted to channel my talents and energy into helping them to actually make a difference. 'He smiled then. 'And it feels good.'

Olivia's dark eyes sparkled, and once again he noticed their incredible flecks of amber.

'Do you honestly think we are making a difference at the Goods Shed?'

'Absolutely! Sustainability is part of the vernacular of Cornwall now. It's something people live, not just talk about. George's vision for the place was ground-breaking. And we're surrounding ourselves with people who have the skills to do it.' He leant forward. 'Who was it who said that where the needs of the world and your talents cross, therein lies our vocation?'

'Aristotle,' Olivia replied quickly. 'George was always quoting him.' She pursed her lips. 'I'd have thought your talents lay in the law, in helping make the world a fairer place?'

'Perhaps long-term they might.' He settled back against

the cushions. 'But I'm happy doing what I am now. I even think I might be a nicer person for it.'

Olivia let out a low chuckle. 'Perish the thought.'

Jago laughed. 'And you?'

She looked away. 'I suppose my real life is in New York – my career, my friends, everything really.' She fingered the side of her head.

The mood in the room shifted. Jago suddenly couldn't imagine the Goods Shed and the station without Olivia there, chatting with all the members. And yet she, apparently, couldn't imagine living anywhere but New York.

'Well, we'd better make sure we get all this sorted out and then we can both go back to doing what makes us happy.'

'That should help to scratch your intellectual itch.' A mischievous smile flitted across her face.

He couldn't help but laugh. 'Oh, that's been well and truly scratched for the last few weeks.'

Olivia glanced at him and then seemed to realise he was teasing. She yawned widely and got to her feet.

'I think I'd better call it a night, Jago. I'm wiped out.'

Jago stood up, too. 'Sure. Sleep well.'

'You too.' She stopped by his side and leant up to kiss his cheek gently. 'Thanks for everything you've done for me, Jago. And for telling me about what happened to you.'

He nodded. 'I'm glad you know. Thanks for listening.' He watched as she walked down the hallway to her room, closing the door softly, but firmly behind her.

***

Olivia lay thinking about what Jago had shared with her and she realised, more from what he hadn't said, how much the attack had affected him. She was usually attracted to straightforward, easy to understand men who worked hard and played hard, didn't require too much effort on her part and weren't interested in any long-term commitment on either side. The Jago Trevithick she was beginning to know fell into a different category, and although she still wasn't interested in a relationship, she could appreciate an attractive guy when she saw one. And the fact that he'd made it very clear he wasn't relationship material either was even better. Life was complicated enough.

Her mind wandered back to Penbartha. Now she was over two hundred and fifty miles away, she felt she could view things more objectively. That she loved being in the fresh Cornish air, able to appreciate the seasons, the bird life and the excitement of spotting seals on her morning runs, went without saying. Of course, she was doing the same kind of architectural work in New York and Penbartha; helping people to achieve their dreams of turning derelict warehouses into executive apartments, and renovating tired, unloved buildings into warm family homes. But in Penbartha she had the added bonus of her involvement in the Goods Shed. The sense of satisfaction and pleasure she got when a member or tenant shared their latest success gave her a thrill she hadn't anticipated. And they were all using their skills and talents to meet the needs of the world, like Jago had said. What more could you ask for? And for the first time in a long while, as Olivia fell asleep in her London bed, she could feel a tiny nugget of hope unfurl somewhere inside her.

CHAPTER TWENTY-FOUR

'I arrived last night, Penny.' Jago's voice seeped beneath Olivia's bedroom door.

'My dear boy, it's wonderful to have you back so soon. Why don't you come across for drinks this evening? We've got tickets for the Opera House, but it would be super if you could join us for drinks first?'

'That's very kind of you. Are you sure it's convenient?'

'Of course it is, James! We're always delighted to see you. Ali will insist!'

'I'm sure Alistair would rather spend more time at the Opera House.'

'Well, I wouldn't. Shall we say six-ish?'

'Um, Penny. I have a friend with me.' There was a pause and Olivia knelt up on the bed to listen more closely. The sound of two people's low voices filled the hallway, as a decision was made.

'That's sorted then. See you both at six, James.'

***

As predicted, Alistair and Penny were charming and entertaining hosts. Dressed flamboyantly for a gala evening at the Opera House, they waved away Jago and

Olivia's apologies for their more casual attire and ushered them into their apartment. It was at the opposite end of the home décor spectrum from Jago's but suited them perfectly. The walls of their large sitting room were painted dark green, with an original marble fireplace, over which hung a large gilt-framed mirror. Family photos jostled for space with heavy invitations on the crammed mantelpiece. Ornately framed landscape paintings, large, overstuffed furniture, crystal chandeliers and full bookcases completed the eclectic mix of styles which worked well together.

Olivia was not sure if Sir Alistair Browne was what she expected of a high court judge. Tall and broad in his dinner jacket and black tie, he had a full head of steel grey hair which he wore swept back from his forehead. Olivia assumed that his wig kept his hair in place in court, but unrestrained it flopped down over his forehead in an endearingly schoolboy-ish manner and he kept brushing it back impatiently. Yet, after a few minutes of conversation, she could easily imagine him in court, dressed in red robes, his sharp hazel eyes taking everything in over his reading glasses, and his deep, booming voice scaring the life out of defendants, juries, and junior barristers alike. It was obvious Alistair liked Jago and valued his opinion and quickly engaged him in some complex legal conundrum, leaving Olivia to talk to Penny unimpeded.

Penny Browne was a one-off, Olivia decided, liking her at once. Her beaded, long red chiffon dress was form-fitting and beautifully cut. Only slightly plump, she carried it off with her amazing elegance and sheer bon viveur. Her makeup was simply but expertly done, and her ash-blonde hair styled in a sophisticated updo. Olivia got the impression that Penny was a chameleon, adept at putting her theatrical tendencies to great use in blending seamlessly into most situations. Just as she was putting

Olivia at ease now.

'It's wonderful to meet you at long last, Olivia. James was telling me about you and that delightful set-up you've got in Cornwall. It sounds right up my street: full of young, bright creative things, unrestrained by what most people see as the norm.' She sighed dramatically as Alistair handed them flutes of champagne. 'I'd fit in much better somewhere like that, wouldn't I, darling, rather than with the bunch of stuffy old judges and their even stuffier wives that I have to put up with here?'

'You fit in with everybody, my darling.' He kissed her cheek gently. 'But best of all with me.'

'Silly old fool.' Penny flapped her husband away with a smile and ushered Olivia to the sofa. Olivia caught Jago's eye, and he winked at her, a curiously intimate gesture that distracted her for a moment.

'James tells me you want to talk to me about the seminar he took me to. As his aged aunt, cheeky boy. I could easily pass for his slightly older sister in the right light.'

Olivia smiled. 'I'm interested in your take on it. What sort of people were there?'

'I should imagine they were the usual sort you get at these investment events. All incredibly rich individuals eager to make even more money, with as little effort as possible.' Penny thought for a moment, swirling her champagne around her flute. 'And according to the chap sitting next to me a few of them were what they call Angel Investors. Are you aware of the term?' Despite Olivia's nod, Penny explained what she understood about the concept.

'Oh, I do wish I could remember the chap's name! He had a slight Scottish accent. And he reminded me of Ronnie Corbett. Not that he was small, or even particularly funny, but the way it took him forever to get to the point of a story was very irritating. I'm sure I took his business card and put it somewhere – I must have a good look for it.' Penny glanced about the room distractedly for a moment before returning to her theme.

Olivia took a deep breath and prepared to wait.

'Apparently, this chap does lots of work as a business angel. He has a particular contact down south somewhere who's got him involved in excellent young business opportunities and makes him superb returns.' Her eyes drifted off towards the ceiling for a moment. 'What he likes about this advisor is that he's involved in businesses that have a social or environmental impact. Ethical investments if you like.'

'Does that make him feel better about having so much money?' Olivia asked politely.

Penny laughed. 'I can see you and I are going to get on famously Olivia. He seems to see this chap as some kind of economic messiah. He eases his social conscience and makes him even more money.'

'Not to mention the whopping tax breaks that are no doubt on offer for this type of investor. Oliva couldn't keep her cynicism out of her voice.

Penny patted her knee. 'Indeed. Anyway, this advisor was getting him such good results that my chap no longer even bothered meeting the young businesses he was investing in. He just handed over the money and waited until he received returns.'

Olivia's scalp prickled. She glanced at the art deco clock that adorned the marble mantlepiece. Time was running out. 'Do I sense a "but"?'

'Of course you do.' Penny was blunt. 'Apparently, all was going swimmingly until sometime last year when the returns suddenly weren't so good. The invitation to this seminar was his advisor's way of making up for the losses his clients had suffered. It was only for the favoured few and offered a great return on investment.'

'Did he ever say what this guy was called?'

Penny scrunched her face in thought. 'No, he was very discreet about his name. Obviously wanted to keep all the investment opportunities for himself. Southwest Something or other.'

'And your chap?' Olivia finished her champagne.

'I'll go through my handbag and look for his card.'

'That will take at least a week if it's the black cavernous one, my darling.'

'I usually take a smaller bag on a fortnight's holiday.' Alistair appeared at Penny's side, having caught his wife's last sentence.

'We need to get moving, Olivia.' Jago added. 'And let these fine people get to the Opera House.'

'It's been lovely to meet you both.' Olivia gave them a friendly smile.

'And you my dear. We must meet up for longer next time. Have dinner perhaps?' Penny turned to Jago. 'How long are you here for, James?'

'Only the weekend, I'm afraid. Then we have to get back to Penbartha.'

Alistair slapped Jago on the back and kissed Olivia, before addressing her directly.

'I hope to see James back at the Bar soon, keeping all us old buffers on our feet. There aren't many barristers with his sense of justice and advocacy skills these days. Anyway,' he caught sight of the clock, 'we'll be in touch and sort something out. Now Penny, we really must go.'

***

'So, what do you reckon?' Jago asked, while they waited for their starters at a tapas bar in Holborn.

'It all sounds feasible, but until Penny remembers her "chap's" name, or finds his business card we haven't really got a lot to go on, have we?' She frowned. 'You were there too. How come you didn't get talking to him?'

'He only had eyes for Penny, I'm afraid, and she was having a wonderful time playing the role of a wealthy investor.' The waitress filled their glasses with rioja.

'We just need something to link this seminar back to someone or something in Penbartha,' Jago said, once she had gone. 'A link is key to being able to make any progress.'

A thought struck Olivia. 'I know you didn't get anywhere with Carless Venture Developments themselves, but what about the photographer who gave you the contact? Have you tried him again?'

Jago nodded, frowning. 'Baker's out of the country on a photoshoot for the foreseeable future, according to his voicemail.'

'So, what's next?' Olivia's voice rose. 'We can't just do nothing!'

Jago reached across to touch her arm. She could feel the warmth of his hand on her skin as she looked up at him. 'I think we have to be patient, Olivia. And hope that Penny comes up trumps, while we lie low here.'

'Have you heard from Trenow?' She gripped his fingers, suddenly nervous.

'Only briefly. There's not much going on with the murder enquiries either. The guy who attacked you on the walkway is still sticking to his ludicrous story. Trenow and his team have spoken to Jess's family and close friends, and they all have alibis for Monday night, which is now the confirmed time of death. Apparently, she was seeing someone new, but she kept it all very close to her chest.'

'Is there any news on Sarah?'

''Fraid not.'

Olivia turned wide, fearful eyes to Jago and withdrew her hand. 'And was any mention made of Willow and Fraser?' She closed her eyes, dreading the response.

'Yes.'

Olivia peered through her fingers. 'What? What was it? Tell me, Jago.'

She had to wait while the waitress placed bowls of olives, bread and oil on their table.

'Okay, okay, I'll tell you. Calm down.' He held up his hands. 'Apparently, Willow and Fraser have made major advances into village life.'

'They have? How? Why?'

Jago chuckled. 'It's good news. Alice was feeling guilty that none of the villagers were making much of an effort to get to know Willow and Fraser and so she and her husband organised a small get-together at their house on Monday evening, and about five couples were there. And their stories all check out according to Trenow.' He looked at her closely. 'Are you crying? I thought you'd be happy.'

'I am happy.' She sat back to wipe her eyes with her napkin. 'Well, relieved more than anything. I was so worried about them both.'

'Well, they are definitely in the clear for Jess's murder. But you know what that means, don't you?'

She froze, then forced the words out. 'The killer's still out there.'

Jago nodded. 'And Trenow's under enormous pressure to make an arrest.'

CHAPTER TWENTY-FIVE

Once again, sleep evaded Olivia. Her body was battered, bruised and exhausted, but her mind wouldn't switch off. Jago's warning words about Trenow buzzed around her head and she was busy sorting through everything she knew about each murder, searching for a link, but it was just out of reach. There had to be one. And other than her, it was obviously someone connected to the Goods Shed. But who?

Sighing with frustration, she went into the kitchen in search of some iced water. Jago had beaten her to the fridge and stood with the door open, his back to her, wearing only pyjama trousers.

He spoke over his shoulder, without turning. 'Can I get you anything?'

'Just some water, please.'

He handed her a bottle, with his back still to her. Which she thought was odd and then realised. 'I'm not frightened of scars, Jago.' Her voice was gentle.

Still, he didn't move. 'You might be of mine.'

She mentally steeled herself. 'Try me?'

He turned slowly, his eyes never leaving Olivia's face.

Her gaze travelled downwards, past his broad shoulders, to his well-defined chest sprinkled with fine dark hairs and then on to his toned stomach, where a patchwork of wide and livid, shiny scars, the largest of which spread in a large, crude zigzag from just beneath his breastbone across to his left side and then back across to beneath his navel. Olivia did not flinch, just put her hand out to touch him, but he grabbed hold of it, as if anxious for her not to get any closer.

'We all have scars, Jago.' Her voice wobbled. 'They're the stories of our lives. Only, for some of us they are on the inside and can't be seen. We just have to learn how to live with them as best we can.'

He held on to her hand tightly, his eyes scanning her face uneasily. 'Aren't you repulsed?'

Olivia looked at him, suddenly aware of an unfamiliar, but very pleasant feeling spreading through her. 'Not at all. They're part of you.' She took a step forward and inhaled his warm scent. Then she bent her head and lightly kissed the tip of the largest scar, feeling a shudder run through his body.

'Olivia,' his voice was husky.

'Shh.' She lifted her head and kissed the corner of his mouth. 'It's fine. I'm fine.'

Jago put a hand on either side of her face, pulled her close and kissed her back. Olivia felt her body arch towards his, enjoying the warmth and solidity of his skin, and trembling with long-forgotten sensations.

He broke off to pull back and stare into her eyes. 'Are you sure this is what you want?'

She leaned up to kiss him again, shivering with anticipation. 'Ever the lawyer I see.' She could feel his mouth smiling against hers. 'Yes.'

At which point Jago gave up any pretence of restraint and, picking her up, carried her to his bedroom and kicked the door closed behind them.

***

Jago watched Olivia as she slept beside him, her curls lying loose and rich against the white pillows. The bruises on her face were fading slowly and turning from dark purple to green around the edges. The dark circles under her eyes seemed paler and the small stress lines that had become a permanent feature between her brows when she was awake had disappeared. He brushed a strand of hair gently out of her eyes, not quite able to believe she was there, in his bed with him. He gazed up at the ceiling and, for the first time in a long while, took his feelings, which he usually kept safely locked away, out and examined them.

Dating, relationships and women went against every one of his self-imposed rules, but he was drawn to Olivia in a way he didn't understand. Anyone could see that she was attractive, but there was so much more to her. She was funny and quirky, different, and he liked that about her. They didn't even know each other that well, and from what he did know, they were complete opposites but there was already an unspoken understanding between them that made him feel comfortable. His body now knew hers. The scent of her skin, the dark depths of her eyes and all the slight curves of her body. Even though they'd both said they weren't remotely interested in a relationship, there was a definite spark between them. Perhaps they could just have fun until she went back to New York. They were both adults and knew the score.

Jago inhaled the sweet scent of her hair as it tickled his bare chest and tucked her body closer to his. He knew that Olivia hoped the murders, the problems with the Trust and the potential land deal were separate issues. His legal brain told him they were more than likely linked, even though there wasn't any evidence to prove a connection. They hadn't even been able to find out who was behind the plans for the retirement village yet. But he felt the net was tightening. Now he was just afraid of what, or who, it might catch.

Jago traced his fingertips along the outline of the small Celtic tattoo at the top of her right thigh. Olivia had explained that she'd had it done in a moment of utter homesickness at university. The Dara Knot represented inner strength and courage, and he hoped that she still possessed enough to get through the ordeal she was facing.

***

'Penny. Good morning. How was the opera?'

'Oh frightful! I simply loathe this modern stuff. But Ali likes it, so I persevere.' She leant forward and kissed his cheek. 'I can't stop, James, I'm afraid. I'm just off to meet a girlfriend at Fortnum's for coffee.'

Jago thought Penny looked dressed for afternoon tea with the queen and told her so.

'Oh, you dear boy!' Penny batted his compliment away. 'You realise it's 10.30, don't you?' She peered more closely at him. 'Are you still in your PJs?'

'Yes. We were having a bit of a lie-in. Olivia has got a lot of sleep to catch up on.'

Penny nodded knowingly. 'And how's that dreadful bruise of hers? I didn't like to mention it last night.'

'That's very kind of you, Penny. It's improving, thank you.' He met her questioning look with silence.

She rallied quickly. 'Well, I just popped in to let you know that I've found that chap's business card.' She rummaged in her pocket and handed it triumphantly to Jago.

'Gordon Munroe.' He read out. 'Investor and Philanthropist.'

'I said he was Scottish, didn't I?'

'You did! And thank you so much for finding it.'

'My pleasure. Remember me to him if you get to meet

up, won't you?'

He kissed her cheek. 'Absolutely. Enjoy your coffee.'

'I'm sure I will. James.' She handed him an envelope. 'We thought you might like these. We've got a clashing engagement, unfortunately.'

Jago closed the front door and returned to the bedroom. His heart heavy. He had half-hoped that Penny wouldn't find the card until later in the weekend, giving them some time to enjoy being together, for Olivia to relax and heal. But he knew that once Olivia knew about the existence of Gordon Munroe, she would be desperate to meet him.

Fortunately for Jago, Gordon Munroe was out of the city and not available to meet them until Monday morning. He was relieved, Olivia frustrated. The envelope from Penny cheered them both. It contained tickets for the latest musical which had just opened in London to rave reviews and sell-out audiences. Having seen it on Broadway, Olivia was keen to see how it translated on to the London stage and was delighted to be back in theatreland after her months in Cornwall. Afterwards, they ate at a tiny bistro in Covent Garden and Jago could tell she was enjoying being in a bustling, anonymous city again.

But by Sunday evening, the novelty of being back in a city was wearing off for both of them. Jago was acutely aware of the constant noise of traffic, which was so loud at times they had to raise their voices to make themselves heard. Even the air in the parks tasted of exhaust fumes and, as an endless stream of people constantly passed them, he longed for the fresh air of Penbartha again. And judging by the expression on Olivia's face as she talked about it, so did she.

***

On Monday morning Olivia was ready for their meeting

with Munroe much earlier than necessary. She paced up and down the apartment, constantly looking at her watch and chewing at her fingernails. Jago sat, quietly reading the newspaper, and trying to ignore her.

'Are you sure I look alright?' she asked for the fourth time, pulling at her jacket. 'I don't know if this is really my thing?'

Jago peered over the top of his newspaper and studied her from top to toe. As a consequence of Olivia realising that she only had jeans and casual clothes with her, they had made a hasty but painful visit to Oxford Street where Jago discovered they had something else in common. Olivia hated clothes shopping almost as much as he did and would much rather spend time in a bookshop than a designer store. She eventually chose a navy, fitted trouser suit and a white, round-necked shirt. Her only concession to the personal shopper trying to help her, was the pair of navy suede, high-heeled pumps and some silver costume jewellery She had swept her hair up into a neat chignon, and Jago noticed that she was wearing makeup which concealed what remained of her bruise. He also realised that it was the first time he had seen her wearing makeup since she'd been back in Penbartha. And whereas he thought she was beautiful and natural without it, with it she looked sophisticated, business-like and classy. And he told her so.

She laughed grudgingly. 'Well, I guess it was either this or borrow one of Penny's frocks.' She twisted round to look at her rear view in the mirror and Jago went back to his newspaper.

His peace was short-lived.

'Can we go now?' She checked her handbag for her notebook for the umpteenth time.

Jago sighed and folded his newspaper. 'Okay. You are driving me crazy!'

She stopped and looked at him. 'I'm sorry, Jago. It's just

that finding out what this guy has to say is so important to me.'

Compassion triumphed over frustration, and he pulled her towards him, kissing the top of her head.

'I know it is. And I'm sorry I've been impatient with you. Let's go now and walk the long way round to his club.'

'It will take me forever to get there anyway in these bloody heels,' she grumbled. 'It's okay for you; you keep your suits and shirts here. I feel like I'm wearing someone else's clothes.'

He ran both hands through his hair in frustration. 'Stop moaning woman, and come on.'

The walk filled the time nicely and as they made their way down the southern side of Lincoln's Inn Field, past the Royal College of Surgeons and the Hunterian Museum, Olivia was completely unaware of the admiring looks she was getting from passing businessmen, solicitors, and barristers late for court. Jago puffed his chest out a little, held on to her hand firmly and walked with his head held high.

He didn't need to ask Olivia what she thought of the Members Club where Gordon Munroe had arranged to meet them. Her face said it all. With pinched nostrils and narrowed eyes she withstood being ignored by the concierge and followed Jago silently across the plush foyer and into the Morning Room, where their host was waiting for them. Jago cast a look around him, noting the red velvet club chairs and matching sofas all discreetly grouped around dark tables; the long windows framed with rich velvet drapes. There were few people in there, being barely ten o'clock, and the assistant manager led them to the furthest, darkest corner. Gordon Munroe obviously didn't want to be seen or overheard.

'Your guests are here, Mr Munroe, sir. Would you like me to arrange coffee?'

Gordon Munroe rose from his chair to shake hands,

first with Jago, more reluctantly with Olivia. Jago noticed the hesitation and was immediately annoyed.

'I'm not sure they will be here long enough, Robert . . .' he began.

Jago turned a frosty smile on the assistant manager. 'Coffee would be lovely, thank you, Robert. Both white, no sugar, thank you.' He turned back to his host and waved at the chairs. 'May we?'

Taken aback, Gordon Munroe nodded and sat back down quickly. He was a small, dapper man in his late sixties or early seventies with closely cropped, dark grey hair, black eyebrows, and a small, neat moustache. He wore a pale grey suit and rimless glasses. Behind them, his small eyes travelled slowly up and down Olivia's body. Jago clenched his fists.

'Mr Trevithick, I assume?' Munroe sat back in his chair and ignored Olivia.

Jago swallowed. 'Yes, and this is Olivia Wells. As I mentioned in our call the other day, she might be interested in the land proposal in Cornwall that was discussed at the seminar last week.'

'Oh, yes. That sounded most attractive, didn't it? I must say I'm interested too. It looks like my advisor has come up trumps again.'

'My friend, Penny, said you had made quite a few successful investments in small Cornish businesses.' Jago's voice was calm but melodic, the voice he used to get the most out of witnesses in court. And the concerned expression on his face invited people to confide in him.

'Penny?' Munroe looked vague for a moment. 'Oh, Penny. What a delightful woman! Is she a friend of yours?'

'Yes. And meeting you has inspired her into making some small investments of her own.'

'Really?' Munroe practically preened himself. 'Well, she did seem interested in my philanthropic work.'

'You did an excellent job of convincing her of both the

altruistic and financial benefits of such investments.' Jago stole a quick look at Olivia, whose face was a picture of bored neutrality.

Munroe frowned. 'In which case I'm surprised she hasn't asked me herself.'

Jago leant forward. 'She's a very busy woman, Gordon. And a wealthy one. She leaves it to me, as her lawyer, to check these things out for her. I'm sure you understand?'

Munroe nodded knowingly. 'Oh, I do.' He leaned back in his red velvet chair and regarded them both over steepled fingers. 'So you want me to give you the details of my advisor who deals with my Cornish investments?'

Alleluia, thought Jago. But nodded.

'Why don't I tell you a bit about the investments I've made so far?'

Jago and Olivia exchanged a swift glance. Stalling tactics.

'That would be fascinating.'

There was a slight pause as a waiter delivered and served coffee. Munroe sipped from his cup and then placed it carefully on the table in front of them.

'My background is in the oil industry,' he began proudly. 'And I'm a corporate man through and through. It didn't do me any harm though. I've worked all over the world and am now happily retired.'

Jago recalled Penny's description of his verbosity. He glanced at Olivia, who was rolling her eyes, and grimaced.

'Yet there's always been a part of me that really admires people who go it alone, without the support of a company and come up with all the ideas themselves. I was looking for something to do with my money, faced with such lousy returns from the bank, when I met this advisor in London, who put me in touch with a few investment opportunities which gave me excellent returns. Then he got involved with various creative businesses in Cornwall.' He reached forward and refilled his coffee cup once he realised that Olivia wouldn't do the honours.

'It sounds intriguing.' Jago commented, feeling Olivia bristle with frustration beside him.

'It is. And I don't know if there's something in the water down there, or what it is, but they seem to come up with amazing concepts and ideas that are just crying out for more experienced businesspeople to invest some time and effort into.' The pride on his face was unmistakable.

Jago nodded.

He swallowed the rest of his coffee. 'I like to think I'm contributing to the Cornish economy, so I've invested in quite a few small business start-ups based there . . .'

'Really?'

'Yes, there's an ethical fashion business, which is doing really well, some digital media companies, and some more environmental concepts that I've invested in. My man is keen on those kinds of things, and one has to do one's bit for the planet, don't you think?'

Jago wasn't sure if he was being deliberately vague or really didn't know where his money was going. 'And what's your involvement in the businesses now?'

'Oh, very little, these days. I trust my advisor implicitly. Now I just get the paperwork, cast my eye over it and if it appeals to me, I give him the nod and transfer the money over.'

'And it's this guy who invited you to the seminar about the retirement village?'

Monroe nodded. 'Yes, it was a special opportunity for some of my advisor's most active clients to get involved from an early stage in a very exciting investment opportunity.'

'It certainly looked most impressive.'

'It does. And an excellent opportunity for those of us whose most recent investments haven't been so successful.' Munroe paused for a moment. 'My advisor is most conscientious and eager to do the best for his clients.'

I bet he is, thought Jago. 'But no investment is ever one hundred per cent safe, surely?'

'Absolutely not. No risk, no reward. That's the philosophy of investors.' Munroe seemed to remember the purpose of the meeting. 'So, you want the name of my contact?'

This was turning into Groundhog Day. Jago stole a quick look at Olivia, who had clenched her jaws together and was breathing carefully through her nose.

'If that's possible.' Jago leaned back in his chair and crossed his legs, the picture of nonchalance.

'What's in it for me?' Munroe's small eyes gleamed.

Jago's expression didn't flicker. 'I might be able to pass on some valuable information about one of your investments. It may not make you money, but it could save you a lot. Which is the next best thing, isn't it?'

Jago could tell he had piqued Munroe's interest. The prospect of losing money was obviously not an attractive one. Even to a philanthropist.

'The company's name is Southwest Invest.' He offered.

Nice try, thought Jago. He remained silent, looking at Munroe with one eyebrow raised, an often used move when waiting for witnesses to divulge a vital piece of incriminating information in court.

'And my man's name is Callum Armstrong.'

***

Olivia's heart somersaulted and a sharp tingling sensation ran right through her. *Callum! Of all people.* She forced herself to sit on her hands. But her face was on fire and her stomach icy cold. She tried to swallow but couldn't. Images of Callum's friendly, round face and his jocular manner flashed through her mind. And yet all this time he had been plotting behind her back, behind Jago's back, behind everyone's back.

Olivia watched as a waiter showed another couple to a nearby table and took their order. She realised she didn't know much about the accountant whom she thought had always been on her side in the trustees' meetings. She'd assumed he'd lived in Cornwall for a long time, as he'd been one of the Goods Shed's longest members. The family photos on the walls all showed his children and wife having fun on the beach, but then as she closed her eyes and recalled the bomb site that was his office, she could see a larger photograph featuring a younger Callum and family grinning in a capsule of the London Eye, the distinctive London skyline behind them.

While her calmer side was telling her it could just have been a holiday snap, her frantic gaze settled on Jago. He was staring straight ahead, and other than a muscle ticking in his jaw, his face was completely unreadable.

Even Gordon Munroe noticed their reactions and raised his black eyebrows. 'Is the name familiar?'

'We know someone of that name.' Jago paused. 'He's an accountant, isn't he?'

Munroe laughed with delight at that and rubbed his hands together. 'Not the Callum Armstrong I know. Being an accountant of any type is far too tame for him; he's more go-getting and dynamic than any risk-averse accountant I've ever met, and I've met a fair few, I can tell you. No, the Callum Armstrong I know enjoys the high life: designer labels, exotic holidays and so on. He hasn't even shown any signs of wanting to settle down; has a different, more beautiful woman on his arm every time I see him.'

Olivia felt her scalp prickle sharply, and she narrowed her eyes at Gordon Munroe as another thought occurred to her; one so horrible and ridiculous that she tried to dismiss it instantly. But it wouldn't go away. She bent down and pulled her notebook out of her handbag. In it were notes from the trustees' meetings she had attended and her sketches and doodles of all those present. She turned the pages quickly, aware of Jago's puzzled stare, until she found a good likeness of Callum Armstrong.

'Is this him?' She handed the notebook over to Munroe, and he looked at it with interest. His small eyes hovered over the sketch of Callum, his round, smiley face, and bright eyes behind the rimless glasses.

'It's an excellent sketch.' He finally conceded. 'And this chap does look like an accountant. But he's definitely not the Callum Armstrong I know.'

He carried on turning the pages and looked up questioningly at Olivia. A belt tightened round her chest. 'Help yourself,' she offered.

Munroe smiled at some of the caricatures and sketches she had drawn, and then stopped at one particular page, frowning.

Olivia held her breath, her pulse pounding in her ears. *Please, no,* she begged silently. *Please, no.*

Munroe carried on slowly turning the pages until he reached the last one and then turned back to an earlier one. Olivia held her breath. Like a sea mist clearing, everything was beginning to make sense to her and from the look on his face, to Jago too. Munroe's eyes darted from the page to her and Jago and back again to the page. He stared at it for a full minute before coming to a decision.

'You said you may have some information for me on one of my investments?'

Jago inclined his head, not taking his eyes off Munroe.

'Well, I hope it's more accurate than what you've told me so far.' Munroe carefully placed the notebook down on the table between them and stabbed his finger at one particularly detailed sketch.

'This chap is definitely the Callum Armstrong I deal with.'

Olivia and Jago both followed Munroe's finger to an intricate, lifelike drawing of a good-looking man with smiling green eyes, a clean-shaven face and a floppy blond fringe.

    Martin Lambert.

CHAPTER TWENTY-SIX

Olivia sank to the floor of the apartment, trying to control the war of emotions breaking out inside her. Shock and anger at Martin's betrayal battled with a sharp stab of grief for the loss of yet another person she'd trusted.

Jago strode out of the bedroom, having changed into more casual clothes and carrying his overnight bag. He hunkered down in front of Olivia and put his hands on her shoulders, forcing her to meet his gaze.

'Are you okay?'

She avoided his eyes, trying to swallow the panic that was taking flight in her stomach. 'I need space to think all this through, make sense of it all.'

'We can do that together.' His voice was calm and comforting. 'There's no need to run this time.'

She closed her eyes and concentrated on her breathing, like she'd learned and then looked at him. 'I don't understand it. Why would Martin use Callum's name to do business when he could use his own?'

'Maybe because he knew what he was doing was illegal?' He squeezed her shoulder. 'This puts a very different spin on things. Even if we leave the planning proposals to one side for a moment, Martin is up shit creek. The deliberate use of someone else's identity, without their permission for personal gain, is a serious crime. Martin could be looking at a minimum of six years for this alone.' He stood up, his face tough and determined, his lips a thin white line; he was back in barrister mode. 'Not to mention the deleterious effect this could have on Callum's reputation and career.'

'I can't believe Martin would do this to Callum. I can't believe he'd do this to any of us. I trusted him. George trusted him!' Her voice broke as his words sank in. 'What are we going to do?'

'I think we need to get back to Penbartha as soon as we can. Do some damage limitation with Callum. And talk to Trenow.' He looked at her. 'At least I do.'

Olivia scrambled to her feet and glared at him. 'I hope you're not suggesting that I stay here?'

He looked away. 'I thought I could drop you at my parent's place on the way home?'

'No way.' Her jaw was set. 'This is my inheritance, my responsibility, my mess. There is no way I'm not coming.'

Jago thrust his hands deep into his jeans pockets and glared back. 'It's only four days since Trenow said you could be in danger. What's changed?'

'The whole Trust could be at risk, Jago. I need to come. I've already lost Mollie and George. Now I risk losing the one thing they placed in my protection. If Martin and the developers get their way, this retirement village could be built, and time will move on. And before long it will be as if Mollie and George never existed at all.' A sob caught in her throat. 'Do you understand why I can't let that happen?'

'Yes, but I don't think it's worth risking your life over it.'

Realisation slowly dawned. 'Martin may be a liar and a fraud. But for him to go from that to a cold-blooded double killer is a bit of a giant leap, isn't it? Even for you?'

Jago's warmth disappeared in an instant. 'Okay. We

haven't filled in the gaps yet. We still don't know who was behind your attack. Or who killed Libby and Jess.' He ran his hands through his hair until it was back standing in its usual spikes. 'And we don't know where Martin is.'

'He's in Leeds.'

Jago did a double take. 'I'm sorry?'

'Martin's in Leeds. He texted me to apologise for not being in touch and to say that he was going straight there from Plymouth for a few days, on business.'

His voice hardened. 'Did you tell him you were here?'

'Obviously not. I'm not stupid.' Olivia rummaged through her bag and then thrust her mobile at him.

'I don't think you're stupid. I just don't know how much you shared with him.'

'Very little.' The back of her nose stung as tears sprang up. She dashed them away quickly. 'Like I said before, I'm not big on trust.'

Jago's blue eyes held hers. 'You've had some bad luck with your choices. But you need to let it go and move on.' He reached out to touch her, warily, as if expecting her to turn away, but she forced herself to take his hand.

'This is exactly why I prefer being on my own. Looking after myself. Fighting my own battles.'

He put a finger under her chin and lifted it up. 'You can't live like that Olivia. And you're not on your own anymore.'

A small thrill tried to fizz through her, but she pushed it away. 'In which case, you won't mind me coming with you.'

***

They left London before rush-hour and made good time along the M4 and M5. By the time they'd reached Swindon, Jago had convinced her that Gordon Munroe would not be alerting Martin to the fact that they were on to him.

'He may be greedy and arrogant, but he's not stupid,'

Jago commented. 'I could see the cogs of his brain whirring when I told him the police would soon know if he contacted Martin and would see him as an accessory. Not to mention what Martin and his cronies might do to him if they thought he was on to them.'

'You think he has cronies?'

'This thing is all too big and professional for Martin to be masterminding it. There were four or five directors mentioned on the Companies House register. Even if they are all bogus, I reckon the actual people are out there somewhere. And the guy the photographer told us about wasn't Martin, was he?'

Jago stared grimly ahead at the motorway as he drove.

Olivia's heart sank. 'I can't believe Martin's caught up in something like this. Not willingly anyway.'

'Let's face it, Olivia. He's greedy. And possibly lazy. A fatal combination in my experience.'

'But he's done so much to help the Goods Shed members. Identified their weaknesses and helped them get the business side of things in order and secured excellent funding for loads of them. There's no way he would have ripped them off.'

Jago raised an eyebrow.

'They all speak really highly of him, Jago. And remember it was the investors who approached him, looking for the opportunity to help local businesses, not the other way round.'

'Okay, he only rips off rich people who can afford to lose lots of money and who will probably be too ashamed to go the police and admit they have been scammed? That's all right, is it? That's how people get away with it. A greedy person is in the best position to know how another one ticks, and what buttons to press.'

'But they were genuine investments in the early days. Munroe said he had some good returns.' She couldn't help defending him.

'And then he got greedy. It looks as though once Martin got these angel investors on board and had won their trust, he could then set up bogus businesses and secure investment for them without them insisting on even the basic checks. He probably used the new investment money to pay bonuses to the angels for a while and keep them sweet. Until his money ran out. Munroe admitted that a few of them had lost money, but they accepted that level of risk. Perhaps that's why Martin eventually came up with the planning proposals. A last attempt to make money and get his investors off his back?' He banged his fist against the steering wheel. 'I've seen it all before, Olivia. On different scales.'

She leant back against her seat and pursed her lips. 'But since I've been in Penbartha, he's worked so hard making contacts. He's always following up leads and attending networking events. You've heard him talking at the trustees' meetings.'

'I have, yes. But have any of his so-called efforts converted into actual new members? Or more business?'

She dodged the question. 'He always said it would take time for all his work to reap rewards.'

'For someone who has lived in big cities all your adult life, Olivia, you have an amazingly innocent streak.'

Olivia glanced at him sideways and wondered about all the things Jago must have seen and heard in his career to make him so cynical.

'And although this is going to shatter all your illusions about him, you have got to accept that Martin is involved in the retirement village plans.'

He was right, but Olivia wasn't giving up just yet. 'I thought people had the right to be presumed innocent until proven guilty in this country?'

'They do, but the evidence against Martin is mounting nicely. Would you like me to go through it again?'

'No.' Olivia stared out of the passenger window onto

the dark motorway. 'I get that it looks like he's involved with the land proposals and may be guilty of fraud, but you've got to admit there's not a shred of evidence to suggest he's guilty of murder. And,' she turned to him then, 'I know for sure that he was in Plymouth the night Jess died because he spoke to me from there and I could hear the ferries in the background. And he gave me an alibi for the night Libby died.'

Jago's grip tightened on the steering wheel. 'I remember. And was it a credible alibi?'

She saw the clench of his jaw. His eyes were narrow as he stared ahead at the road, and she wished for a moment she could read his mind. Then was glad she couldn't.

'To be honest, Jago, I remember nothing about that night.' She felt heat flood her face. 'It's a complete blank. Which I don't understand, as I'm sure I hadn't drunk much, but my head was sore as hell the next day.'

'Did you tell Trenow that?'

'No. I was too afraid.' Her voice was small. 'But I'm sure nothing happened between us, and Martin did admit that we hadn't had sex.'

'So, he's only in the frame for major fraud and deception. Not rape. Or murder. How very honourable of him.'

'Oh, come on. I think he was genuinely being kind to me that night, as I was so upset about arguing with Libby. Why on earth would he tell the police that he'd stayed if he hadn't? Why would he protect me that way?'

Jago turned briefly to her then, his eyes flashing. 'Do you really need me to spell it out for you?'

***

'So what do you know about his background?' Jago asked over a cup of coffee at the service station.

Olivia refused to look up from stirring the pretty

pattern on top of her cappuccino.

'Not much. I don't ask people about their families, as a rule. In case they ask me to reciprocate.' She lifted her head and her gaze challenged Jago to say something. He remained silent.

By Exeter, as they left the M5 for the A30, Olivia began to relax, and she could see Jago's grip on the steering wheel loosen. They breathed out simultaneously as they passed the road sign declaring they were in Cornwall.

'Nearly home,' Jago said, the relief in his voice audible. 'There's something in the air in Cornwall that helps you breathe more easily and think more clearly, don't you think?'

Olivia glanced at his face, looking for an edge to his words, but saw only a genuine smile at the pleasure of being back in his home county. And she understood completely. Even after all her years away, there was still something about Cornwall that pulled at her.

'Don't you ever think of Penbartha as home?'

She knew he was challenging her now. 'I did when I was younger. Without a doubt. But over the years I've been away I've sometimes wondered if people think I left because I thought Penbartha wasn't good enough. You know how people can be.' It was a very quiet confession.

'From what I've heard, people admired you for doing your own thing and following your dream.'

Olivia shrugged. 'Penbartha doesn't feel the same without George and Mollie.'

'It won't always be like that. It will get better. And I'll be there for you,' he paused. 'Until you go back to New York.'

'Really?'

'If that fits in with your plans?' He took his eyes off the road for a moment as he indicated to move lanes. 'Look, Olivia. This wasn't just a dirty weekend for me. Nice as it was. We're a team now.'

Once again, a little thrill buzzed through Olivia. This

time she let herself enjoy it for a while before pushing it
away.

***

A sign for Launceston flashed by in the fading light and she
shifted in her seat. 'Do you mind if we leave the dogs with
your parents for a few more days?'

Jago stared ahead. 'Don't you want them back in
Penbartha with you?'

'More than anything. But I can't risk their safety again.
I'd never forgive myself if anything happened to either of
them.'

'But you're prepared to risk yourself?' His despair was
audible. 'Fine. We'll come back and collect them as soon as
we can.' Jago's left hand rested on her knee, and he
squeezed it gently. 'It will all work out, Olivia. Trust me. At
least we have a couple of days before Martin's due back
from Leeds.'

***

By Truro, it was pitch-black, and Olivia was fast asleep.
Jago drove past the signs to Penbartha and headed along
another creek. He turned off a lane, past some iron gates
and then right onto a rough track. They eventually
rounded a corner and arrived at a cobbled parking area by
the water's edge. He pulled up and cut the engine.

'Where are we?' Olivia's face peered out from the
blanket Jago had wrapped round her.

'At my house. I just need to check on a few things here.
Go back to sleep.' He helped her inside and by the time she
was beneath the soft white duvet, her eyelids were firmly
closed.

***

Next morning, they found Callum in his cluttered office, looking, as usual, as though he might drown in paperwork.

He hugged Olivia and quickly tipped a load of files, balanced precariously on two chairs, onto the floor and signalled for them to sit down.

'I'm glad you're both here. I've just finished updating the schedule of repayments for the works on the Goods Shed and we're on target. And the café is looking great.' He beamed at them. 'And all has gone quiet on the trustee's front. So good news all round.' His face sobered quickly. 'Although this awful business with Jess has cast a cloud over everything.'

Jago nodded. 'I'm sure it has. But do you mind if we talk to you about something else?'

Callum nodded enthusiastically. 'Go ahead.'

'It's going to sound a bit left field, I'm afraid. Did you ever live in London?'

Callum blinked. 'Um, yes. Years ago. After university, I did my professional qualifications with one of the big accountancy firms in London. But then I met Rachel who was desperate to get back to Cornwall. So as soon as I could get a decent job down here, we moved.'

'How long ago was that?'

Callum leant back in his chair and contemplated the ceiling while he thought. 'Ten, fifteen years ago? Before we had the kids, anyway.'

'Did you know anyone from the Goods Shed before you came to work here?' Jago asked.

'Not really, no.' Callum looked closely at Jago. 'What's all this about?'

Jago tried a placatory smile. 'Bear with me and I'll explain soon. Can you just think very hard about whether you knew anyone here, or was even connected with here?'

Callum went back to examining the ceiling. 'I found out about the Goods Shed through Edgar. I knew him from a

Cornish Business alliance I was involved with.'

Olivia sat forward. 'What was that?'

'Oh, it was a networking thing for small businesses, mainly in the finance and legal sectors. We'd meet once a month and offer mutual support, swap stories and recommend each other to clients, if it was appropriate.'

'Was there any literature about your services?' Jago shot a puzzled look at Olivia's question.

Callum pulled a face. 'I seem to remember there was some kind of not-very-glossy brochure that listed us all and our various specialities. But that was about all.' He rubbed at his receding hairline. 'Can you please tell me what this is all about? You're worrying me.'

'One more question.' Jago promised. 'And then I'll explain. How long ago was this brochure in circulation?'

'Well, I've been here two years; I joined the Business Network about ten years ago.' Callum spoke his thoughts. 'Probably five or six years ago?'

Jago nodded.

'Now, will you tell me what's going on?' Callum's tone had lost its usual jocular note and his face looked stern.

'Look, there's no easy way of telling you this, Callum, but we think someone's been using your identity to commit fraud.' Jago spoke quietly but calmly.

'What?' Callum's chair tipped so far back it nearly went over and he struggled to right it.

'We think somebody in London has been using your identity, not your profession or anything, but your name and possibly your location. If you think about it, it's easier than ever to set up an email address in someone else's name and communicate as that person. What checks do we ever carry out when we meet someone?'

'Who the hell would want to steal the identity of an approaching middle-age, receding accountant from Cornwall?' Callum's attempt at a joke hit home hard with Olivia.

'It's a long story and we'll tell you all about it in due course, we promise. But it's probably best you don't know any more just now.'

'Olivia's right. We're involving the police, so just carry on as normal and don't say anything to anyone. Not even your wife, if you don't mind. The fewer people who know, the safer it will be.' He paused for a moment. 'I assume your business bank account is entirely separate from your personal accounts?'

Callum blinked. 'What? Yes, yes. I have one account for the business and then my wife and I have a joint account with another bank. It's all completely transparent. I'd better not be in any trouble, Jago. This could ruin my business. I could be struck off.'

'Not at all. I'm sure you'll be fine. Everything is traceable nowadays with internet banking. That's one advantage of it. But, and I realise this may sound a little melodramatic, trust no one at the moment. At least until the police have been in touch.'

'I'm an accountant, Jago, I don't trust anyone.'

***

Relieved to have had their trust in Callum validated, Jago and Olivia went to the Signal Box for a late lunch, courtesy of Alice. She was so pleased to see them, she immediately nipped to the Bakehouse to pick up some of their favourite foods.

'Everyone is so glad you are back, Olivia, and you Mr Trevithick,' she twittered as she handed them brown paper bags containing their lunch. 'Things have been rather gloomy around here, but you being back gives everyone hope.'

'Really?' Surprised tears rushed to Olivia's eyes.

'Of course. Everyone knows how important this place is to you and appreciates how hard you work at it. And you understand how everyone else feels about it. Especially the locals. I must dash. I'm due to show some prospective members about at 2.30 p.m.'

Jago eyed Olivia over a wholegrain baguette. 'So how does that make you feel?'

She pulled an agonised face. 'It's an enormous responsibility and I'm not sure I'm worthy of it, or up to it.' She couldn't hear his response, as his mouth was full of baguette and salad.

They were just sitting down together on the sofa, ready to plan how to approach Trenow with their recent information, when a knock came to the door.

'Come in,' Jago called, getting to his feet.

Edgar Moore appeared in the Signal Box, puffing from the exertion of climbing the wooden stairs. His pale eyes looked watery, and he wiped his large nose with a slightly greying cotton handkerchief.

Olivia leapt to her feet and led him to the sofa.

'Edgar,' she admonished him. 'You shouldn't have walked all this way by yourself. We could have come to you.'

'You're very kind my dear. It's no wonder George thought so much of you. You've always been so loyal. To him and everything he believed in.' Edgar sighed. Every line of his body seemed to sag and shrivel.

She fetched him a glass of water, which he drank thirstily.

'I'm so sorry,' he muttered, his eyes fixed on the floor, as if he were talking to himself. 'You're a decent person, Olivia, and I can't live with myself anymore . . .'

She stared at him in horror, her mind reeling with possibilities. 'Edgar! What do you mean?'

Jago put his hand on Olivia's and signalled for her to let Edgar speak.

'It's about Martin. Martin Lambert. I'm afraid he's not all that he seems.'

Any relief Olivia may have felt at those words was washed away by the anguish on the old man's face.

'And I'm also afraid that I may not have been as honest as I could have been about how long I've known him. But his mother came to me some years ago and asked me to help him start again down here.'

She bit her lip.

'He'd got into the wrong crowd. From a young age. And the crowd he was in got more wrong, and more dangerous as he grew older. His mother blamed herself. She'd married unwisely, completely taken in by the charms of her husband, who soon turned out to be an alcoholic and a gambler. They never knew when the bailiffs would turn up and take away what little they had left. And she thinks that's what made him so desperate to make money, become so greedy. He's a bright boy, but lazy, so he would always go for the easy option. He got involved in various scams in London and was constantly robbing Peter to pay Paul. Why pay for anything upfront when you can get it on tick and worry about paying for it later?'

Edgar paused and blew his nose noisily. 'Then he got mixed up with some very dangerous people in London. His mother approached me and begged me for help. She wanted me to help Martin make a new start down here, as far away from his London cronies as possible. So he came down and George met him. We both saw a potential in him as a business advisor. He has a superb business brain and George knew that was what the members needed. Plus, Martin looked like a successful business entrepreneur, with his car and his watch and his fancy clothes, and George thought he could be a good role model for some younger members. Show them what was achievable.' He nodded at the wince that crossed Olivia's face. 'I'm afraid I wasn't entirely truthful with George about Martin's past. And we've all been conned, one way or another.'

Olivia refused to look at Jago.

'Martin did really well to begin with and I was foolish enough to believe he'd left his London life behind him. But old habits die hard.' He paused for a moment, seeming to steel himself. 'I recently learned that not only has he kept in touch with his old cronies, but he's also actively involved with them again. And he's behind one of the most treacherous pieces of business I have ever known.' His head bowed again. 'I'm afraid I've betrayed both you and your godfather, Olivia.'

Olivia couldn't bear to put Edgar through the ordeal of having to explain it to them. 'If you're talking about the proposals for the site of Penbartha station, we know about them, Edgar.'

His pale eyes blinked. 'You do?'

'Only recently.' She surprised herself by how calm she sounded. 'So Martin's in this with his London connections?'

Edgar's relief at not having to go into detail was short-lived. 'It would seem so. And they are dangerous men.' He shuddered. 'And Martin's getting desperate. I'm worried he'll do something reckless.'

'Are they putting pressure on you to ease the way on the planning permission front, in your role as a councillor on the Planning Committee?' Jago's tone was curt.

Edgar wiped his eyes again. 'Yes, they are. Even though I've told them there's nothing I can do. They just won't accept it.'

Olivia was incensed that anyone would try to intimidate an old man. 'Do you know where Martin is now, Edgar? Is he in Leeds?'

He turned a puzzled face to her. 'Leeds? Who knows? All I know is that he's running out of time. He's out of his depth and I'm afraid. For him and me.'

'We need to take this to the police, Edgar,' Jago said firmly. 'Do you want me to come with you?'

'Please.' He struggled to his feet. 'Can we go now? I

really need to get this off my chest once and for all.'

Olivia helped the old man to the door and down the stairs. 'Can I just ask you one more thing, Edgar?'

'Yes, my dear. You're still being kind to me. Despite everything.'

'What exactly is your connection to Martin? He never spoke about it.'

Edgar's body sagged again. His head went down so he couldn't look at her. 'He wouldn't, my dear. It means nothing to him. Not like it did with you and George. He's my godson.'

CHAPTER TWENTY-SEVEN

'I ended up feeling sorry for the old boy by the time Trenow had finished with him,' Jago reported over breakfast the following morning. It had been late when he'd picked Olivia up from the Coach House, where she'd spent the evening with Cassie and Kitten, and he couldn't face going through the whole sorry tale again.

'Do you think Edgar knew anything about Martin using Callum's identity?' Olivia munched on her toast.

'Not at all. He was horrified when that came out. But he admitted that Martin had shown a keen interest in the Business Alliance when they met in London, some years ago.'

'So now poor Callum's been dragged into it as well.'

Jago chuckled. 'Don't feel too bad about it. Once the police assured Callum, he was not in any trouble he threw himself wholeheartedly into helping them with the fraud side of their investigation. Apparently, he's always fancied getting involved in forensic accounting.'

'Good for him.' Olivia finished her tea. 'I feel awful about involving so many people in this whole sorry mess.'

'Don't. Callum and I both are enjoying exercising parts of our brains we haven't used for a while.' Jago popped the last triangle of toast into this mouth and spoke round it.

'Are you now going to accept that Martin is behind this land proposal?'

She held up her hands. 'I accept that it looks like it, Jago. I just don't understand why. I know you think it's because he's just greedy and lazy, but he's not an out and out bad person. Those guys in London that Edgar was talking about must be putting him under real pressure to make him behave like this.'

Jago looked in amazement at her. 'I think you're missing the point here. Someone has murdered two women connected with the Goods Shed, in the most horrible, cruel ways; another has gone missing; several members of the Goods Shed have left for unspecified reasons; Willow and Fraser have had issues with suppliers and customers, and there was an arson attack on the café.' He reeled off the list without pausing for breath. 'Not to mention the broken window at Tresillian, your attack on the walkway, and all this business with the retirement village. What, or who, do you think is the common denominator?'

Olivia pushed back her chair and faced him, shoulders back, hands on her hips. 'Why do you keep insisting that the murders have anything to do with all the other things, Jago? As I've already pointed out, there's not a jot of evidence to link Martin to anything but the land proposals, is there? And let's not forget that you're the one who is so keen on evidence.'

Jago couldn't help being impressed. Most people backed down when he used that tone of voice in court. But not Olivia. He hardened his heart in his efforts to get her to face reality.

'Okay, okay. Let's break it down a bit more. Members leaving, Willow and Fraser's issues, the hostility of some trustees. Then we have the fire at a vital time for the refurbishment of the ticket office, and to top it all, a certain someone is trying to arrange the sale of the entire site behind your back.'

'And my learned friend's point is?' She raised her chin.

A muscle began to twitch in Jago's cheek. 'My point, Olivia, is that it doesn't take Einstein, or Rumpole, or even Miss Marple, to work out that someone wants you out of here. Either willingly, if you agree to sell and go back to New York, or by force if they decide to use violence to persuade you, or by arrest if the police take the easy way out and charge you. Because once you are off the scene there will be no one to fight for the site and it can be sold for development.' He spoke the last sentence slowly and carefully, making sure she got the meaning of his words.

He watched as her head lifted and her chin tilted. She was silent for a few moments and then took a long, slow breath.

'Fraud is not in the same league as murder. And while I accept that it looks as though Martin is involved with the proposals for the retirement village. I think we need to give more consideration to what Edgar was saying about those guys in London. Who knows what pressure they're putting him under? Or what they might be doing without his knowledge?'

Jago opened his mouth and then closed it again, deciding not to mention what Edgar had told him about Martin encouraging him to believe that Olivia was behind all the problems at the Goods Shed. It was a while before he spoke again.

'Okay,' he said. He forced himself to stay calm. 'Let's put that to one side for the moment and just look at the facts. Martin's alibi will be worthless with all this proof about his dishonesty. Which leaves all the evidence the police have got firmly pointing at you. Who knows how long it will be before Trenow bows to the pressure he's being put under and charges you? Do you fancy twenty years in prison for murder? Possibly more?'

Olivia sank back onto her chair and turned away from

him to study the view of the creek from the window. After a few moments he gingerly placed his hand on her shoulder, half expecting her to shake it off. She didn't.

'I just don't understand why you're so quick to make excuses for Martin Lambert.' His exasperation was audible. 'It's okay to be wrong about people, Olivia. We all make mistakes.'

She continued looking out of the window, concentrating on a cormorant diving for a fish. Only when the bird reappeared, fish in beak, did she turn back to him.

'But it's not just me who got it so wrong about him. It wouldn't be so bad if it was. George did too. I always thought he was a superb judge of character. I trusted his judgement implicitly. That's why I probably let my guard down with Martin more than I would have done normally. George was obviously taken in by him as well. That's what really hurts.'

'Shh. Come here.' Jago gathered her into his arms and held her. 'I understand why you're so upset about George being conned too. But he would have faced the facts, Olivia, and dealt with it. And so can you.' He stepped back so he could put a finger under her chin and tip her face up to look her squarely in the eyes. 'You're a fighter, Olivia. A survivor like me.'

'I don't feel like a fighter. More like a hamster on a wheel.'

'Well, if you are, you're a bloody tough hamster. Remember what you've been through. Your past has made you who you are today.'

***

Jago suggested they went along to the café to see what progress had been made. Kitten met them, dressed in a pair of decorator's paint-spattered overalls, and a Mrs Mop style headscarf, holding back hair that had a decidedly blue tinge to it.

'Olive!' The younger girl threw herself down the steps of the building and into the arms of her friend. 'Come and have a look at everything we've done.'

As Kitten's questions came thick and fast, with no gaps for answers, Olivia and Jago allowed her to drag them inside. It now looked very much like the vision for the café as a modern, streamlined eatery with a vintage twist that she and Kitten had worked on so tirelessly. It was also full of vaguely familiar people, all working away happily, some singing along to the radio that was playing quietly on a windowsill.

Olivia gazed round, open-mouthed. 'I can't believe you've got so far in such a short time.'

Kitten just grinned. 'Well, the cavalry arrived.'

'The cavalry?'

'Yes.' Kitten pulled Olivia and Jago round by their hands, pointing out what had been done and by whom.

'All these villagers have hidden talents,' Kitten began, 'but John, Alice's husband, has been a complete star. He's an ace electrician and cabler, and he and his men have laid all the cables for the computers and Wi-Fi and finished the electrics. Along with a smoke and burglar alarm. Andy, whose brother is a member of the Goods Shed, and his mates have used their days off to clean all the panelling that was damaged by the fire and then fix it to the walls and paint it. And Dave, the postie, has helped paint all the walls and ceilings.'

Olivia held a hand up to silence Kitten as she admired the eau de nil tongue-and-groove panelling on the lower walls and the clotted cream colour of the walls above. Industrial pendant light fittings, sprayed in matching eau de nil, hung from a white ceiling.

'Those are fab, Kitten.' Olivia's eyes were wide. Jago had never seen her lost for words before.

'And look at the floor!' Kitten squeaked, dropping to her

knees and stroking the ceramic tiles, which looked just like wood. 'Bill, who's Jim's brother, is a tiler by trade, so he got them at a great discount and laid them for nothing. And John installed the underfloor heating for us to free up wall space; it will mean we can sweep up the mud and dust from dogs and walkers and mop the floor.'

'It's great.' was all Olivia could manage. Her eyes travelled to the basic structure for the L-shaped counter which had been installed between the kitchen and the main area, giving a grand focal point to the room.

'Because of all the help we've had, Rocky and his guys have been able to get on with the furniture.' Kitten followed Olivia's gaze. 'He's varnishing the railway sleepers for the counter at his workshop, and then he can install them. And he's found some local slate for the tops.' She led the way through to the kitchen where two men were busy with a jumble of wires.

'Olivia, this is John. Our sparky.' John shook Olivia's hand vigorously and then Jago's. 'And this is Luke, one of his men.' More hand shaking followed.

'I can't thank you enough for all you've done.' Olivia looked overwhelmed by all the people helping.

'When we heard about the fire and realised the impact it would have on the opening date, Luke and I were happy to help, weren't we?' Luke nodded silently and left the talking to John. 'This café will be a right treat for the village and a great meeting place for all our different clubs. I know from my Alice how much you've done for us, with coming back from America and all. So we wanted to do our bit. To show our thanks.' He turned his face in Kitten's direction. 'Even if that one is a bit of a tyrant.'

Jago saw the tears forming at the corners of Olivia's eyes and he moved over to her, but once again, Olivia surprised him.

'Thanks, both of you.' She brushed away a tear. 'I'm overwhelmed by everyone's kindness.'

John shrugged off her thanks. 'You're one of us, Olivia. Part of the Penbartha team.'

Proper tears began to fall then, and Jago pulled her gently by the arm.

'Thanks, John.' He caught the other man's eye, who nodded and grinned. 'Let's see what else this slave-driver has been doing.'

The rest of their whirlwind tour took in the new, bright lavatories, fitted and decorated in a traditional Great Western Railway style, and the platform overlooking the walkway, and which would form part of an outside seating area in the summer. A local blacksmith was just finishing fitting the last of the wrought-iron railings to the platform edge to secure the area, and another two men were up ladders, busily painting the canopy that overhung the platform.

All Olivia's attempts at thanks, as she walked around, were brushed away with brusque Cornish forthrightness. 'It will be good for the village' and 'we want to do our bit' was the universal response, leaving Olivia teary-eyed with gratitude.

They ended up in the small office off the kitchen, that Kitten had commandeered as mission control, for Olivia to sign off on some stationery orders. A sudden commotion in the main café heralded the arrival of Rocky, who rushed into the office, knocking over two piles of paperwork and a broom, and enveloped Olivia in a bear hug.

'Olive! Am I happy to see you!' Jago and Kitten, looking on as Rocky held his dearest friend at arm's length and scrutinized her face, exchanged a small smile. From the look on Kitten's face, she was as confident of the true nature of the friendship enjoyed by the two dark curly heads in front of them as Jago was. He contemplated his feelings towards Rocky for a moment, and though he was slightly envious of his shared history and long friendship with Olivia, he felt nothing of the white-hot rage he experienced whenever he thought about Martin and his supposed alibi. He zoned back in on their conversation, just as three more villagers arrived and began cleaning windows.

'I can't believe all these people have done this for us, Rocky. It's so incredibly kind.'

Rocky beamed at her, his white teeth dazzling against his piratical dark looks. 'Not for us, Olive. They've done it for you. You're part of this village, remember; always have been and always will be. No matter where you are. You don't stop being part of a family just because you're not always with them, do you? And they wanted to show how much they appreciate everything you've done for the village. It's their way of saying thanks.'

Much to Jago's delight, Olivia disentangled herself from the group hug, edged over to him and slipped her hand into his, a gesture not unnoticed by Kitten and Rocky. He felt ridiculously proud and suddenly didn't want to think about Olivia returning to her old life in New York.

Jago snaked his arm around her waist and bent his head to whisper into her ear. 'Now you know all these people think you belong here, are you going to believe it too?'

She rewarded him with the biggest smile he had ever seen cross her face.

CHAPTER TWENTY-EIGHT

Jago sat in his Signal Box next morning, contemplating his relationship with the woman who had suddenly become such a big part of his life. It was clear to him that Olivia still planned to return to New York once everything was sorted and he accepted that was probably for the best. They were incompatible in so many ways. He was logical and measured. She was instinctive and creative and more swayed by her gut feeling and intuition than anyone he had ever met. But it was that passion, energy and determination that pulled him towards her. He enjoyed the way she teased him, called him out on his ego and challenged him on all sorts of issues. He hadn't ever before experienced the kind of feelings he had for Olivia. They were different, deeper, compulsive.

Jago stood up and walked over to the window. He wasn't used to thinking about how he felt when he was with someone. He was much better at analysing his thoughts rather than his feelings, and the change in him made him smile. He'd obviously been spending too much time with Olivia, relishing every moment of the time he had left with her. He didn't like the thought of her leaving, so he turned his attention to the other matter that was bothering him: his own future. He had a great home here, the best commute ever, and a job he enjoyed. So what was he missing? He was an active trustee, helping the Goods Shed members, supporting George's vision and doing his bit for the environment. But, and he was only just prepared to acknowledge it, his sense of justice was beginning to itch again. He knew that Olivia was aware of it from the way they'd talked, and he knew that just idly scratching it would not work. The troubles in Penbartha and his regular chats with Alistair, encouraged by Olivia, had made him think long and hard.

Footsteps jolted him back to reality. The arrival of a plump vision in white and taupe linen followed a light tap on the door.

'Cassie,' Jago greeted her warmly, 'we don't often see you down this way.'

She looked round nervously. 'I just saw Olivia going down the drive to Tresillian with Kitten, and I thought I'd grab the chance to have a quick word with you. In private.'

'Sure. She's had to do an emergency dash to pick up client folders so she can email stuff over to Joey. And then she's meeting Willow for lunch.' He waved her to take a seat on the sofa. 'Can I get you anything?'

Cassie didn't reply for a while, taking ages to arrange her usual layers of flowing linen around her before she sat down. 'Er, no thanks.'

Jago pulled up a chair opposite Cassie and looked at her closely. 'C'mon, Cassie. What's up?'

Her eyes bounced around the Signal Box, from the desk to the clock, to the windows. Then she folded and unfolded her taupe scarf, smoothing it out on her lap and re-pleating it carefully, not meeting Jago's gaze.

'Cassie?'

The older woman eventually raised tired green eyes to Jago's face. *She looks old*, Jago thought, older than he had ever noticed before. Her greying hair, usually so beautifully coiffured, was unwashed and lay flat against her head, and her soft face was lined and pale. Jago felt his pulse quicken. 'What's wrong? Are you ill?'

She shook her head slowly. 'No, although I've told Kitten I've caught some kind of bug. Just to get her off my back.'

Jago broke his cardinal rule of remaining silent in order to encourage the other party to feel inclined to fill it with chatter that could be useful.

'What is it, Cassie? Please tell me. Is it about Olivia?'

'In a way, but before I tell you, can I ask you something?'

He nodded. 'Ask away.'

'You might not think this is any of my business, but I feel responsible for Olivia now, especially since George died.'

'I understand.'

Cassie fiddled again with her scarves, refusing to meet his gaze.

'And I realise I haven't always been fair with you since George died. For silly reasons I'd rather not go into now.' Her voice, gentle at the best of times, was barely audible. 'And I really don't want to interfere in your personal life, Jago.'

'Shall I help you out here?' Jago asked, a small smile on his face. 'Are you asking me if my intentions towards Olivia are honourable?'

Cassie looked up, her face not altering. 'Are they?'

Jago's bright blue eyes grew serious, and he rubbed his cheeks with his knuckles for a moment before speaking. 'If it will help allay your worries, yes, I care about Olivia. We haven't really talked much about the future because there are so many other things going on at the moment. Whether she'll let me look out for her is another matter. You know Olivia.'

A soft, hand reached out and grasped his. 'Thank you. Olivia and I had a long chat the other night. Not about you and her. Just things in general. She seems calmer, happier, even with all this stuff going on. Her eyes were bright again, and she was talking more about the future than the past. She hasn't done that for a long time.'

Jago was surprised at how happy Cassie's words made him feel.

'I just need to know she has someone else in her corner,' she sniffed. 'I don't think I've done a very good job.'

He squeezed her hand. 'Don't be daft, Cass. You've been great to Olivia. She adores you.'

Fat tears appeared under the lids of Cassie's eyes, making them glitter and sparkle. Jago realised she must have been a real beauty in her prime. 'Olivia told me you're a barrister. I think I need your help.'

The tears began to fall, sliding down the rounded cheeks, dripping off her chin and leaving dark marks on her taupe linen top.

Jago fished around in his desk for a spare clean handkerchief and handed it to her, cursing the fact that he was still hopeless around weeping women. 'Please don't cry. I'm sure nothing is that bad. We can sort it.'

She sniffed loudly for a moment and then blew her nose before taking a deep breath. 'I've let her down, Jago. Just like her own mother did. And I've let George and Mollie down too. I'm so ashamed of myself.'

Any happiness Jago had been feeling ebbed away. 'Just tell me, Cassie. I'll do whatever I can to help you.'

'It's about Martin. Martin Lambert.'

He stiffened. 'What about him?'

Cassie scrabbled in her pockets for another tissue and dabbed some more at her eyes before she turned them once more on Jago. 'Is it true that Jess was poisoned?'

Jago's eyes widened. 'I think that's what the post-mortem revealed,' he hedged. 'But I haven't heard any more than that.' He paused for a moment. 'Why do you ask?'

'I heard it was an unusual poison that they couldn't identify at first.'

He shrugged, unsure what he could reveal.

'It's just that I know about herbs and plants because of working with Mollie for all those years. She taught me so much, and I loved it.' Cassie's voice steadied.

Jago raised an eyebrow.

'So I know which herbs and plants are most effective at poisoning someone.' The green eyes challenged him. 'Like aconite.'

He flexed his fingers. 'Aconite?'

'Yes. It's from the plant Monk's Hood. Mollie kept it for her rheumatism. She was in so much pain, and there was nothing the GP could ever give her that helped at all. So she made her own liniment with aconite. It was the only thing that gave her any relief, and I used to help her.'

'What's that got to with Jess being poisoned? You've lost me there, Cassie.'

Her face paled again. 'Few people realise how toxic aconite can be,' she confided. 'I'm not sure even Olivia knows, as Mollie was always so careful about how she stored it. We kept it locked in a drawer in the big cabinet in the krowji.'

Jago remained silent.

'But Martin came round a few weeks ago and was asking lots of questions about herbs and so on. He said he was having trouble sleeping and wanted to know if I had any natural remedies to help him. I did, so I gave him some valerian and told him to stick to the dosage I suggested, as it can make you very drowsy, and to avoid alcohol completely. He promised me he would, and I didn't really think any more of it.'

Jago made himself walk over to the window and look down at the walkway below for a moment. Was this yet another coincidence, or was it one of the last pieces of the jigsaw puzzle? He turned slowly back to Cassie.

'And what happens if you take too much valerian, or mix it with alcohol?'

Cassie looked surprised at the question. 'Well, you'd probably sleep really heavily and have an awful headache the next morning. A one-off excess shouldn't cause any long-term problems though.'

Jago recalled Olivia's description of how she felt the morning she'd found Libby's body and sat back down next to Cassie, frowning.

'And did you talk about aconite with Martin after that?'

'Yes.' Cassie's voice rose again. 'We just got chatting, and he asked me what the most poisonous drug was that Mollie kept in the krowji. And I opened my big bloody mouth and told him all about how toxic aconite is and that if you swallow it unknowingly, you could be dead within a couple of hours.'

Jago could not suppress the flicker of anticipation deep down inside that told him that proving his case was just within reach. It was a feeling he hadn't had for a very long while, and he'd forgotten how good it was. He took a deep breath and chose his words carefully.

'Are you saying that you think Martin poisoned Jess?'

'It's a bit of a coincidence, isn't it?' Cassie stumbled to her feet and paced up and down the room. 'We have that nice cosy chat about aconite; he'd already been in the krowji several times and knew we keep all the herbs in the big apothecary cabinet. And he's watched me fetch the keys to all the locks at Tresillian from my kitchen drawer loads of times, when he's walked across to the house with me to see George or Olivia.'

Jago snapped into lawyer mode, his analytical brain examining this fresh information for snags. 'Do you know where Martin is now?'

'Leeds or Liverpool or somewhere. At another business conference. He's not due back for a couple of days. That's why I'm telling you now. So we have time—'

'Are you absolutely sure he's away for another few days? I need you to be certain, Cass.' He didn't bother to disguise the concern in his voice.

Cassie nodded.

'Right. You and I need to speak to Inspector Trenow.' His heart sank as she started weeping again. 'You won't be in any trouble, Cassie. You weren't to know what he would do with the information you gave him. And perhaps there's nothing behind your suspicions. But until we know what's going on, please don't mention this to anyone else. Particularly Olivia. The less she knows about this, the better. Believe me.'

***

Olivia packed her client files into her work holdall and waved Kitten off. She could feel herself smiling and realised that for the first time in a long while, in spite of everything, she was happy. She was still on a high from the delight she'd felt the previous afternoon at the station café where she'd been swept away by everything going on there. If that wasn't an example of community spirit in action, she didn't know what was. She'd forgotten the pleasure of belonging and of sharing genuine laughter with like-minded people. A tiny bubble of hope had floated across her stomach at the thought that perhaps she belonged in Penbartha after all and could stay a little longer. The bubble had grown overnight and swelled even more with an exciting call she'd just received from Historic England, with a very interesting offer. Joey had brought her back down to earth with an email requesting an urgent update on a client's drawings, but she was working out different ways to keep everyone happy, herself included. She wouldn't let herself think about Jago and where he fitted into all this just yet. Being with him felt right, and that was good enough for her now.

Her phone pinged with a text from Willow, saying she'd been struck down with a stomach bug and was cancelling their lunch. Just as she was tapping out her reply, another text arrived. It was from Martin, saying he'd got back from Leeds early and would she like to meet him for lunch in Falmouth to chat over some good news for the Goods Shed?

Olivia checked that her reply had gone to Willow and then thought hard about what to say to Martin. Remembering Cassie's words to her at the beach, she meandered down the garden to the quay and surrounded herself with sea and nature, as Mollie had always done when she needed to listen to her inner voice. Turning back to the view, she could imagine George and Mollie sitting there quietly with her and for the first time since George had died, she could feel the invisible thread that connected the three of them. Feeling their hands in hers and concentrating on her thoughts, the answer came. 'You can do this.'

Fifteen minutes later, Oliva was driving into Falmouth with a renewed sense of purpose. As much as there was a large part of her that didn't want to face Martin alone, she knew it was the right thing to do. Jago was always telling her that running away wasn't an option anymore and she needed to face things head-on. And that was exactly what she would do, starting from now. She needed to figure out who was behind the proposals for the retirement village and the most obvious way of doing that was to talk to Martin.

In an attempt to take her mind off what lay ahead, she allowed herself to think about untangling her feelings about New York and Penbartha. It surprised Olivia how much she'd missed the village and the people in it, after just a few days in London. Previously, she'd always assumed it was George and Mollie she missed. But now she realised it was much more than that. Everyone had welcomed her back with open arms, unquestioningly, for her own sake. And now, when she thought about her life in New York, it seemed too busy, too noisy, too hectic. A major promotion was hers for the taking, but for the first time, Olivia allowed herself to question whether it was what she really wanted. It would involve more client schmoozing, which she did not enjoy, more chasing staff to get their bills out, which she hated. Less creativity . . .

Yet, she remembered, as she drove into the carpark at Martin's apartment, depending on what happened with the police investigation she might not have a choice. In the meantime, she needed to concentrate on her lunch with Martin. He had suggested they eat at a restaurant, so she wasn't worried. Besides which, Martin had only ever shown genuine kindness to her. *And*, a little voice kept whispering in her ear, *George could never have been so entirely wrong about a person.* She would be fine. Even so, as she stood outside Martin's apartment door, she whipped out her phone and tapped out a quick message to Jago.

'You're looking well,' Martin opened the door before she rang the buzzer, leaving her with her mobile still in her hand. He greeted her with a warm hug and ushered her into his modern harbourside apartment, in the most recent and expensive development in town.

'Thanks. And it's such a beautiful day, it feels as though summer is on its way.' She smiled at him, dropped her mobile into her bag and followed him through to the sitting room, where bifold doors led to a balcony with spectacular views across the harbour. Through the open doors she could smell the salt air on the soft sea breeze and hear distant voices floating up from the harbour beneath them.

She wrinkled her nose as she walked across the recently vacuumed rug to the window. 'What's that funny smell?'

Martin sniffed the air and frowned. 'Oh, that. I've just had the rugs cleaned. Cream wasn't the most sensible choice. Now, shall we sit outside for coffee?' He led the way through the doors at the end of the room and gestured towards the rattan furniture, already covered with smart navy cushions.

Olivia made herself comfortable, her heart beating only slightly too quickly as she watched the sunlight dancing on the water below.

Martin reappeared with a tray bearing coffee paraphernalia. He poured the coffee carefully, and then regaled her with amusing stories about the business conference he had just attended and the people he'd met. Olivia listened carefully, her mind working on two levels at the same time; taking in the words that were coming out of his mouth and analysing what she already knew. Despite his usual entertaining style, she couldn't laugh.

'Are you alright, Olivia? You're looking pale.' He pushed back his floppy hair. 'And you haven't said anything about what you've been up to while I've been away.'

She pulled more curls across her yellowing bruise. 'Nothing much. Still juggling the demands of Joey and getting the café ready for its grand opening.'

'Cassie said everything's on target.' He drank quickly and refilled his coffee cup.

'For now, yes. But I still haven't made any progress with appointing a manager.' She crossed her fingers beneath the table. 'And then the other day Joey called and offered me a raise if I go back before the end of next month.'

'Really?' His green eyes flashed. 'A good one?'

Olivia nodded. 'Very good.'

'Then you'd be mad not to take it, wouldn't you?' His eyes rested on her face. 'And you must be really missing all your friends over there.'

Olivia held his gaze. 'For sure. And my life would be so much easier out there, with no one else to worry about.'

'Absolutely! You and I are kindred spirits, Olivia. We're not the sort who want to put down roots and stay in one place. We need to move about and see the world. It's how we're made and why we get on so well.'

Olivia's fingers fumbled as she picked up her cup, spilling coffee over the table. Martin snatched at a napkin to wipe the spill up and then crossed his legs, smoothing his chinos over his knees. 'And,' he continued, 'I feel I owe it to George after all he did to help me out. So, I've been thinking of ways I can help *you* out. In my professional capacity.'

Olivia's heart quickened. 'Really?'

'Perhaps. As long as we approach it from a business point of view rather than an emotional one. I know Penbartha station has enormous sentimental value for you, but given all the grief and sadness that's tied up in it, don't you think you might be better off just selling the entire site? And then you could have a clean break from it all and just go back to New York and make a proper life there.'

Olivia's heart sank. But when she looked at Martin, he smiled an open, encouraging smile and she felt a glimmer of hope. Perhaps George had been right all along about him, and he'd got a plan that would mean they could continue redeveloping Penbartha station?

'And the Goods Shed and everything would carry on as it is?' She sat up straighter, her expression hopeful, 'Just without me?'

'Well, I'd have to look into it more, as it's not really my area of expertise.' He tidied the coasters into a neat pile. 'But we have to face facts, Olivia. I don't think it's likely that anyone will take it over as it is. It's not really a money-making enterprise at the moment, is it?' He waved away her attempt to interrupt. 'I know it doesn't need to make money just yet, but we're in the twenty-first century. Businesses need to turn a profit to survive.'

'What would happen to the members?'

'There will always be similar places in Cornwall the members could move to.' He pressed on, and she bit her lip. 'With a bit of luck, you might be able to sell the land for redevelopment. Perhaps for housing?' He sent her a look. 'Then you'd be doing your bit for the Cornish housing shortage.'

Olivia gulped and tried to lighten her voice with a small laugh. 'Demolishing our beautiful buildings and replacing them with modern boxes goes against everything we stand for environmentally. I can't see the trustees ever agreeing to that. Can you?'

He smiled reassuringly. 'I'm sure you've got the power to wind up the Trust if you want to. And the trustees can't do anything about it. Then you could give everyone notice and do whatever you like.'

She couldn't stop herself. 'I still don't think a new housing estate would go down at all well with the villagers, do you?'

'But it won't be your problem then, will it? You'll have made a fortune, so just leave Cornwall and enjoy your money in Manhattan.' He smiled. 'C'mon Olivia. When you first came to Penbartha you were all for moving back to New York as soon as you could. And now I'm offering you a win-win scenario. Sell the site, invest some money in a similar enterprise elsewhere without the responsibility, and go back to your life in New York.'

A sense of unease started to build up inside and she hesitated. Martin was looking at her like she was a stranger.

'What's up Olivia? This isn't like you.'

'I need time to think about what you've said.' A look of irritation flitted across Martin's face, and she hurried on. 'Besides, I think all these discussions might be completely immaterial, Martin. The police won't let me go very far at the moment, with the murder investigations.' She spoke slowly. 'And if they do suspect me, do you honestly think they'd let me sell up and profit from such an awful crime . . .' she trailed off.

An alarm beeped on Martin's phone, and he shook himself like a dog. 'Lunchtime. Instead of going out, I'm going to cook today.'

A prickly sensation ran down her arms. 'I thought we were going to try that new seafood place at the top of the quay. The food's had great reviews and the views should be wonderful.'

'No,' he spoke firmly. 'There was an amazing farmers' market where I was in Leeds, and I picked up some local fresh produce.' He smiled at her. 'And I've got wonderful views here.'

Olivia forced herself to smile back. 'Okay, lunch here sounds lovely.'

'Fantastic! You lay the table while I cook.' He spoke over his shoulder as he walked into the kitchen. 'We're having three courses. Everything you need is in the low unit.'

With Martin busy in the kitchen, Olivia set about finding the right mats and cutlery to set the table. He was very particular about the use of mats and coasters. She knelt down beside the blond wood buffet unit and began sorting out what she needed. Unsurprisingly, everything was in its place, neatly stacked in size order. She pulled out a few mats and then reached towards the back of the cupboard for the rest of the set. Her fingers brushed against a piece of paper which she pulled out. It was a letter, addressed to Martin, that had fallen down the back of the drawer above it.

'The cutlery is in the left-hand drawer,' he called from the kitchen. 'I've moved a few things around.'

'Okay! But I'm still sorting the mats,' she called back, her eyes busy scanning the letter. It was from a letting agency, informing Martin he would be facing official enforcement action for non-payment of rent. Olivia stared at it, puzzled. She was sure Martin had told her he had bought the apartment as an investment opportunity.

'Have you found it?' he called again, and Olivia hurriedly opened the drawer and rattled the perfectly arranged cutlery.

'Yes!' She kept her voice light and shoved the letter back into the cupboard, groping her hand round to feel if anything else was there. Her fingers grasped another, thicker wad, caught down the back of the drawer. She tried the drawer, but it was locked and so she went back to easing the bundle from out of its resting place, pausing now and then to rattle the cutlery. It eventually came free, and Olivia shoved it under another pile of mats and concentrated on setting the table.

'How are you doing?' Martin popped his head around the door and nodded his approval at the neat way she had arranged cutlery, glassware, napkins, and plates.

'We're having pasta, so I'll serve up in here in warm bowls.' He whisked the china from the table.

'Why not just use this lovely large pasta bowl and we can serve ourselves?' she suggested.

'It's a special lunch, Olivia, and I want to do it properly.' He looked at his watch. 'I'll put the pasta on and then we can start with the first course in about ten minutes. Is that okay?'

'I'll just pop to the bathroom and wash my hands before we eat.' She spoke to his back, and hurriedly crossed to the buffet unit, grabbed the bundle and her handbag and escaped to the bathroom, carefully locking the door before sinking on to the lid of the lavatory.

The wad of brown envelopes was folded over and secured with a thick elastic band. She carefully pressed them flat. The printing on the envelope showed they were from Treliske hospital, but they had been put back in, so the address didn't show through the cellophane window.

A memory of something flashed through her mind but she pushed it away, wondering if Martin's mysterious illness could be connected with his money worries. She looked at the envelopes for a few moments and then at her watch. Time was ticking on. She carefully eased the first letter out, opened it, her eyes on the top of the letter. A chill spread through her veins.

The letter was addressed to George, calling him for a check-up on his aneurysm repair. As was the next, the next, and the next. Olivia flicked manically through the letters until she had read all six of them. All letters and reminders calling George for his check-ups. None of which he had received.

Her world tilted and the space between her shoulder blades burned and prickled as the words on the letters blurred in front of her. Cassie's voice telling her how helpful Martin had been taking George's post down to him every day and Keren Tremaine's suggestion that he might simply have become forgetful in old age echoed round her head. Olivia gasped as the reality of what Martin had done hit her. Hot coffee and stomach acid burned the back of her throat. She fell to her knees, flung the lavatory seat up and heaved and heaved violently into the bowl until there was only bile left. She leant back, pressing her hot face against the cool marble tiles of the bathroom walls and tried to concentrate on her breathing. In, out. In, out. In, out.

There was a tap on the door. 'You okay, Olivia?'

'I'm fine.' She forced herself to sit up and speak normally. 'Just touching up my makeup.'

'Don't be too long.' She heard his retreating footsteps. 'Our first course will be ready in twenty seconds.'

Olivia collapsed back against the wall, thoughts and visions whirring round her head. Who could do a thing like that? To an old man? Who had shown him nothing but kindness and help? What else would someone like that be capable of?

CHAPTER TWENTY-NINE

Olivia's heart crashed against her ribcage as she considered the terrible possibility that she was alone with a murderer in his apartment. How could she have been so stupid to have come on her own? Wild thoughts chased each other round her brain. Had Jago even read her text yet? She snatched her mobile from her bag and gave an anguished moan. Her earlier text hadn't gone. She stabbed at the send button and then threw the phone back into her bag while she tried to think. Was there any way she could get out and just run? Then she remembered the letters, George and how he had died alone. And her resolution not to run anymore. It was time to stick around and fight.

An image of Zev, an ex-navy SEAL and her self-defence instructor in New York spun into her mind. As she concentrated on his face, she pushed herself up from the warm floor tiles, holding on to the basin for support, and made herself drink from the cold tap. Raising her eyes to the mirror, she caught sight of a wild-eyed, dishevelled face. *That's no good, Wells*, she told herself grimly. Tidy yourself up and think carefully about what you're going to do. Keep calm and channel that anger.

When Martin called again from the kitchen, her mind clicked into gear, and she was ready. She strolled into the living area, her back teeth clamped together, and a false smile fixed on her face. As she took her seat at the table, she messaged another five short words to Jago, praying that the internet coverage, not known for its reliability in this part of the harbour, would hold out. She slipped her mobile into the open front pocket of her handbag, the record button activated.

Martin came in from the kitchen holding two plates aloft. 'Bruschetta!' He placed the plate in front of her with a flourish. Olivia stared at the small, white square platter bearing slices of lightly toasted French bread topped with chopped cherry tomatoes, red onion, and fresh basil leaves, all drizzled with caramelised balsamic vinegar. She remembered that when she used to pick the round, red fruit in Mollie's greenhouse, the scent would make her stomach quiver with anticipation and the smell of the leaves would linger for ages on her fingers. She picked up her fork and speared one tomato, holding it to her nose. These weren't the rich, sun-warmed tomatoes of her childhood that smelled as good as they tasted; these were cold and devoid of taste.

Olivia played with her food, pushing the tomatoes around the plate, but not eating them. Her head was full of George, the memories of how he had been so full of life, so positive, how he had been a godfather, father, and grandfather all rolled into one. And if it hadn't been for Martin's cruel actions, how he could still possibly be here today.

He swallowed his last mouthful of food, dabbed at his mouth with his napkin and placed it carefully by his plate. 'Are you ready for the main course?'

'In a minute, Martin.' She took a deep breath, seizing the moment to give Martin one last chance to come clean. 'Did I tell you George didn't attend any of his follow-up appointments for his aneurysm repair at the hospital?'

Martin's eyes flickered for a moment and then held

hers. 'Why on earth not?'

Doubt, mixed with a morsel of hope, sliced through her. Could he really be that devious? She tested the ground. 'Perhaps he didn't receive his appointment letters.' She didn't take her eyes off his face, acutely aware of his reactions. 'Perhaps someone intercepted his post?'

Martin blinked, collected the plates up and got to his feet. 'Really, Olivia? That's a bit extreme, isn't it? He was an old man, getting forgetful. He probably just forgot to go.' He carried on to the kitchen.

Olivia stayed at the table, fiddling with her cutlery, and looked around the room, while she tried to calm her thoughts. Far from the casual disorder of Tresillian, everything was neat. The expensive pieces of furniture were placed just so, the modern artworks perfectly straight on the walls and the sleek, silver media centre exactly parallel with the skirting board. Even the books were arranged in alphabetical order, and the few trinkets he had were placed at a precise distance from each other on the mantelshelf. Martin's obsession with tidiness was getting more extreme and she wondered if keeping his external world in such perfect order helped him control the cruel and chaotic thoughts that must be going on inside his head.

'Penne pesto!' He reappeared with two bowls piled high with pasta. 'I even made my own sauce, with fresh wild garlic and basil leaves I picked up at the farmers' market. Parmesan?'

Olivia nodded and waited for him to grate fresh parmesan onto her plate before splashing red wine into her glass.

'This Barolo is just fabulous. It's a big wine and I know you'll like it. Try it.'

She swirled the ruby red liquid around the large glass and lifted it to her nose. She inhaled a deep fruity, almost cherry and plum bouquet, and sipped it. A warm sensation spread through her veins, and she closed her eyes.

'Mmmm.'

Martin tucked into his pasta. 'Try it with the food. It will enhance the flavours.' He took a big forkful of pasta and followed it with a gulp of wine to prove his point. He smacked his lips and waved at Olivia's bowl with his fork.

She speared a piece of penne smothered in fresh pesto with her fork and lifted it to her nose. The sharp smell of pesto made her sneeze, suddenly and violently.

'It's the wild garlic.' Martin assured her, handing her a large cotton handkerchief. 'It tastes wonderful.'

Olivia dabbed at her eyes and nose, and watched him eat for a moment, her pulse quickening. This was getting too big for her.

'Martin, I'm not in the mood for playing games. If I'm honest with you, will you please just be honest with me?'

The room seemed to still and the air grew heavy.

He placed his cutlery carefully on the side of his bowl and returned her gaze, his mouth a flat line. 'What's this all about?'

'I know about the proposals to demolish Penbartha station and the surrounding buildings, and build a retirement village,' she began and brushed away his attempts at interruption. 'Jago and Rocky met a publicity photographer on the walkway, who was the soul of indiscretion. Told them all about the plan and the seminars in London.'

Hope glinted in his eyes, and he leant forward. 'Don't you think it's the perfect place for a retirement village that charges the earth?'

She shook her head. Withdrawal slid across his face, like a blind being pulled down. Within seconds, it was completely closed.

'Everything would have worked out if you'd just sold up and shipped out.' He straightened his napkin and then gripped it in his fist. 'But you just couldn't let go. And you ignored the warnings. All of them.'

Memories of the fire, the problems at the Goods Shed and the attack on her and Zennor flooded her mind. For a moment she was so shocked she couldn't speak.

'You did all those awful things? To me? And Zennor? To get me to sell up?'

He laughed mirthlessly. 'Not me in person, obviously. But yes.' He reached out a hand and pushed back her curls to reveal the bruise on her forehead. 'So, he did get to you. Useless bloke's disappeared off the face of the earth, so I didn't know. But you still haven't got the message, have you?'

Olivia stared at his hard face. The cold, unfamiliar face of a dangerously changeable stranger.

'Why are you doing this?'

Martin sighed and took another sip of his wine. 'I'm in trouble. Serious trouble. And I owe a lot of money to some very nasty people, and if I don't pay it back soon, my life won't be worth living. Selling Penbartha station is my ticket to a new life.'

Olivia could hear the fear in his voice. A tiny part of her almost felt sorry for him.

'How on earth did you get yourself into this mess?'

'That's none of your business,' he snapped. The switch in his mood was so abrupt Olivia shrank back from him. 'I didn't have a fairy godfather to grant my every wish like you did! In fact,' he spat, 'my own godfather is completely fucking useless. All you had to do was sell the station and my cut from the developers could have got those bastards off my back for good, and there would have been enough left over to set myself up nicely somewhere else. But no, your misguided sense of loyalty to some dead old people—'

Olivia gasped at the cruelty behind his words. 'So your original plan was to get George to sell the site? By hook or by crook?'

The muscles in Martin's neck bulged and his fists clenched at his sides as he nodded.

'And you intercepted his post.'

He nodded again. 'He didn't leave me with a choice, Olivia. I tried to get him to understand the benefits of selling, but he just wouldn't see sense. He kept going on about leaving a legacy for you and for the village. It was just as well he died when he did. I might have had to do more to hasten him on his way otherwise.'

A fist clenching sensation hit her stomach. 'How can you say that? He was a harmless old man! And he was all I had left.'

'Perhaps, but I knew he was leaving you everything in his will. Edgar told me. You could be very wealthy. I'm fighting for survival.'

'And you thought I'd just agree to sell up?'

'Of course I did! George was forever telling me how clever you are. I automatically thought there was no way you'd want to bury yourself in this god-forsaken place when you could just take your money and run back to your fancy life in New York.'

'How wrong you were.' Olivia's chin rose.

His green eyes flashed with anger. 'You've changed, Olivia. You're not the ambitious, career-minded girl you were when I first met you. You've gone soft, let this place get to you, spent too much time with Kitten and her grungy friends.'

'So what if I've changed?' She challenged him. 'I've realised what's important to me. But I'm still a problem solver and I want to help you. We can go to the police, explain everything. They'll offer you protection.'

'It's too late for that. I'm in too deep.'

Olivia's stomach lurched. 'What are you going to do?'

'I need you out of the way. If you're accused and convicted of murder, you'll be out of the picture and the trustees will be only too happy to sell the land to distance themselves from you.'

All the random thoughts that had been whizzing around her head for the last three weeks, the vague, loosely connected facts, were slowly beginning to link up and shift into place to form a clear picture. Like the Penbartha sea mist slowly clearing, Olivia was seeing things properly.

'So you murdered Libby and made it look as though as I'd done it.'

He clapped his hands together slowly. 'Well done, Olivia. You've finally got there. Yes, I murdered Libby, but only because I had no choice.' His voice was cold and calm. 'If you'd just agreed to sell in the first place, I wouldn't have needed to bring her in on my plan. She was obsessed with me and would do anything I asked.' A cruel glint filled his eyes. 'But then she went soft and said she didn't enjoy making you look so bad and wanted to apologise and explain. By then she was too much of a risk and had to go. Removing her from the scene just killed two birds with one stone. And setting you up for it was child's play.'

Olivia closed her eyes against the cruel words. 'So why give me an alibi?'

'Think about it.' His face twisted. 'Giving you an alibi gave me one too and put the police off the scent.'

'And Jess?' Her voice was a whisper.

'It turned out she was easy to play too. And more than happy to comfort me over Libby's death. I just wound her up before that last meeting and you played into my hands so nicely by arguing with her, it was obvious people would think you'd killed her too.'

'And you poisoned her?'

Martin nodded, but there was another, more frightening emotion behind his eyes that she couldn't identify.

'Cassie is very knowledgeable about garden poisons and very easy to get information from. A bit too susceptible to a younger man's charm if you ask me.'

Olivia looked down at the brightly coloured food on her plate. And swallowed.

'And Sarah?'

'Who knows? She apparently overheard me talking to Libby a few times and put two and two together when she died. She's a feisty little thing. Even challenged me over it. But then she did a runner, and I can't find her anywhere.'

'So she's not dead?' Olivia couldn't keep the hope out of her voice.

'Not unless one of my contacts has found her.' He looked at his watch. 'And now you're going to eat the same lovely dish that I prepared for Jess. But this time I know exactly how quickly the poison will work, so I can get you out of here before you make a mess of my soft furnishings.' His eyes flickered over to the sofas where the smell of cleaning fluid was the strongest. 'And rain is conveniently forecast again for later.'

She looked at him. 'And how are you planning to explain my death to the police?'

'I'll tell them you came here and confessed to Jess's and Libby's murders and that you were so overcome by grief and remorse that you couldn't take any more and took your own life.'

'That's ridiculous! They won't believe you.'

'Why not? You lied about your alibi.'

She faltered. 'I did not.'

'You did, by omission. And you've always claimed you can't remember what happened the night Libby died. I can tell the police I gave you the alibi because I was frightened of what you would do to me. And that's why I've been keeping away from you. You're unpredictable. Unstable. I'm sure I've still got some of the valerian you drugged me with that night. I could tell the police I found it in your handbag.' His eyes darted round the room; his pupils dilated. 'Yes, that's what I'll tell them. It was you. All of it.

And now you can't cope with what you've done.'

Olivia's skin prickled. 'You really think I'll willingly ingest poison?'

'Why wouldn't you? What have you got left now? Your godparents were the only people who cared about you, and they're both dead. You're lousy at choosing friends, and even your own parents choose to live on the opposite side of the world. And if you're still not convinced,' his breathing quickened, 'I think I'm quite a bit stronger than you, aren't I?'

She wasn't on her own. Despite what Martin said, she had Rocky and Cassie and Kitten. And the villagers who had made it clear to her she belonged in Penbartha. And there was Jago. He had made her realise that she was no longer fulfilling her godparents' legacy out of duty, but because she wanted to. And although she had refused to let herself think about their relationship, for the first time in a very long time, Olivia had found herself looking to the future rather than backwards to the past. A waft of sea breeze through the balcony doors brought Olivia a sudden clarity of thought. She remembered Mollie telling her that one of the biggest hurts of grief is the words that are left unsaid. And she still had a lot to say to the people she cared about.

The ice in the pit of her stomach suddenly transformed into hot coals of rage as adrenaline coursed through her body. Her future was worth fighting for, and Martin's past deeds needed avenging. Thinking fast and looking for a way to buy time, she filled her wineglass to the brim.

'Your plan won't work, Martin.'

Panic flitted across his face. His eyes, already slightly wild, bulged. 'What do you mean?'

'I put in a fast-track application to Historic England.' Her chin rose. 'I heard today they've accepted it. And given us specialist status because of the links with Brunel. You'll never get planning permission now. Whatever happens.'

Her hands only slightly shaking at the lie, she raised her glass at Martin.

The low fire of greed and jealousy Martin had been harbouring for years blazed and engulfed him. Red-faced and furious, he scrambled to his feet and grabbed her wrist. Olivia jerked away, deliberately sending her glass and the bottle of wine flying. Dark red wine gushed everywhere. Across the tabletop, onto Martin's white shirt, cascading on to the huge cream rug.

He froze and watched open-mouthed as the wine pooled like fresh, warm blood where it lay. Olivia watched the wine drip steadily on to the rug. Unable to control his obsession for neatness any longer, Martin let out a howl of rage and dashed into the kitchen for a cloth.

That was all the time she needed to swap their plates. In the five seconds before Martin returned and started dabbing furiously at the wine stains, Olivia had started picking at her food. By the time he had poured table salt over all the red patches and returned to his seat, she was still pushing the pasta around her bowl, her head down and her hands trembling.

Still angry and flustered, Martin began eating his food furiously, shovelling pasta into his mouth with his fork.

'This is all your fault, Olivia. You could have avoided it if you hadn't been so bloody obsessed with doing your duty.' He pointed an empty fork at her angrily, his mouth full of food.

'I don't think so.' She forced herself to stay calm. 'But we need to talk about it. Find a way forward for both of us.'

He stabbed angrily at more pasta, and wolfed it down, his eyes never leaving her face. 'There is no way forward for both of us. It's either me or you.' He took another gulp of wine. 'You're not as clever as George claimed, are you? Not even bright enough to swap the bowls while I was out of the room.' His mocking eyes followed hers to his nearly empty plate, then to her barely touched one and finally rested on her face as horrid realisation dawned.

He launched himself at her, his furious breath scorching her face. 'I'm much bigger than you. The poison won't work as quickly. I've got time.' Both his hands clamped round her throat, his thumbs pressing against her windpipe as he lifted her off the floor and forced her across the room.

Spots flashed across her eyes, and she kicked out wildly at his crotch, but he twisted and took the impact on his thigh. She tried screaming but only a faint choking sound came out. Gasping and gurgling, her lungs burning, she clawed at his fingers, at his hands, at his arms. Clawing and clawing, trying to loosen the pressure on her throat, but his clammy hands squeezed and squeezed. She glanced up into his manic, bloodshot eyes and knew this was the end. She tasted blood as her lungs screamed for air one last time. Everything darkened. Then went black.

***

Olivia gagged. The pressure around her throat had loosened, and she lay sprawled on the wine-soaked carpet, alongside Martin's sweating body which was writhing as he scratched desperately at his neck. Retching at the sickening stench of sweat and red wine, Olivia snapped back into reality.

With an image of Mollie from all those years before clear in her mind, she stumbled into the kitchen to fetch warm water and salt. Her shaking hands rattled the glass against the tap, water spurting everywhere. She staggered back to Martin, who lay still and motionless on the floor.

'Drink . . . need to be sick . . . get rid of it!' Her throat spasming, Olivia's voice was little more than a croak as she fell to her knees and tried to force his mouth open to pour the solution in.

With a howl, Martin reared up, and knocked the glass

out of her hand. He grabbed her by the hair and dragged her through the balcony doors, impervious to her twisting and kicking out at him. He pulled her across the balcony and forced her against the rail, his breath foul and hot on the back of her neck.

'I know you can't swim and the water's really deep here. I'll say I tried to stop you jumping but couldn't.'

Martin forced Olivia's body forward and upwards until her feet were flailing off the ground and all she could feel was the hard metal of the rail digging into her stomach. She opened her eyes fearfully, terrified that all she would see was the murky harbour water twenty feet beneath her.

At the sight of the water, something clicked in her brain, and she stopped struggling. Surprised by the sudden loss in momentum, Martin loosened his grip on her throat. Olivia hooked her foot behind her and twisted it round his ankle. Jabbing both elbows backwards with all her strength into his groin, she managed to topple him, and they crashed headfirst over the railing together.

As Olivia slammed into the harbour, her throat filled with cold, murky seawater, sucking all the breath out of her, and she was back in that fierce ocean with Aidan, clawing for the surface, struggling for air and light. But this time, as she felt the air on her face, it wasn't Aidan she was searching for. Her old swimming instinct kicked in. She tried shouting for help, but no sound could escape her damaged throat. So treading water, she hunted frantically for a sign of Martin beneath the surface, ducking repeatedly under the turbid water, looking for him.

Something cool and pale brushed past her and she grabbed at it blindly, following a slippery hand up an arm to a body. She tried to pull his head clear of the water with her last ounces of strength. But Martin was heavy and still, the poison doing its work and she couldn't bear his weight. She kicked out with her legs and her lungs worked furiously, trying to drag in air, but it wasn't enough. She needed more. The muscles in her arms and legs burned, and Martin's body began to sink, pulling her down with him. She slipped below the surface with no energy left to kick.

Perhaps this was it. She'd accomplished what she'd set out to do and now everyone would manage without her. It wasn't what she wanted, she had so much more to look forward to.

Was this how Aidan had felt all those years ago? How long would it be before the pain stopped?

She drifted further and further away until a feeling of watery peace descended.

CHAPTER THIRTY

THREE WEEKS LATER

Jago stood on the edge of Penbartha creek watching the dogs playing on the shoreline, his hand shielding his eyes from the sun as he checked on the weather. It was a beautiful morning, despite the early hour, and the startlingly blue sky arched high above the creek and the pastureland opposite. He lifted his head and breathed in. Yes, there was a definite hint of the coming summer in the air. The chill had disappeared from the breeze, and he could already feel the warmth of the sun seep through the skin of his bare arms. It looked like it was going to be a glorious day.

Jago whistled to the three dogs, eager to get back to Tresillian and Olivia.

Since that fateful day, he had rarely let her out of his sight. He would never forget the scene he and Trenow had found at the harbour when Olivia's message had finally come through. Even when they had dived into the water, he had thought they were both dead. And whereas he was indifferent to Martin's fate, he hadn't been prepared for the surge of raw emotion he'd felt when the paramedics had strapped a barely conscious Olivia onto a stretcher and blue-lighted her to hospital.

Thanks to Olivia's foresight in activating the recording device on her mobile phone, the police had been able to listen to Martin's confession and hear exactly what had gone on afterwards. Unfortunately, in Jago's opinion, because of Olivia's actions, Martin had not died. He was at the start of a long and painful recovery in a secure hospital and when he was better would stand trial for a litany of criminal offences. Whatever the outcome, Jago knew that Martin Lambert would not be inhaling the fresh Cornish air for a very long time. If ever. And while Jago might have believed that Martin deserved to die that day, he was content to know that Olivia wasn't battling with her conscience over it.

Olivia had recovered well. After a fortnight of proper sleep, the dark shadows under her eyes had disappeared, her skin regained its healthy glow from being outside in the spring sunshine and freckles now dusted her nose. She looked like a tremendous weight had been lifted from her shoulders. Jago remembered the Olivia he had met when she'd first come back from New York; stressed and unhappy, her eyes dark and sad. Now she was relaxed and chattered with everyone as she rushed around, preparing for the café's opening, energy and enthusiasm fizzing from her and her deep laugh infecting everyone. She was laughing more – proper laughter that made her eyes sparkle and her cheeks glow. And he realised this was the real Olivia, now the stresses and sorrows were behind her. She was happier, more carefree.

The grand opening of the café wasn't the primary source of his preoccupation now. Jago had spent the last three weeks trying to deny that there was anything serious going on between them, and unpicking his jumble of emotions, but he had to face facts. He had never felt like this about anyone. He'd thought Lucy was the love of his life for a long time, but now he couldn't even remember what she looked like. He was more concerned that Olivia had been in a quiet, reflective mood all week. He'd sensed her withdrawing from him, speaking more and more to Joey on the phone, and excusing herself to speak to him in private. And from the way she'd encouraged him with his own plans to return to London and the Bar, he realised they were both preparing themselves for their new lives, thousands of miles apart.

***

Olivia sat in her favourite spot on the old granite quay at the edge of the creek, listening to the water flowing past, and felt a calm descend. She had deliberately made time every morning to sit there and let her mind wander. It was the perfect place to lose herself in her thoughts. Today, the early morning air smelt of salt and hope and new beginnings. The last few weeks and months had been filled with grief, trauma and one crisis after another, but now, as she stared into the familiar cloudless sky, she felt different: peaceful.

She had escaped with surprisingly few injuries. CT scans had revealed two cracked ribs and several minor fractures of the cartilage in her larynx, caused by Martin's attempted strangulation, and they had kept her in hospital for three days to make sure no complications arose from her injuries. After her release, the pain in her throat had slowly diminished along with her headaches and swallowing difficulties. The awful bruising and scratches had faded, and she no longer wore a scarf to hide the marks. The only lasting physical effect of the attack was on her voice, and that had improved from a painful, scratching to a deeper and definitely more husky sound than it had been before.

Olivia knew she'd done the right thing in saving Martin's life. She didn't need vengeance; she needed to know that he would face justice for all his crimes, and although it wouldn't bring any of his victims back, their families could feel some kind of closure. She sighed to herself. Closure was such an American word, and yet it said it all. The letting go of what once was.

She had done a lot of soul-searching since she'd come out of hospital. She knew she was at a crossroads. She could return to New York and run away from her grief and sadness, or she could be strong and embrace the love that was all around her here in Penbartha. She realised she had been grieving in one way or another since she was ten years old, starting with Aidan's death and her parents' rejection of her. Libby's murder and her fight for the future of the Station Trust had been her way of focusing her attention away from her grief over the deaths of George and Mollie. Martin had been right about that. Now it was time to concentrate on her own happiness and make some tough decisions about her career and her life.

Until a week ago, she'd been uncertain. Then early one morning, while she'd been walking the coastal path, she knew instinctively what she wanted from her life and where she wanted to be. She'd told Martin that she preferred the person she'd become in Penbartha and realised the words she'd spoken on impulse were true. She'd had a week to make plans and there were still some tough conversations ahead, but today was about the opening of the Waiting Rooms and she would enjoy every minute. She let herself savour the turquoise expanse of water in front of her, its surface sparkling under the strengthening sun, and waved to a paddleboarder and her dog making their way slowly up the creek to the village. She was smiling as she went up the garden to get ready for the big event.

Gentle wafts of fresh coffee and beeswax greeted them as they stepped through the double doors to the Waiting Rooms. Olivia looked around with delight. It was already a hive of activity with everyone bustling about, stringing fairy lights around the platform canopy, the wrought-iron railings and across the walkway in both directions. The ladies from the sewing group were looping their beautiful, handmade bunting through the trees lining the walkway and zigzagging it across the platform. Inside the café the new waiting staff and extras hired for the opening day, all recruited locally and wearing their new uniforms, were rushing around, getting instructions from Cassie.

Olivia looked for Kitten, automatically seeking her brightly coloured hair to identify her among the throng of helpers.

'Sorry, Cassie,' she interrupted. 'Have you any idea where Kitten is?'

'I think she's in the kitchen,' Cassie replied, a mysterious smile on her face.

Olivia eventually made it to the kitchen after being stopped every five seconds to answer a question or put something right and popped her head round the door. She immediately saw Harry, the young and passionate chef, head bent over the Daily Specials Board which was being painstakingly inscribed in a chalk pen by another person. Two fair heads together.

'Oh, sorry, I thought Kitten was in here.' Olivia spoke to the backs of the two bowed heads.

One head lifted slowly and turned, an enormous smile on their face. 'She is.'

Olivia's mouth fell open. Not only had Kitten eschewed her usual bizarre outfits in favour of the new Waiting Rooms uniform, which showed off her small, dainty figure, but the pink, blue and green highlights had disappeared entirely, and her hair was back to her natural honey blonde colour, still cropped short but now curling delicately round her face. She had removed all the piercings, apart from two in each ear. For once, people could see beyond the wacky appearance and concentrate instead on her sharp cheekbones, upwardly slanting olive eyes and wide mouth. A face that was both interesting and attractive.

'Oh, Kitten. You look fabulous!' Olivia gasped. 'I can't believe you've been hiding behind all that makeup and hair dye for all these years.'

Kitten shrugged off the compliment with her usual forthrightness. 'I guess I decided it was time I grew up a bit and made my point in other ways. And besides, Rocky said I'd scare the customers off if I didn't tone it down a bit.'

Olivia privately thought Rocky probably had a point but didn't say so. 'Well, I think you look wonderful. And I'm touched that you would go to these lengths for the sake of the Waiting Rooms.'

Kitten's eyes shone with a familiar zeal. 'Ah yes, but it's not just about the Waiting Rooms is it, Olive? It's a whole new beginning for lots of people. One of our new suppliers has just told me that if everyone who lives in Cornwall spent just an extra fifty pence a week on local produce from a local supplier, it would add ten million pounds to our economy every year. Wouldn't it be amazing if we could help that happen?'

'We will,' Harry said, in the fervent tones of someone newly converted to a cause. 'You've done a grand job of sourcing all these suppliers, and I know from speaking to them they are all delighted to be on board with this venture.'

Olivia smiled and moved on quickly before Kitten warmed to her theme, satisfied that the kitchen and menu were under control. As she walked past the main counter, Sarah, happily returned to Penbartha as soon as she heard the news of Martin's arrest, was giving reminders to the newly trained baristas on how to use the enormous and rather scary-looking stainless steel coffee machine. The counter was home to various slate platters and glass dome display dishes that looked increasingly enticing, filled with the delicacies that were being brought down from the Bakehouse. Alice's sixteen-year-old niece, Clemmie, proud in her first work uniform, grinned at Olivia as she tested the till for the last time. Olivia smiled back and checked her phone once more to make sure that all the invites had gone out to the local newspapers, lifestyle magazines and the Cornish radio stations. She had left no outlet for publicity unexplored.

By 10 a.m. everything was in place. Staff were on standby; they had primed the coffee machine and the waitresses were ready with smiles to greet customers. Olivia and Kitten hugged each other nervously and then turned together to face the excited staff.

'Right. Here's to the Waiting Rooms! Good luck everyone. Let's open the doors.'

***

By 8 p.m. the spring dusk was turning to darkness, and the starry sky and loops of twinkling lights and lanterns dancing in the trees spotlighted the walkway. Happy guests clinked glasses and teacups, and the distant creek glittered in the fading light. The local boats had joined in the village celebrations, and were decorated in bunting and fairy lights, reflecting a dazzling patchwork of colours on the water. Music floated on the breeze, champagne fizzed, and the whole place had a magical feeling like an enchanted forest, buzzing with happy people. The plan had been to open quietly at 10 a.m. for a day's trading, and then have a massive party in the evening for all the locals, friends and anybody who had helped them in any way. But it had turned into one all-day long celebration. Everything had gone to plan, all the journalists had loved it and promised to write amazing reviews, and the villagers had turned out in droves.

By sunset, most people had moved out onto the platform and walkway to make the most of the balmy evening and party atmosphere. The enticing scent of wild bluebells and laburnum in the hedgerows floated through the air on the evening breeze. Only a few of the more elderly villagers, including Mrs Chynoweth, stayed in the comfort of the sofas inside the Waiting Rooms, sleeping off the excesses of the free champagne.

Olivia took a moment to look around at all the smiling faces spilling out from the station onto the walkway. Everyone she knew in Cornwall seemed to be there. She'd made a great fuss of all the villagers and members of the Goods Shed and they were all still there, mingling together and proclaiming it as the best community event ever held in Penbartha. Fraser and Willow had finally arrived after a busy day trying to keep up with the demand of orders from the café and were being showered with praise for their wonderful bakery. All their other suppliers, who between them had provided everything on the menu. Meat, fish, salad leaves, cream, butter, jam and even the organic dog treats for canine customers, had come from every corner of the county to support the opening celebrations. Rocky was being inundated by potential clients wanting his advice. Alice had filled page after page of an appointments book with the names of people who wanted Olivia's architectural services. Callum and Paula and their respective families were taking a well-earned break after spending the day showing people and prospective members around the Goods Shed, before pointing them toward Alice for further information and membership application forms. Only when the enquiries had ceased did Alice relax, and Olivia was delighted to see her and John dancing slowly together with a group of their village friends on the walkway.

Edgar had sent along a crate of champagne along with his apologies and a note of congratulations. Olivia was sad that he hadn't attended personally but understood how difficult it was for him. Ross Trenow had shown up with his wife, a shy and quiet woman who was nothing at all like Olivia had imagined, but quickly decided she would like to get to know. Kitten and Cassie were still working hard, making sure everyone had plenty to eat and drink and had found kindred spirits in Jago's parents, who had joined in and were busy topping up people's glasses with champagne. They had brought along the three dogs to join in the evening celebrations.

Olivia pushed back her curls which were hanging loose around her shoulders and realised she was feeling good. Alive and happy. She could still smell the sun-warmed flesh on her arms from a day largely spent in the spring sunshine, seeing to customers, friends and guests and her skin tingled comfortingly. She took a moment to soak up the merry scene in front of her and file it away for her memories. She would never forget this day for as long as she lived, and she could feel the spirits of George and Mollie beside her on the platform. She had fought for their legacy. First, out of a sense of duty, then it had quickly become out of choice and her belief in their shared vision. She'd had the determination and the creativity, but most importantly she had accepted help from people who loved her.

All day, Olivia had felt a long-forgotten energy flowing through her. She looked down the walkway towards the creek and smiled. She would never tire of this view. Ever. Her eyes sought out Jago among the throngs, his silver head and broad shoulders visible above most of the other guests in his characteristic upright stance. Dressed in faded Levi's and a paisley patterned blue shirt that accentuated the colour of his eyes, he was engaged in deep conversation with Ross and Lara Trenow. But he raised his head and looked in her direction as if sensing her gaze and the slow smile he sent her fizzled down her spine.

Within minutes, Olivia felt familiar arms slip round her waist from behind and she leant backwards into his solid warmth.

'Hey,' he whispered into her ear. 'How are you doing?'

'I'm good.' She turned in his arms and traced the line of his smile to the corner of his mouth and kissed it. 'Everyone is being so kind. The suppliers are all delighted with the information we've provided about them on the back of the menus, and local artists have asked us to consider displaying their work on the Waiting Rooms' walls.'

He returned the kiss. 'And I've had loads of enquiries about sourcing railway memorabilia as everyone loves all the original details you've included here. I will be very busy until I go back to London.' He waved in the platform's direction. 'Even the old porters' trolleys and vintage cases and trunks seem to have gone down well.'

'I never thought it would generate so much more work for everyone this quickly.' Her eyes shone. 'It's just what Penbartha needs.'

'Hey, you two. Come and dance!' Kitten and Rocky grabbed their hands and pulled them down on to the walkway which had been morphed into a makeshift dancefloor. They danced slowly among their friends until they saw their chance and slipped away together, closely followed by their dogs.

Olivia looked round at the magical scene in front of her and grinned suddenly, feeling much younger and less serious than usual. More her real self.

Jago kissed her and she could feel his lips curve into a smile under hers.

'Happy?' He pulled away slightly so he could look at her.

'Very.'

'And now you can go back to New York with a clear conscience.'

She shook her head, and Jago brushed a thumb gently down her cheek. 'Hey, come on! We can make this long-distance thing work.' His blue eyes sparkled. 'I've got a confession to make. Although I'm going back to the Bar, I've decided not to go back full-time. I don't want to leave here permanently. I've cleared it with my clerk, and I'll just be doing the occasional big trial.'

'Really?' Her eyes widened.

'I don't want to get caught up on that hamster wheel again. Life's too important. And it will give me more time to see you.' He grinned. 'I'll have paid for the whole of that Chilean hydroelectric plant before we know it.'

'No, you won't.'

'What?' Jago was stunned. 'I thought we'd agreed.'

'We did.' Olivia caught hold of his hand. 'It looks like we've both been doing a lot of soul-searching. And there was one thing Martin said to me that was absolutely true.'

Jago raised an eyebrow. 'There was?'

'He said that I'd changed since I came back.' She didn't go into detail. 'And I have. I've let people in, let them help me. I'm part of something much larger than I could ever have imagined.' She kissed him. 'I've got a confession too. This is where I want to be. This is my home, Jago, and it always will be.'

He blinked, grinned, and then blinked again. 'So, you're staying?'

She nodded. 'Does that fit in with your plans?'

He didn't reply, simply picked her up and spun her round in delight. Then he stopped suddenly. 'What about Joey?'

'Joey's cool with it.' She smiled. 'He says he understands completely. I've agreed to do some work for him, but remotely. Jess was right. I can't be true to what we believe in here, and then keep dashing across the Atlantic, can I?'

'So what will you do here?' His eyes narrowed. 'Is Rocky involved in this? He's been acting very strangely around me lately.'

Olivia laughed. 'You know how Rocky hates secrets. But yes, I'm going into business with Rocky, doing retrofits and so on. And I made the most incredible contact at Historic England when I talked to them about listing the buildings here. I'm joining a national campaign by architects to prioritise retrofit over demolition and rebuild. I couldn't have found a more perfect role, and I'm really excited about it.'

Jago pulled her close, his fingers twisting into her silky curls. 'I reckon you and I make a good team, Olivia Wells. Don't you?' His blue eyes held hers.

A thrill ran through her as she grasped the subtext of his words, and her smile grew.

'Yeah, I reckon we do.' She moved closer, pressing her body against his and kissed him again, feeling a sense of calm descend over her body.

'You're not planning on running away anywhere just yet then?'

She snaked her arms around his neck and looked at him as she shook her head. 'You were right. I've been running away all this time. And I need to stop. I'll still run. Every morning probably. But I'll always come back. I promise.'

Jane believes she was always destined to be a crime writer. As a child she was an avid reader of the *Famous Five* and any other mysteries she could find at the local library. Her first commercial success came when she was eight years old, with the publication of a letter to the Bunty comic about her grandfather digging up a small handgun and two gold hoop earrings in his garden and suggesting they were connected to an unsolved murder. From that moment she wanted to be a writer.

Small things like life, career, marriage, motherhood and illness got in the way, but that initial ambition never died. After years of secret scribbling, lots of reading and one other small success in flash fiction, Jane began writing *A Deadly Inheritance.* The Covid pandemic eventually focused her mind on finishing her novel, and she enjoyed writing as a means of escape from the grim reality of what was going on in the world.

A Deadly Inheritance is the first book in a new series and combines Jane's love of Cornwall, murder mysteries and her interest in the environment, sustainability and creativity.

Love crime fiction as much as we do?

Sign up to our associates' program to be first in line to receive Advance Review Copies of our books, and to win stationary and signed, dedicated editions of our titles during our monthly competitions. Further details on our website: www.darkedgepress.co.uk

Follow @darkedgepress on Facebook, Twitter, and Instagram to stay updated on our latest releases.

Printed in Great Britain
by Amazon

13466622R00203